Christianity After Communism

Christianity After Communism

Social, Political, and Cultural Struggle in Russia

EDITED BY

Niels C. Nielsen, Jr.

Westview Press
BOULDER • SAN FRANCISCO • OXFORD

Copyright © 1994 by Westview Press, Inc.

Published in 1994 in the United States of America by Westview Press, Inc., 5500 Central Avenue, Boulder, Colorado 80301-2877, and in the United Kingdom by Westview Press, 36 Lonsdale Road, Summertown, Oxford OX2 7EW

Library of Congress Cataloging-in-Publication Data
Christianity after communism : social, political, and cultural
struggle in Russia / edited by Niels C. Nielsen, Jr.
      p.   cm.
   Includes bibliographical references.
   ISBN 0-8133-2365-7
   1. Russia (Federation)—Church history—20th century.
2. Christianity—Russia (Federation)—20th century.
3. Christianity—Russia (Federation)—Forecasting   I. Nielsen,
Niels Christian, 1921–   .
BR936.C48   1994
274.7'0829—dc20
                                                    94-29700
                                                    CIP

Printed and bound in the United States of America

(∞) The paper used in this publication meets the requirements
     of the American National Standard for Permanence of Paper
     for Printed Library Materials Z39.48-1984.

10   9   8   7   6   5   4   3   2   1

Contents

Preface

This book consists of the presentations given at a conference on Religion in Eastern Europe After Communism, held in Houston, Texas, April 25-27, 1993. The conference was sponsored by Reunion Institute, the Houston Graduate School of Theology, the Institute of Religion, the program in religion at the University of Houston and the Wessendorff Foundation. The American participants are specialists in Slavic studies in the United States. Three lecturers, Fathers Janusz A. Ihnatowicz (Roman Catholic), Vladimir Ivanov (Orthodox), and Dr. Alexander Zaichenko (Protestant) have taught in Russia. The English researcher, Dr. Philip Walters, is director of Keston Research in Oxford, England, at an institute which reported on religion in Eastern Europe for decades in the communist period.

The topic of the conference was not the past but the future: What has happened to religion since the demise of communism in the former USSR? This is the question addressed by our authors. All of our author-participants share the conviction that something new and of crucial significance for religious life has happened and is happening in Russia. Too little information is available about it in English. With the demise of communist ideology and its atheistic propaganda campaigns, religion now has a more open role to play in social and political, as well as personal, life. Of course, neither in the past nor in the present is its influence simply positive. Today, old conflicts have surfaced—often in bitterness and religious intolerance as state-sponsored suppression of the churches has ceased. Unshackled from Marxist rule, nationalism has proved highly divisive and has led to violence—most terribly in Yugoslavia. Paul Mojzes' chapter about Yugoslavia, the only one describing the conflicts engendered by the end of communism outside the former USSR included in our volume, makes this point.

It was considered of first importance by the conference organizers that presentations come from different points of view within the Christian spectrum of churches and beliefs. The analysis presented in this book centers on Russia (with one exception, Yugoslavia) and includes Orthodox, Roman Catholic, and Protestant interpretation. Also important are the rapidly changing situations in the non-Christian areas of the former USSR.

With the end of communist persecution, Islam and Buddhism are reasserting their presence along with shamanism, and there is missionary activity by Hare Krishna, a form of Hinduism. There are also interesting and significant new developments in other areas of Eastern Europe, for example, former satellite countries such as Bulgaria, Poland, and East Germany. That these subjects were not included in this volume does not mean that they were considered unimportant. They simply were beyond the scope of the conference and its necessary limitations of size and time.

Because of their topics as well as the respective authors' interests, the chapters of this volume differ in style and approach. Some presentations are descriptive and analytic. Others are more prescriptive and theological. This variety itself should lead the reader to an individual evaluation of the present religious situation. Suddenly, church leaders as well as individual believers found that their situation was very radically changed. There was new freedom for activity but also an acute lack of funds. Ideologically, old disputes have flared in unexpected ways.

The evaluations of Father Ivanov and Dr. Alexander Zaichenko, both from Moscow, give very divergent judgments about present religious developments in their country. Ivanov, a church historian, reflects as an Orthodox priest faithful to the Moscow Patriarch. Zaichenko, a high-ranking economist who continues to write in his field for international journals, earlier was among President Gorbachev's advisers. He is one of the few intellectuals active as a free churchman. After he finally secured a Bible in 1985, he was baptized in 1986. Like Ivanov, Zaichenko's point of view is that of an informant giving his own perceptions of the situation. For the audience at the time of the conference, his comments were particularly engaging. Historically, it is evident that Protestant sectarianism has provided islands of ethical consciousness in the past in Russia. Zaichenko's hope that privatization will lead to millions of individual proprietors developing a religious and ethical consciousness seems an optimistic projection in view of the present upsurge in Mafia-like profiteering.

The translations of Patriarch Aleksi's address to a group of American rabbis during a visit to New York City and the material from Metropolitan Ioann of St. Petersburg are included because they bear on the growth of anti-Semitism in Russia today. They are diametrically opposed to each other in viewpoint, one informed and tolerant, the other obscurantist and dangerous. Although the Patriarch has restricted the Metropolitan's right to speak publicly for the Orthodox Church, the Metropolitan, in a show of unity, did not at once, in reply, openly attack the Patriarch.

Both American specialists, Professors Steeves and Daniel, provide important information on contemporary developments. Steeves tells of the efforts to organize Christian political parties, narrating the difficulties of sustaining any clearly identified Christian consensus and influence. Daniel highlights not only the vitality of the new religious press which has developed under glasnost' but also the variety of viewpoints among Christians writing for it as well. Philip Walters of Keston Research at Oxford, England, enumerates a number of positive developments. His information, like that of Professor Pankhurst who is a sociologist, comes from extensive recent travel in the region as well as a host of important contacts from before and after the end of persecution.

The only chapter included in the volume whose author was not present at the conference is that of Dennis J. Dunn; he was in China at the time of the meeting. Dunn's wide historical knowledge of both political and religious conditions in Russia has been reflected over the years in the range of his publications. The two chapters by seminary educators, Walter Sawatsky and Father Ihnatowicz, come from contrasting confessional points of view. Ihnatowicz recently taught at the new Roman Catholic seminary in Moscow. Sawatsky's account of conflicting visions in theological education, also from firsthand contact and travel, reflects significantly on the future as well as the past. His counsel was especially valuable in arrangements for the conference; special thanks are due to him. Paul Mojzes, editor of *Occasional Papers on Religion in Eastern Europe,* has long researched developments in Eastern Europe. His chapter provides information for the reader's further reflection on the contrasting pattern of events in the former Yugoslavia and the former USSR.

Niels C. Nielsen, Jr.

About the Editor and Contributors

Patriarch Aleksi II, Patriarch of Moscow and All-Russia, is ruling head of the Russian Orthodox Church.

Wallace Daniel is chairman of the Department of History at Baylor University in Waco, Texas.

Dennis J. Dunn is professor of history at Southwestern Texas State University in San Marcos, Texas.

Janusz A. Ihnatowicz is chairman of the Department of Religion at the University of St. Thomas in Houston, Texas. Father Ihnatowicz recently taught at the Roman Catholic Seminary in Moscow.

Metropolitan Ioann of St. Petersburg is the leading hierarch of the Russian Orthodox Church in St. Petersburg.

Vladimir Ivanov is professor of church history at the Orthodox Seminary in Moscow.

Paul Mojzes teaches at Rosemont College, Rosemont, Pennsylvania.

Niels C. Nielsen, Jr., professor of philosophy and religious thought emeritus at Rice University, Houston, Texas, is author of *Revolutions in Eastern Europe: The Religious Roots* (1991).

Jerry G. Pankhurst is associate professor of sociology at Wittenberg University, Springfield, Ohio.

Walter Sawatsky teaches at Associate Mennonite Biblical Seminaries in Elkhart, Indiana.

Paul D. Steeves, professor of history at Stetson University at DeLand, Florida, is editor of the *Russian Encyclopedia of Religion*, which is now being published volume by volume.

Philip Walters is director of Keston Research, Oxford, England.

Alexander Zaichenko conducts research at the National Institute of Science in Moscow and writes for the magazine *Delovie Lyudi*.

Introduction

Niels C. Nielsen, Jr.

The End of the War Against Religion

Very few if any among specialists—historians, political scientists, or sociologists—anticipated the speed with which totalitarian rule would collapse in Eastern Europe. The 1989 People's Revolutions, two centuries to the year after the French Revolution, marked the end of communist power in the satellite countries of the Soviet Bloc. The Berlin wall was opened to the West, and East Germany, Poland, Czechoslovakia, Hungary, and Romania all were freed from communist rule. Bulgaria and Albania soon followed. Who would have prophesied that nonviolent popular uprisings could achieve such success? Only in Romania was there bloodshed. It was in this setting that the greatest persecution of religion since the end of the Roman Empire abruptly came to an end.

It is hard for Western democrats to be completely objective in evaluating the developments which brought about the historical watershed. Overcome by nationalism, the Soviet Union itself soon ceased to exist and was replaced by fifteen independent republics. For societies as well as individuals, the course of events signalled a historic watershed. George Weigel, in his book, *The Final Revolution,* argues that much of academia along with the Western press have missed the deeper meanings and forces at work in the end of the Cold War.[1] A moral and religious revolution preceded and explains the overthrow of communism. It was a religious movement, not simply concern for political democracy and a market economy, that brought revolutionary change for both societies and individuals, Weigel believes.

This much is clear: religious liberty was part of the new civil order along with popular elections and a market economy. Mass atheism, imposed from above, had been a new twentieth century phenomenon. Believers suffered through communist anti-religious campaigns for nearly half a century (three quarters of a century in Russia); suddenly they found that they were no longer second-rate citizens. They now could attend church free of threats of job loss or educational discrimination against their children. Of course, there is a diversity of religious legacies and churches in Russia and the so-called satellite countries: Poland, East Germany, Czechoslovakia, Hungary, Romania, Bulgaria, and Albania. Historians are still appraising the diverse ways in which church and state, religion and culture reacted to persecution in the communist era. But religious faith does not return simply with the end of persecution. Even in its demise, communist totalitarianism has left a far-reaching negative legacy.

Communist persecution had been justified ideologically under the guise of class morality and the dictatorship of the proletariat. Totalitarian rule began with violence: churches were attacked from without in a campaign of terror and murder. When religious institutions still commanded a lingering popular allegiance, regimes attempted to subvert and control them from within. Shortly before the Second World War, under Stalin's rule, all but a very few sanctuaries had been closed throughout the USSR. Even though persecution relented somewhat during the Second World War as Stalin looked for support against the Nazis, communist anti-religious dogma did not change. After the war, in the late 1940s and early 1950s, atheism was imposed with ruthless terror on the satellite countries whose conquest was sanctioned at Yalta when the dictator met Roosevelt and Churchill.

Now, atheism has fallen from power throughout Eastern Europe almost as if it had never threatened or dominated in public life under communist rule. Of course, the change of ethos did not take place without struggle. With the sudden restoration of freedom of conscience, in most countries religion is expected to play a more active role in the renewal of public morality under the rule of law. Naivete about revolution in the name of freedom could last only briefly. Not to be minimized are new challenges and perils: an articulate ideological nationalism as well as economic chaos. The vacuum left by the demise of communist rule has been filled not just by pluralistic democracy and respect for law, but by new and divisive ideologies of blood and soil which defy any religious sense of brotherhood or universalism. Nations whose borders were established by politicians after the First World War, Czechoslovakia and Yugoslavia, have divided, the one peacefully, the other in a tragic civil war.

As the years passed, under communist rule, belief in God had became a more vital option as the Marxist dream of a new society had proved bitterly uninspiring and without appeal. It was not really surprising that religion continued to live on even in the face of all the brutal attacks upon it. In a number of the satellite countries, Christians were in the forefront of the uniquely peaceful revolutions which without violence overthrew Marxist rule. In the so-called Revolution of Light in East Germany, protesters left church buildings holding candles, showing that they carried no weapons. The Velvet Revolution in Czechoslovakia soon followed, joining humanist and Christian motivation and support. During the decade long struggle of the Solidarity (Christian) labor movement in Poland, violence came exclusively from the communist regime. Only in Romania was the fall of a Stalinist dictator accompanied by bloodshed and massacre. It came in response to the peaceful defense of a Reformed minister by both Orthodox and Protestant citizens.

An earlier communist optimism and fanaticism declined, and it became clear that dialectical materialism had not renewed community morals or personal ethics. On the contrary, the Marxist doctrine of class struggle had subverted both. Even in situations in which religious institutions stood in need of radical reform, human concerns about suffering, death, and immortality did not disappear. They surfaced with renewed tenacity in the late communist era. Moreover, they were not simply intellectual but were carried in power in folk piety. The "Babushka" phenomenon in Russia is an example. Grandmothers who cared for young children taught them to pray, inculcating belief in God even while the state championed atheism.

Even while Stalinism was still politically dominant, a slow but growing revival of interest in religion among intellectuals (extending over more than a quarter of a century) made evident that faith in God could not be destroyed simply by economic change as Marx and Lenin had supposed.[2] For pragmatic reasons, President Gorbachev felt forced to come to terms with the international and social role of ecclesiastical institutions as well as believers' faith commitments. In order to enlist popular support for his program of reform and renewal from persons who continued to trust in God, he went to Rome and met with Pope John Paul II. It was a symbolic gesture which had already been extended to the Orthodox when he met with Patriarch Pimen, the impotent leader of the national church, in Moscow. The regime could no longer conceal that communist totalitarianism had defaulted on its promise to fulfill life, either individually or in society.[3] An ideology which initially had attracted idealists now served only ruthless self-interest as part of a power struggle. It had become exhausted as a life philosophy decades before it fell from power shortly before the end of the century.

Religion's Role

In Russia today, a thousand year long legacy of Christian thought and life is being looked to again after seven decades of communist materialism. Historically, the celebration of the millennium of Christianity in Russia in 1988 can be seen as a watershed event in which new freedom for religion began to be signaled even before the 1989 peaceful revolutions in the satellite countries. Many of the communist leaders ruling the USSR had become convinced that faith in God could not be destroyed. This, in turn, probably contributed to President Gorbachev's decision not to suppress the popular uprisings in Eastern Europe. Increasingly, before the change of state policy, the communists had found it very difficult to identify any genuinely outstanding novelist or poet who was still dogmatically anti-religious. Boris Pasternak and Alexander Solzhenitsyn, the Nobel prize winning literary figures best known in the West, represent only the tip of the iceberg of a continuing literary interest in religion.[4] Of course, it is too simple to speak just of the disappearance of religious rites and symbols under communism. Its rule did not bring the end of religion as Leninist-Marxist theory had supposed. Paradoxically, a sense of the sacred lived on in pseudo-religious atheistic forms which included national group ceremonies, holidays, a favored party of the elect—the Proletariat—and expulsion of heretics, all premised on the promise of utopia. The newly instituted totalitarian state reverted to archaic forms of civil religion which were both brutal and self-defeating. In retrospect it is clear that the result was not the elevation of the common life but degrading of any work ethic or common concern for justice.

Philip Walters in his chapter in this book emphasizes how difficult it is to achieve fresh religious orientation and revitalization. In the West, the late twentieth century is often described as postmodern. In Russia, questions about the meaning of the postmodern often seem irrelevant when the Enlightenment has been so long rejected in dialectical materialism. For decades no entrance into the modern world had been allowed except in Marxism. Fortunately, now in the post-communist era, a number of the leading Russian intellectuals, including philosophers and theologians, write less defensively. Beginning from earlier pre-communist paradigms and thinkers, they all are attempting to reconstruct and reinterpret them positively, for example, the pre-revolutionary religious philosophy of Vladimir Soloviev. Unfortunately, Soloviev is little known or followed by the Orthodox hierarchy and clergy.

Popularly, religious faith has fresh appeal, as it comes from a long national but suppressed legacy. During the communist period, the Orthodox Church hierarchy in the Soviet Union was extensively under KGB state control and excessively manipulated and oppressed. The opening of secret police files in Russia as well as other countries has shown that a larger than expected number of church leaders in most countries throughout Eastern Europe (with the exception of Poland) were collaborators at various levels. Russian bishops even have spoken of the sin they took on themselves in order to maintain institutional life, in short, to keep at least some sanctuaries open. The options were limited. Observers who have not lived in the area have great difficulty, even to the present, in appraising the compromises which clergy felt obliged to make with communist officials. Still, the very existence of functioning churches was in itself a protest against totalitarian atheism. Prayer and worship were the one area of life which the communists could not subvert and control fully.

Amid reopened as well as newly constructed sanctuaries, priests have become busy with a flood of baptisms, too many of which, they note, are without adequate catechesis and teaching. Day to day institutional and pastoral life is being renewed. But only a minority of the population is related to institutional religion in any significant way in Russia (apart from baptism), although it has wide popular appeal. Whereas in 1988 a Soviet-American survey showed that only 10% of the population believed in God, five years later the estimated figure was over 40%.[5] Although there has been some recent decline in the number of professed believers from 27% to 24% in Moscow according to the study, throughout the country there is still evidence of what has been described as a "religious boom."

Nauka i religija (Science and Religion), the formerly atheist magazine, reports a survey by S. B. Filatov and L. M. Worontschova from the analytic center of the Russian Academy of Science, with the following results: 41% of the population say that they believe in God as compared with 29% in 1990.[6] The sources of the new conviction are listed as 29% from television, newspapers and magazines, 31% from literature, 21% from Scripture and other religious literature, 21% from relatives and friends, and 9% from the church, preaching and conversation with clergy. It is clear that leading personalities have been influential. Fifteen percent of those queried mentioned Solzhenitsyn, 14% the literature and art specialist of the Academy of Science, D. Ligachev, 13% the physician and heart specialist, N. Amosov, 11% the television journalist, V. Molchanov, 10% Patriarch Aleksi II. The pop singer A. Pugatcheva, General Gromov, and the rock singer B. Grebenchikov were included in the list.

The Orthodox Historical Legacy

The Orthodox Church historically played a highly important role in creating community in the past, for example during the more than two centuries of Mongul rule. A Russian is never more himself than when he is in his own national church, it is said. Nation building was a building of faith. With respect to the future of religion, the question is asked: Is Orthodoxy the answer? Can it rechristianize the land? What should be the role of past traditions in the new context of freedom for religion and democracy? A thousand years of Christian history loom large in the Russian outlook which is so powerfully determined by tradition to the present. The communists tried to destroy the past and were unsuccessful. To affirm the Russian past is to affirm Eastern Orthodoxy, its apologists claim. The country had only very brief periods of accepted religious pluralism and tolerance at the beginning of both the nineteenth and twentieth centuries. Actually, Church leaders were meeting in a reform council in St. Petersburg at the very time that the communists seized power. Today, as our authors report, there are manifold forces seeking to renew their community's life in order to fill the ideological vacuum left from the demise of dialectical materialism.

Not surprisingly, the appeal of a nihilistic consumer oriented mass culture being imported from the United States and Western Europe is seen as a negative threat to spiritual life. The new capitalist forms of life entering the country from the West are doing little to help the masses economically or morally; their standard of living continues to decline. Politically liberal democrats fear that the country could turn even more sharply to the right—to the brown and to the red—led by nationalists and former communists, if the economic situation degenerates still further. Paradoxically, although Marxism's claim of economic determinism has been rejected, the future depends significantly on economic reorganization and renewal.

The Orthodox claim for hegemony in the present situation is a simple one: the thousand year history of Christianity, half of it before the birth of Protestantism, is one that ought not to be undervalued. They, more than any other party, have indigenous Russian resources for the revival of religion.[7] The traditional story recounts how Prince Vladimir, the ruler in Kiev, deliberately chose Orthodoxy over Roman Catholicism and Islam after his legates had been dispatched to visit centers of all three religions. It was the worship in Saint Sophia Church in Constantinople which impressed them most of all. Deciding to accept Orthodox Christianity, the ruler and his court were baptized in the Dnieper River at Kiev in 988, and his kingdom became linked with Byzantium. The new tie brought learning and culture as well as religion, and Christianity was welcomed as a civilizing force.

Orthodoxy remained dominant even when Kiev's rule collapsed, overwhelmed by Muslim armies who invaded from the East. The Church, more than any other factor, had a unique role in preserving Russian identity in the period of Tartar occupation. Under Muslim conquest, its bishops still were allowed significant autonomy to rule over the Russian Christian community. Liberated from foreign invader shortly before the discovery of America, the Tsarist state and the Orthodox Church were linked in a union of throne and altar until 1917. At least since the time of Peter the Great, this meant control of the church by the state, one which has continued in a singularly perverse way under the communists. As Father Ivanov points out in his chapter in this book, Orthodox leadership now seeks to find freedom from this kind of polity while at the same time retaining a significant social role in culture.

This much can be said in defense of such a revised polity in an inclusive territorial church. Led by the Patriarch, it is the one great national institution with enough spiritual vitality that it could yet inspire a new revived Russian culture, reinvigorating ethical sensitivity. Russian Orthodoxy belongs to the inclusive "church type," to use the terminology of the German historian of social ethics, Ernst Troeltsch. On principle, it is distinguished from the more exclusive "sect type" orientation, the so-called gathered church of Protestant evangelicals.[8] Orthodoxy seeks to minister to the whole Russian people and not just to a limited group of believers. Whereas its leaders earlier cooperated with Protestants like Billy Graham, they are now more defensive, opposing sectarian proselytizing of Orthodox Christians (which they distinguish from preaching and conversion of unbelievers).

Renewed Nationalism

Today, it would be naive to suppose that the Russian Orthodox hierarchy and clergy have become fully democratic or progressive in the present period of change. Communist officials made deliberate efforts to keep both clergy and believers isolated from the modern world, confining practice to the sanctuary. In the early period of their reign, the communists favored the so-called "Living Church" in an effort to displace the Patriarchate. The attempt failed as believers looked to the Orthodox hierarchy for leadership. Of course, there is a wide spectrum of beliefs, from moderate to conservative in the church hierarchy. In the post-communist period, both clergy and laity include significant groups of right wing and Panslavophile sympathizers.

Political democracy and pluralism premise not only individual freedom of conscience, but the disestablishment of religion with a significantly secular area of public life in which citizenship is not determined by religious confession. Can the ideal of a free church in a free society be attained realistically? It is not yet fully clear how religious believers will react to the new democratic structures in which they live and work or what their long term role will be in the post-communist order. Within the churches themselves there is still isolation and defensiveness against modern culture, particularly as associated with the West. This much is evident: a belligerent nationalism preserved in a variety of ecclesiastical traditions mocks the universal and ethical teachings of Christianity.

For centuries there has been controversy between Westernizers and Slavophiles. The doctrine of Moscow as the Third Rome, developed by clerics following the fall of Constantinople in 1453, intensified the Orthodox rejection of Roman Catholicism as well as the Protestant Reformation. Russian messianism persisted into the communist era in secular guise. Now it has a renewed expression in reactionary nationalism. Unfortunately, the earlier ecumenical rapprochement that developed under persecution in the communist period has declined visibly. Right wing hierarchs such as Metropolitan Ioann of Leningrad, whose sermon is included in this book, reassert Russian nationalism, characteristically in dogmatic intolerance and anti-Semitism. Of course, ecclesiastical differences continue to have divisive power as linked to newly aroused nationalisms. To date, the violence has not been as great in Russia as in Yugoslavia, thanks to new secular democratic forces and leadership. To be sure, it has not been absent as in the 1989 People's Revolutions (with the exception of Romania) in the former satellites. Nationalism, the overwhelming force that broke up the Soviet Union, gave a sense of history as it helped to keep religious belief alive amid communist persecution. Now, it threatens to overwhelm democratic forces in alliance with "fundamentalist" right wing reaction and obscurantism. As will be noted in greater detail by our authors, nationalism has led to major Orthodox schism in the Ukraine in addition to intensifying Orthodox-Roman Catholic hostility. Greek rite Roman Catholics, the Uniates, who were forced by Stalin to merge with the Orthodox, now have been given their independence. Their struggle to recover church buildings has led at times even to physical violence. In Yugoslavia, although some few ecclesiastical leaders have worked for peace, the Orthodox and Roman Catholic Churches have contributed to division throughout the land and continue to be engaged on different sides in the civil war.

The Evangelical Influx

From the low church side, evangelicals are pressing in from the West and joining indigenous Protestant efforts at evangelization. Leaders like Billy Graham were already visiting the country and preaching on a joint platform with the Orthodox before the fall of communism. Now they are less welcome as the Orthodox Church seeks to preserve its jurisdiction. Will the Protestant model of Christianity become numerically important in Russia? The American Methodist theologian, Thomas Oden, after teaching in Moscow, expressed regret that there has been no major Protestant era or legacy in Russia.[9] He found a lack of orientation toward religious self-criticism and the sense of freedom which he hopes will develop in the future. However, it is not primarily Protestant theologians but activist evangelicals who are seeking to make converts. In the past, there have been a number of Protestant groups in the former USSR. Century old communities of Mennonites and Lutherans are largely made up of ethnic groups, primarily from earlier immigrations. They were tolerated as self-governing ethnic communities with their own distinctive traditions. Baptists, Pietists emphasizing freedom of conscience and the separation of church and state, entered the country only in the latter part of the last century.[10] Pentecostals are of even more recent origin, as their movement did not begin in the West until early in the twentieth century. Dissident sectarians like the Old Believers and later the Baptists, as the economist Alexander Zaichenko points out in his chapter in this book, often did very well in business in Tsarist times. But, of course, they did not develop an inclusive model for the society as Zaichenko seeks to do today.

Even in the communist era, Protestant agencies, generally with the cooperation of Orthodox Christians, worked to make Bibles available in Russia. Now Bibles are being supplied in the millions along with other religious literature, after the fall of communism. Orthodox leaders have pressed the government to restrict entrance visas given to religionists from abroad. Billy Graham held an evangelistic campaign in Moscow, and worship services from the Crystal Cathedral in Garden Grove, California are carried in the country by television. How much such American Protestant activity will achieve lasting influence, how much it will run into the barriers of nationalist sentiment, is not clear. In June of 1993 the Russian Parliament passed a new law regulating the freedom of religious confessions.[11] Mainline and Neo-Protestant indigenous bodies, with the support of human rights advocates abroad, sent formal letters of protest to President Yeltsin about the proposed legislation. Yeltsin refused to sign it, and when he shut down the Parliament by force, the legislation was no longer on the table. In all probability, it will be revived.

The proposed legislation was said to reflect the wishes of Patriarch Aleksi II. The spokesman for it in the Parliament was the conservative Russian Orthodox priest, Wjatscheslav Polosin. Polosin himself charged that the White Brotherhood which prophesied the end of the world on November 24, 1993 is sponsored from abroad; actually, it is an indigenous Orthodox heresy. The proposed legislation divided religious organizations into two groups, foreign agencies and indigenous ones. Organizations from abroad which have been in Russia before the new law goes into effect would be less restricted than ones which, subsequent to its enactment, seek to enter the country. Ominous was the fact that Gleb Yukunin, a long imprisoned dissident and an Orthodox priest who served as a liberal member in the Russian Parliament, has questioned its wisdom. The law was written in such a way that it could have been enforced loosely or more strictly.

Religion and Culture

It remains to be seen how the different religious parties, including Jews, Muslims, Buddhists and humanists as well as a variety of Christians, will relate to society as well as to each other in the future. It is important in the new political and cultural situation that religious symbols should be revitalized but not absolutized in a kind of integralist fundamentalism. The folk piety which significantly helped to sustain religion in Russia under communism now lives on amid a more literate, educated populace than when communism came to power. At the same time, religious groups all are free to educate openly as they were not before. This much is clear: a simplistic return to the past will prove unproductive as much as sectarian exclusivism and social irresponsibility.[12]

Renewed interest in religious art, architecture, and literature as part of national history had intensified even before the change of government policy. Church buildings, which the communists defaced and destroyed by the thousands, are being reconstructed and new ones built. Not just the structure of Orthodox church buildings but their iconography most of all makes clear how much Christians in the Eastern tradition live out of symbolism and story. Of course, Muslim symbolism is nonpictorial. From the Orthodox Christian point of view, Western theology is often intellectually overdefined. In reply, Protestants and Roman Catholics ask at what point cultus and symbol require critical reflection and analysis. This, indeed, is the question of the Enlightenment which was not raised often enough in the pre- communist period in Eastern Europe. Moreover, whereas the Roman Catholic Church gave up its prohibition of mass in the vernacular at the Second Vatican Council, celebration of the Russian Orthodox liturgy continues in Old Slavic.

The tasks of reconstruction are enormous. Not only must church leaders give attention to overcoming the legacy of past compromises made in collaboration with old communist regimes. At the same time, they confront new urgent questions about anti-Semitism and the relations between world religions, Christianity and Islam for example, as well as between the Eastern and Western churches. Obviously there is no one simple pattern in Eastern Europe, but causes and movements in the new setting. Political and ecclesiastical boundaries were determined earlier by the borders between language groups and nations as well as by political circumstances. Tragically, the sanctioning of old conflicts by a continuing sense of the sacred makes them even more fateful today. To cite the example of the former Yugoslavia, the nation was located in the border area between the Latin and Greek churches, a division which had made for century long conflicts. Religion's role, although often disappointing, remains crucial, Paul Mojzes argues in his chapter in this book. In religion as in other concerns, lasting solutions must come significantly from within the area and its constituencies, he believes.

The Threat of Restorationism

Not surprisingly, a restorationist vision favoring traditionalism and nationalism lives on in the monarchism which is not limited to Russia alone. It has advocates in the former Yugoslavia and Romania. A Dutch scholar who converted to Orthodox Christianity and studied at the Theological Academy in St. Petersburg recently suggested that the democratic orientation of President Yeltsin's reforms should be regarded positively, but only as a preparation for the restoration of tsardom.[13] Although restorationism may seem to solve political and religious problems to such partisans, it creates many others.

Development of a fundamentalist Eurasian ideology in Russia today under the leadership of a new right continues earlier Panslavophile developments in a reactionary pattern.[14] Such anti-Western, anti-American, and anti-Semitic ideas are being disseminated popularly in a variety of publications and have a high priority in discussions among intellectuals since the demise of the Russian Empire. In fact, a number of the conspirators who attempted a coup against Gorbachev's rule espoused this ideology which is highly mythical in its orientation. Opposition is directed not only against perestroika and Gorbachev's version of a common European house which was essentially a strategy of Westernization, but against all liberalism and democracy.

Russian nationalism and the longer Russian past, of course, are closely linked in the new Eurasian ideology. In terms of history, it even looks positively on the Tartar dominated era and Muslim fundamentalism in its antisecular and anti-Western articulation. The revolution of 1917 as well as the recent overthrow of the Soviet system are attributed to an international conspiracy: they resulted from a Jewish-Masonic plot. In this perspective, the recent demise of the former Soviet Union is viewed as a catastrophe of world political dimensions, not so much because of the end of communism, but the end of empire seen in geographical terms. Actually, the movement is oriented more on geography than on blood ties of Russian nationality alone. Not surprisingly the outlook first was articulated in a variety of emigré settings in Western Europe before the Second World War.

To date, proponents of the Eurasian ideology have not captured the leadership of the Russian Orthodox Church as represented by Patriarch Aleksi II who seeks to encourage a milder form of nationalism. But popularly it does give grass roots support to the anti-Semitism which earlier came down "from above" and now has grown up "from below" as a popular explanation for the collapse of the Soviet Union. Not surprisingly, priority is given to community rather than individual conscience. The Eurasian ideology provides an explanation, albeit a very mythical one, for the course of events in the area in the last half of this century. Basic is the concept of a European-Asian cultural realm, one which long has been threatened on both sides by East and West. The Panslavophile mythos is not new, but only takes new forms and its exponents are paranoid about new conspiracies. Universal and natural law as well as the secularity of the Enlightenment as propagated in the West are condemned.

Non-Christian Religions

The former Soviet Union had over fifty million Muslims living within its borders. With the collapse of the USSR, the future of Muslim-Christian relations has become of growing importance, politically as well as religiously.[15] Today, republics with major Islamic populations are independent states, still seeking new identities. Will traditionalism turn into fundamentalism or will there be a neutral area for politics in public life? Recently there has been an attempt to establish Buddhism exclusively under state rule in Mongolia. How much will earlier models of intolerance, now joined to nationalism be transcended? This is a question for the Christians as much as for Muslims and Buddhists. Christian-Muslim warfare is long-standing in the Armenia-Azerbijan area. In Yugoslavia today, Islam is attacked vehemently by Serbian "Orthodox" nationalists.

In the situation now free from communist repression, Orthodox-Jewish relations have reached a crucial stage. Today, the paranoia which led to murderous pogroms by the Cossacks under the Tsars has not relented. A nine or ten year old pupil in a newly opened Moscow Sunday School asked by a Western visitor what she thought about the Jews answered, "I hate them!" Asked if she had ever known a Jewish person individually, she replied, "No, I don't want to."[16] Jews now are blamed for the communist past on the premise that the majority of its revolutionaries were, as Karl Marx, of Jewish descent.

Actually, the presence of Jews is not even necessary for anti-Semitism to develop. Identification of Jews as a nationality was required in passports in the old USSR, and many citizens tried to hide their Jewish ancestry. Now this is no longer necessary, but communist propaganda has left its legacy. The tragic consequences of anti-Semitic hatred was evident in the brutal axe murder of Father Alexander Min', a brilliant Orthodox priest of Jewish descent, and one of the most promising theologians in all Orthodoxy. Min' was assaulted with an axe and killed as he went along the street on September 9, 1990. Patriarch Aleksi II has spoken out against anti-Semitism, citing Soloviev, Bulkagov and Berdyaev.[17] On the other side, Metropolitan Ioann of St. Petersburg has cited the "Protocols of the Elders of Zion" as authentic in a reactionary stance. Alleged to have originated in the first Zionist Conference held in Basil, Switzerland in 1897 and revealing a plot for Jewish world domination, the Protocols have in fact been proved to be a fraud. Surely a test of any authentic revival of Christianity will be whether it can avoid the aberrations of this part of the "Christian" past in the land.

Positively, synagogue as well as cultural Jewish cultural life is being revived with help from abroad; still, recovery is limited.[18] The large part of the Jewish population came into the Russian empire only with the annexation of Polish areas in the eighteenth century. Anti-Semitism with its pogroms was supported by the Tsarist state both indirectly and directly. Communism before perestroika repressed Jewish life and especially emphasized anti-Zionism. Stalin's last paranoia was directed against his Jewish doctors. It is a measure of the dangerous obscuratism which threatens that anti-Semitism should be at all debated in Russian Orthodox circles today and quotations from some Church Fathers cited in defense of intolerance. The Holocaust under Hitler made clear for all the world to see how devastatingly dangerous anti-Semitism remains to the present.

Conclusion

The outstanding danger is that an intolerant ideology, sanctioned by religious nationalism, could replace a simplistic atheistic one. This has taken place most of all during the post-communist era in Yugoslavia where inhumane, barbarian forces are practicing "ethnic cleansing." To the present, the situation in the former USSR has not degenerated as much, although there have been threatening conflicts sparked by religious nationalism and intolerance, notably between Azerbijan and Armenia. What seems most needed now is critical reappraisal of religious traditions in depth rather than any new encompassing ideology. Political democracy requires a significant secular area of non-confessional life in the new era. At the same time, religiously inspired critical judgments and respect for the dignity of fellow humans need to be expressed in actions and not just words.

Realistically, the religious situation is one in which there is a widespread interest in religion, but the degree of revival and conversion in the former communist realm is not yet clear. Faith questions can now be openly discussed and the impotence of the state sponsored anti-religious campaign has become evident. In Russia, throughout the nineteenth century, religion was judged to be obscurantist by a whole generation of skeptical and estranged intellectuals. When it came to power in an ethos of revolutionary utopianism, communism itself turned out to be anti-Enlightenment and totalitarian. Premising a naive materialism, Marxism dealt with questions about the relation of science and religion simplistically from the point of view of a dogmatic scientism. At the same time, throughout Eastern Europe there was not major popular acceptance of Enlightenment insights.

Now following its demise, the question of the relation between religion and civilization has taken a new and urgent turn. One must hope that the twenty-first century will be more humane than the present one with all of its totalitarianism, and that religion, now freed from persecution, will play a positive role. Will Orthodoxy open itself to the new spiritual movements in the society even when they are not within the bounds of the institutional church, or will it remain so concerned with the past that it will not be able to respond positively to the developing post-modern situation?

Notes

1.   George Weigel, *The Final Revolution: The Resistance Church and the Collapse of Communism* (New York: Oxford University Press, 1992).

2.   Jane Ellis, *The Russian Orthodox Church: A Contemporary History* (London: Routledge, 1986).

3.   Patrick Michel, ed., *Les Religions à l'Est* (Paris: Cerf, 1992), pp. 129-145.

4.   Niels C. Nielsen, Jr., *Solzhenitsyn's Religion* (Nashville: Nelson, 1975).

5.   *Informationsdienst Osteuropaeisches Christentum*, Vol. 5, No. 12-14/93, p. 15.

6.   Ibid.

7.   Cf. Walter Sawatsky's chapter in this book.

8.   Ernst Troeltsch, *Social Teachings of the Christian Churches* (1912).

9.   Thomas C. Oden, *The Living God* (San Francisco: Harper, 1987).

10.   J. J. Hebly, *Protestants in Russia*, tr. John Pott (Grand Rapids: Eerdmans, 1976).

11.   *Informationsdienst*, Vol. 5, No. 12-14/93, pp. 3-4, 36-48.

12.   Niels C. Nielsen, Jr., *Revolutions in Eastern Europe: The Religious Roots* (Maryknoll, N.Y.: Orbis, 1991), p. 67.

13.   Theo van der Voort in personal conversation with the author. Cf., Nielsen, *Revolutions*, p. 140.

14.   Karla Hielscher, "Die Eurasian-Ideologie, Geschichtsmythen der russischen 'Neuen Rechten'," *Glaube in der 2. Welt*, Vol. 21, No. 7-8, 1993, pp. 25-30.

15.   Cf., Peter Scholl-Latour, *Unter Kreuz und Knute, Russische Schicksalsstunden* (Munich: C. Bertelsmann, 1992), p. 58.

16.   Erich Bryner, "Dear Readers," *Glaube in der 2. Welt*, Vol. 21, No. 7-8 (1993), p. 2.

17.   Patriarch Aleksi, "Eure Propheten sind unsere Propheten," *Glaube in der 2. Welt*, Vol. 21, No. 7-8, 1993, pp. 40-41.

18.   Gerd Stricker, "Geschichte des Antisemitismus in Russland," *Glaube in der 2. Welt*, Vol. 21, No. 7-8 (1993), pp. 35-40.

1

Religion, Revolution, and Order in Russia

Dennis J. Dunn

When Vladimir had the East Slavic peoples baptized into the Orthodox Christian religion in 988, he provided a basis for a new order that slowly evolved on the Eurasian plain. Orthodoxy became the foundation for the states of Kievan Rus, Muscovy, and the Russian empire. The order that was fashioned was not a perfect order, but it was a society, on a rough and dangerous plain, where people could find, more often than not, a measure of justice, a framework for consistent morality, protection from invasion, a strong government, a viable economic system, a rich religious life, gifted artists and writers, support for the family as the basic unit of society, and, finally, the potential for evolving a society of law, limited government, and free inquiry. That the latter potential remained undeveloped, in contrast to Western Christian society, does not diminish Slavic Orthodoxy as a source of creativity, law, and responsible government. For a long stretch of history it was hamstrung by the tradition of caesaropapism. When it attempted to remove that yoke in the 17th century, the Tsar proved to be too powerful, and Peter the Great replaced the patriarch with a government office, the so-called Holy Synod. In addition, Orthodoxy had to contend against the legacy of Mongol despotism in the state of Muscovy and the culturally divisive and secularizing influence of Western political models and ideologies from as early as the seventeenth century, but especially during the eighteenth and nineteenth centuries.

The Tsars were interested in shackling the Church and society to strengthen their power. The importation of Western military technology, Prussian and Swedish government models, and French and German ideology was undertaken to enhance the absolutism and military prowess of the central government. The growing secularization of Russian society, which Western ideologies especially reinforced, soon created a rift between the religious masses and the intellectual elite, and, eventually, between the tsar and the intelligentsia. The Tsarist government led the secularizing drive, but seemingly was oblivious to the damage that secularization was doing to the concept of a religiously-sanctioned monarchy. Russia could have imported Western Christian ideas, which actually were at the root of Western society, but the history of ill-feeling between Western and Eastern Christianity and the disdain and abandonment of Western Christianity by many Western intellectuals precluded that possibility. Some Russian intellectuals, like Peter Chaadayev and Vladimir Soloviev, urged Russia to turn to Western Christianity, but most intellectuals were convinced that the putative utopia of secular Western ideologies was the only direction for Russia.

As Tsarist Russia pulled away from its religious roots and adopted Western secular ideologies and models, it increasingly found itself with a weakened system of order and civic cooperation. By the end of the 19th century Orthodoxy was still influential, but harmony and amity in Russian society was quickly dissipating. To be sure, Russian society was industrializing and, by the reign of Alexander II, initiating some fundamental reforms, but it was losing its social cohesion, sense of purpose, and shared hope in the future. Russian society increasingly saw class conflicts; social disruption and alienation; disunity; internecine violence; the waging of imperialist wars or policies against Turkey, Persia, Afghanistan, Poland, Japan, and China; and growing ideological movements that claimed to be scientific and progressive but were in fact quite dogmatic and fatuous.

In the wake of the triple defeats of the Crimean War of 1853-55, the Russo-Japanese War of 1904-05, and World War One, the Tsarist government cracked and eventually fell. It had brought on its own destruction in part through its neglect of the religious base and unwillingness to allow the religious institutions to evolve to reform the social order. It consistently showed poor judgment in pursuing war, blocking land reform, and crippling political change. Ironically, the Tsarist government's move away from Orthodoxy brought on disorder that created opportunities for a reformed Christian order. The Orthodox reformers included Vladimir Soloviev, Nicholas Berdyaev, Sergei Bulgakov, and Sergei Frank who found in Christian teaching the basis for a new order built around human freedom. Fr. George Gapon, furthermore, found in Orthodoxy a social program that addressed the needs of workers and peasants.

The weakened condition of the Tsarist state, however, was an opportunity not only for Christian reformers, but also for the radical ideologists who had become so commonplace by the turn of the century. In fact, the secularizing ideologies from the West had conditioned the Russian intelligentsia to favor a non-religious order, indeed, an antireligious order. In truth, many intellectuals blamed Orthodoxy in part for the failures of the Tsarist government. Under those circumstances, it proved to be quite impossible for Orthodox and other religious reformers to provide a framework for a new order. Instead, the day belonged to the ideologists. The violence and strain associated with World War One shattered the already vacuous Tsarist order, stymied the religious reformers, and opened the door to the most extreme ideological movement on the Russian scene, the Communist party of Lenin. Instead of a government that promoted and protected human freedom and creativity, the people of Tsarist Russia had a Marxist-Leninist government imposed on them. It was a cataclysmal change from the waning religiously-based order of Orthodox Russia.

Once the Communists were in power, they implemented two parallel and mutually supportive policies: they continued the Tsarist policy of separating the people from their religious roots, and, secondly, they forcibly tried to remake society to conform to their *a priori* ideological convictions. The consequences of these policies were far-reaching. Communist society came to resemble Tsarist society in its yoking of the peasantry and its drive toward centralization, although the new government was no longer hampered by traditional morality as it went about the process of social engineering. Second, a massive persecution of religion was organized. The Communists acted largely because religion, although weakened greatly by the Tsarist government, was still a powerful force among the people and thus a block to the development of an ideological society that wanted no transcendent power to which individual conscience could appeal to justify deviation from the Party's totalitarian rule. In 1928-29, with the beginning of the First Five Year Plan and the policies of collectivization and industrialization, all religions were violently persecuted. No church, temple, or mosque was left untouched. Third, the persecution and growing secularization of Soviet society led directly to violence, class hatred, paranoia, private and public arrogance and selfishness, irrationality, pessimism, civic collapse, and imperialist policies in Asia and Europe. The Leninist-Stalinist society of the 1920s and 1930s was a mindless orgy of brutality where the best and brightest people perished in a river of blood. The state succeeded in industrializing quickly some sectors of the economy only by foolishly wasting the rich resources of the land and talents of the people. It expanded its influence in Mongolia, China, and Eastern Europe only by expending its treasure and allying itself with its mortal enemy, Nazi Germany. It fashioned an order that appeared strong to the casual outside observer, but was feeding on itself, bringing on weakness and eventual disorder. Only massive force and terror kept Soviet society from flying apart, and under those conditions there was little room for human productivity, creativity, and freedom.

The attack against religion in the 1930s was uncommonly brutal. One first-rate observer at the time, William Henry Chamberlain, the *Christian Science Monitor* correspondent, was shocked at the intensity and vulgarity of the persecution. He concluded that religion in Soviet Russia was quickly being exterminated.[1] The Communists, however, were not satisfied with the results. They were surprised during the 1937 census when some 50 million Soviet citizens, despite years of antireligious propaganda, persecution, and the threat of reprisal and intimidation, announced that they were still believers.[2] Nadezha Krupskaya, Lenin's widow, warned then that religion was still a profound force which was not withering away any too quickly.[3] As a result, the Communists increased their antireligious effort, especially during their alliance from 1939 to 1941 with the other major ideological state, Nazi Germany.

Despite the Communist onslaught, religious belief and institutions persisted. They survived primarily among women and old people, where they were a significant force because of tradition and the attractiveness of religiously-based morality as compared to the politically-based morality of Communism. When the Soviet Union and Nazi Germany went to war, religion obtained a breathing space from persecution and further strengthened its position. The Communists, faced with a direct threat to their regime, looked for any friend or ally. The Russian Orthodox Church was especially cultivated, because it proved itself to be a valuable ally against the Nazis. Stalin allowed the Russian Orthodox Church to elect a Patriarch — Sergei — in 1943 and to start publishing again the *Journal of the Russian Patriarchate*. The Bolsheviks were impressed with the Orthodox Church for four reasons. When the Germans occupied Ukraine and Belorussia, they allowed the churches to be opened, and the people flocked to them. It was clear that religion had not lost much of its appeal despite decades of Communist persecution, propaganda, and indoctrination. Secondly, when the Nazis attacked, the Church leaders called upon the people to defend Holy Russia and the Soviet government, and the people responded. It was obvious that Orthodoxy was a deep-seated force among the Russian people. Thirdly, believers tended to be honest, hard-working, self-disciplined, and responsible, in other words, reliable and valuable citizens. It was foolish to attack them any time, but especially during a time of national crisis. Finally, the Soviet Union's Western Allies, the United States and England, were concerned about religious freedom in the USSR. It was clear that a tolerant religious policy could pay dividends for the Soviets in the West.

As for other religions, their position depended upon Moscow's internal and external policy needs. Jews continued to be hampered, although their treatment improved because they were seen as useful allies against the Nazis. However, Stalin's anti-Semitism worked against this trend. Catholics, not a significant numerical group after the USSR lost the three

Baltic States and western Ukraine, were attacked less than before, and the Kremlin made some marginal efforts to establish a modus vivendi with the Vatican for whatever benefit it would bring either from Moscow's Western Allies or from the Catholic populations of Eastern Europe. The Muslims also obtained a temporary reprieve from Moscow primarily because it was preoccupied with the German threat and religious persecution was a low priority. All the different religious groups did contribute to the Soviet Union's war effort, and the Soviet government realized the counterproductiveness of pursuing antireligious policies while the country was fighting for its life.

After the war and into the 1950s the Soviet government continued with its expedient approach, which meant a particular religion's status depended upon its usefulness to Soviet domestic and foreign policy. The Orthodox Church was tolerated because of its wartime effort, its usefulness in support of Soviet foreign policy, especially peace campaigns, and its leadership's willingness to support Soviet policies, including Soviet antireligious policy. Muslims were publicly put up with because of benefits that such a policy provided the USSR in the Muslim world, but privately the government worked to secularize Muslim life. Jews, for their part, were persecuted because of traditional anti-Semitism and Soviet suspicion of Israel's ability to influence Soviet Jews. Catholics were persecuted vigorously, too. The Ukrainian Uniate Church in Galicia and Transcarpathia was forced to join the Russian Orthodox Church. The Latin Catholic Church in Lithuania, Latvia, and Estonia had some of its bishops and priests arrested. Catholic Churches throughout Soviet-controlled Eastern Europe were also generally persecuted as Moscow attempted in the late 1940s and early 1950s to force the satellites to adopt the Soviet model. Protestant sects were also attacked, and certain groups, like the Pentecostals, Seventh Day Adventists, Initiativniki Baptists, and Jehovah's Witnesses were outlawed.

In short, the general approach of the Soviet government toward religion from 1941 through most of the 1950s was ambivalent — some religions were tolerated and others were persecuted. The inconsistent approach ended in late 1958 when the Soviet government launched a massive antireligious campaign, including arresting clergy, imprisoning believers, and closing churches.[4] The campaign was started by Khrushchev, and it was continued, with varying degrees of intensity, by Brezhnev, Andropov, Chernenko, and Gorbachev. The post-Khrushchev campaign was not as intense or heavy-handed as Khrushchev's persecution, but it was still persistent and only really waned on the eve of the celebration of the millennium of the Christianization of the East Slavs in 1988.[5] One of the most heinous aspects of this persecution was the placing of police agents and collaborators in positions of religious responsibility in all of the major religions of the Soviet Empire, but especially in the Orthodox Church.[6]

The motivation for this onslaught was undoubtedly linked to religion's growth, and the challenge which that expansion implied. Religion grew for two reasons. The inconsistency of the Communist persecution enabled religion to survive and gain a foothold. Secondly, the continuing failure of ideological policies applied to the social, political, and economic order made religion attractive as an alternative source of order. The Communists tried to cultivate deserts, reverse rivers, maintain a huge military backed by heavy industry, change human nature, establish imperialist bases around the world, make Stalinists popular, increase nuclear weapons while avoiding nuclear war, challenge yet coexist with capitalists, and control heretical Communists, especially Chinese deviationists. Violence and terror, although tempered by Stalin's successors, permeated the social fabric. The Communist policies were incredibly expensive, wasteful, and consistently unsuccessful. "Super" status was achieved as a military and space power, but the society could not feed itself and the standard of living remained low. Disillusionment and cynicism sprouted among the people, and arrogance and selfishness among the Communist elite. In the four decades following the end of World War Two, the Communists maintained the system by milking the resources of Eastern Europe, tightening the belts of the Soviet citizenry, using up the rich natural resources of the Eurasian plain, especially the oil and gold, building a huge espionage network to ferret out technical and security information abroad, and obtaining occasional subsidies from the capitalists who were mystified by the ideological gyrations of the Kremlin. The foreign policy of expansion and the domestic policy of censorship and isolation kept the world in a fog about the true weakness of the Soviet Union, that it was essentially a sprawling empire, held together by force but otherwise lacking any tolerable system of cooperation and order. It was an undiagnosed sickman.

The Soviet state's weakness was an opportunity for religion. As the trauma of Stalinism and World War Two abated and disillusionment with Communism set in, religion stood ready to offer itself as a basis for a new order, and it soon found supporters from among two groups that the Communists thought were firmly in their camp or under their control: intellectuals and nationalists.

The intellectuals were attracted to religion after the Soviet government admitted the bankruptcy of Communist ideology by trying to blame Stalin for the corruption, crime, terror, and dismal standard of living that characterized postwar Soviet society. Many intellectuals turned to religion as a legal or desirable alternative to Marxism-Leninism.[7] Most were interested in religion because it spoke to private conscience, fed the human longing for immortality, and clearly articulated a norm for what men and women ought to be. The Communists defined a good person in terms of the person's duty to the party and state. Such an arbitrary and unpredictable standard for goodness was unsatisfying. Religion provided an objective basis for morality and, ultimately, a persuasive justification for sacrificing individual interest to the commonweal. To minds like that of Alexander Solzhenitsyn, religion appeared to be the sine qua non of the social order.

The nationalists looked upon religion as a factor in national identity and a legal, if persecuted, institutional support for a nationalist movement. When the Soviet government encouraged nationalist feelings in the Communist republics of the Soviet Union and Eastern Europe, even to the point of recommending Tito as a possible model, in order to expand the Communist base of power beyond naked force, it simultaneously, although unintentionally, stimulated deep religious feelings. There is no essential link between religion and nationalism, but because of historical conditions nationalism and religion in Russia and Eastern Europe, unlike Western Europe, were indissolubly intertwined.[8] Religious-nationalist forces emerged in Russia, Poland, Hungary, Lithuania, Ukraine, Georgia, Armenia, and, eventually, Czechoslovakia. The Catholic Church was particularly active in Lithuania, Ukraine, and Poland. Islamic nationalist movements stirred, too, in Soviet Central Asia.[9] Religion proved to be more substantive as a ethno-national force than Marxism-Leninism was as a politically unifying force. The Communists had attempted to create a new "Soviet man," but no such person appeared, and religion reappeared after the black night of Stalinism as a mark of distinction among the myriad peoples of the Soviet Union.

The new antireligious campaign that started with Khrushchev and persisted into the Gorbachev era failed dismally, like so many other Communist policies. Religion grew even stronger in the 1960s, 1970s, and 1980s. Religious-Nationalist samizdat publications appeared like Ukraine's *The Chronicle of Current Events*, which was published for the first time in 1968, and *The Chronicle of the Catholic Church in Lithuania*, which was produced for the first time in 1972. The Soviet government tried to suppress these publications, but it could not stop them. Believers in both Eastern Europe and the Soviet Union organized commissions based upon basket three of the Helsinki Accord signed in 1975 and demanded that the Communists allow religious freedom.[10] Intellectuals, nationalists, students, workers, and farmers all demonstrated a heightened interest in religion. The Russian Nobel prize winner for literature, Alexander Solzhenitsyn, openly confessed his faith and denounced the Orthodox hierarchy for not taking a firm stand against the Communist regime. Despite massive force the Kremlin could not solve the religious conundrum.[11]

The religious challenge grew geometrically in the Soviet Union and Eastern Europe in the 1970s. It reached a climax in 1978 when Karol Wojtyla, the Polish bishop of Cracow, was elected Pope. His popularity throughout Eastern Europe, including Ukraine and Lithuania, shocked the Communists. His first visit to Poland in 1979 led to the creation of the Solidarity labor movement and saw over 20 million Catholics rally to his leadership. The Polish Pope shook the foundation of the Soviet empire and challenged the stability and legitimacy of the Communist rulers.[12] And he was not the only threat. The Ayatollah Khomeini, who came to power in Shi'ite Iran a few months after the Pope's election, started a fundamentalist Islamic movement that stirred the 50 million Muslims of Soviet Central Asia.

Solzhenitsyn, John Paul II, and Khomeini symbolized the profound religious challenge confronting a Soviet empire that grew weaker daily. Apathy; despair; class and nationalist hatreds; lack of investment in infrastructure and consumer industries; inefficient agriculture; unproductive labor; stifling bureaucracy; imperialist movements in Afghanistan, Nicaragua, Vietnam, Angola, and elsewhere; an arms race; and disruptions in Eastern Europe sapped the strength of the Soviet Union. The Kremlin developed a siege mentality and tried to hang on, supporting the status quo, but moving closer to collapse. It dealt with the symbols of religious resistance in heavy-handed fashion. It expelled Solzhenitsyn from Soviet Russia in February 1974. It attempted to contain Islamic fundamentalism by invading Afghanistan in December 1979. Finally, it orchestrated, many observers believe, the assassination attempt against John Paul II in 1981.

Although the Communists tried to eradicate the religious challenge through brute force, they apparently never grasped the nature of the religious protest. As Marxist-Leninists they assumed the crisis in the Soviet Union was economic and could be solved by economic means. Shortly after Mikhail Gorbachev came to power in 1985, he announced that he was going to halt the decay and decline of Soviet society through the new policies of glasnost' and perestroika. Glasnost aimed to liberalize Communist society in order to obtain some popular backing in the Soviet Union and the West for the real solution, the policy of perestroika. The latter policy sought to alter the structure of the Soviet Union, especially the economic structure without altering the Communist Party's hold on power. It proved to be a series of half-measures and lectures.[13] It did not encourage the people to cooperate, to work harder, or to sacrifice for the public good. The Soviet Union slipped further into turmoil and confusion everyday. As far as religion was concerned, Gorbachev, as mentioned, halted violent persecution shortly before the Christian millennium in 1988, but the Soviet system remained essentially antireligious.[14] The Soviet leadership seemingly did not consider the possibility that the basis for true reform might start with the spirit of man, that social harmony and cooperation might have to precede economic and political improvement.

The Soviet Union has crumbled. It is impossible to describe with certainty the kind of order that will eventually fill the vacuum of the collapsed Communist empire. It is possible that some of the republics will import new secularizing ideologies from the West, possibly liberalism, capitalism, or "democratism." If they do try to build a new social order upon such "isms," the republican governments will likely discover that they will prove to be a weak foundation, much as Marxism had been. The new Commonwealth of independent States that includes Russia, Ukraine, Belorussia, Kazakhstan, Kyrgystan, Tajikistan, Uzbekistan, Turkmenistan, Moldova, Armenia, and Azerbaijan (Georgia has not joined) was thrown together for immediate economic and security needs. Many of the members have stated that they are developing democracy and market economies, but there is no substantive evidence that such complex processes are underway or even possible and, further, if they were, that such developments would produce long-term harmony and cooperation. The CIS is an unwieldy arrangement not only because of the lack of a central government with all the attendant confusion that implies for monetary, foreign, economic, and military policy, but also because it constitutes a polyglot of ethnic and religious groups who have had a long history of enmity. Boris Yeltsin, a professed Orthodox believer, has bet upon the return of religious values to bring order to Russia. At his inauguration as Russian president he stressed that "the rebirth of the our state will be based on the spiritual emancipation of people, true freedom of conscience, and the complete rejection of any ideological diktat. Religion has a special place in this process."[15] Philip Dimitrov, Bulgaria's prime minister, echoed Yeltsin's view in early 1992 when he stressed that the former communist societies must develop a civil society based upon "shared moral values" because "the whole history of mankind has proven that without God, or a higher moral authority, the things most precious to us humans are often denied to us."[16]

Western specialists, like Jeffrey Sachs of Harvard University and Marshall Goldman of Wellesley College, recommend economic change as the precondition to order and the development of the market system.[17] Such advice, of course, is sound, but it puts the troika before the horse. Mikhail Gorbachev tried and now Boris Yeltsin is trying to initiate economic reform, but with only marginal success. Richard Pipes of Harvard University suggests political reform as the first step, the need to develop democratic parties to end the anarchy in Russia and the Commonwealth nations. He is puzzled by the lack of violence in the former Soviet republics in light of the anarchy, but explains it away by arguing that the people are too tired and they know that Communist violence achieved nothing.[18] The specialists appear less than perspicacious when their abstract formulas and theories crash against the daily reality of Russia and the former republics of the Soviet Union. Non-specialists, like George Bush and Bill Clinton, cannot be blamed for mouthing slogans and simple solutions to the complex problems of Russia and the former republics of the Soviet Union, because they are at the mercy of the specialists and the rigors of daily politics.

They can be held responsible, though, for foreign policy plans that countenance spending public resources on wishful thinking, vain hopes, and ill-considered advice.

What is missing in the foreign policy approach of the United States and the other great powers toward Russia and the CIS is the realization that religion, not economics and politics alone, is very significant and will likely be the basis for the new order that emerges in Russia, Eastern Europe, and across the Eurasian plain. Religion is popular everywhere, and it played a major role in bringing down the Communist order. Lithuania, Estonia, and Latvia — three predominantly Western Christian nations that achieved independence in September 1991 — seem to be fashioning a religiously-based order that could be a model for some of the other republics. Their constitutions stipulate religious freedom and true separation of church and state, and they are firmly based on Judeo-Christian principles. A religiously-based order, combined with religious freedom and toleration, would go far in helping the republics deal with a history of ethnic intolerance and, importantly, building a stable economic and political order.

If religion is the basis for the new order, the process will not be simple or without stress. Russia will reorganize, naturally, on the basis of Russian Orthodoxy, but it will, hopefully, be a reformed Orthodoxy that supports limited government, the rule of law, and religious freedom. Boris Yeltsin promises that kind of society, and young religious leaders in Russia, like Father Gleb Yakunin, are working for that kind of Orthodoxy.[19] However, many in leadership positions in the Russian Orthodox Church are tainted by collaboration or the suspicion of collaboration with the KGB. Father Georgi Edel'shtein believes that the Patriarchate of Moscow is Russia's last surviving Soviet institution.[20] On the first day of the attempted coup, August 19, 1991, Yeltsin appealed to the Russian Orthodox church for support. He explained the seriousness of the situation: "The tragic events of the past night oblige me to turn to you and to all believers in Russia." He urged the Patriarch to use his power and influence over believers to help the fledgling democratic movement survive this test. In doing so, Yeltsin mirrored the actions of previous Russian leaders in times of crisis by instinctively turning to the power of the church and its followers. Patriarch Aleksi II, however, waited until it was clear that the coup had failed before he anathematized all those who had helped organize the coup attempt. Only on August 21 did he throw the full weight of the church behind the Yeltsin government.[21] His action reflected his and some Orthodox bishops' uneasiness about the train of events and added evidence to the conviction among some young Russians that many of Orthodoxy's leaders are agents of the KGB.[22]

If Russia can overcome the problem of tainted clergy, Orthodoxy might very well serve as a basis for a reformed order. Anti-Semitism is growing in Russia today as ultra-nationalists movements like Pamyat' seek to find a scapegoat for Russia's mounting economic problems, but a reformed Orthodoxy could help counteract such tendencies. Orthodoxy, in fact, seems to hold out the best hope for stability and security among the Russians, and not only the Russians.

Belorussia also will probably follow the lead of the Russian republic and coalesce around Orthodoxy. However, Orthodoxy is extremely weak in Belorussia because of the brutality of the Communist persecution, and, for this reason, the burgeoning Catholic Church, estimated to have some 15% of the total population among its followers, might be an attractive partner for Orthodoxy. A Catholic-Orthodox order would affirm Belorussia's interest in the West and certainly propel her into a stronger relationship with Lithuania, Latvia, Poland, and Ukraine, if the latter builds religious bridges to the West.

Ukraine, with the bulk of its population divided among Ukrainian Autocephalous Orthodox, Russian Orthodox (now called Ukrainian Orthodox), and Ukrainian Catholics, is preparing a constitution that includes stringent provisions for the protection of religious freedom. There is also some support for a reunion of the Catholic and Orthodox Churches in Ukraine. Such a development is not likely, but the Ukrainian Catholic Church, which practices Orthodox liturgy but accepts the leadership of Rome, is the most dynamic religious force in Ukraine today and a reunion, even if only part of the Orthodox participate, would enhance Ukraine's cultural ties to the West. It would also undoubtedly help revitalize the anemic Christian Churches in the West where secularization has taken its toll and opened the door to a hydra of ideologies that in the not too distant past have included Fascism, Nazism, and Communism.

Armenia and Georgia will naturally organize themselves around their respective Orthodox faiths. They will probably seek a tie with Ukraine or Russia for that arrangement will provide them security against their Muslim neighbors and a convenient cultural link to the West. Moldova will attempt to build its order around Romanian Orthodoxy, but its large Ukrainian and Russian Orthodox population and its significant Catholic population might lead it to drift into Ukraine's orbit, particularly if Ukraine strengthens its cultural ties to the West and Romania continues with its pseudo-reformist government.

In time, all of the Orthodox republics might find a home in a larger Orthodox union that could stretch from the Sea of Okhotsk and the Baltic Sea to the Black Sea. A new Orthodox order might be organized that could loosely unite Russia, Belorussia, Ukraine, Georgia, Armenia, Romania, Bulgaria, Serbia, and Greece. Religion, seemingly, is the defining reality in Eastern Europe and Russia. We might witness the re-emergence of the Byzantine Orthodox Empire without an autocratic center, but with a European

Union-like unity to foster trade and cooperation. Kazakhstan, where there is a plurality of Slavs and a large Muslim population, will doubtless stay with Russia, because that arrangement is culturally suitable to the Slavs and apparently is the clearest path to modernization. A religiously-based order will, by necessity, encompass general principles that Muslims and Orthodox Christians can agree upon, but there will be ample occasion for misunderstanding in this religiously and ethnically mixed republic. Ultimately, it might be that the republic will be divided between Orthodox and Muslims. Any attempt to change the border now, however, will lead to violence, even though all admit that the Communists arbitrarily drew the borders.[23]

The predominantly Muslim republics of Kirghizia, Tajikistan, Uzbekistan, Turkmenistan, and Azerbaijan will organize around Islam. Eventually, some of them might come together to try to form an Islamic union that could include Afghanistan and, perhaps, Pakistan. Most of them, though, will seek some affiliation with Turkey, Iran, or Kazakhstan, depending on their religious orientation, ethnic affinity, and interest in obtaining access to Western technology. The Farsi-speaking Tajiks would logically form some kind of relationship with Iran, while the others, who are Turkic-speaking and mainly Sunnis, would seek out Turkey. The Azeris, of course, are mainly Shi'ites, but they seek Turkish support, because of their conflict with Armenia. Ethnic and religious violence, however, as demonstrated recently in the Nagorno-Karabakh region of Azerbaijan and the Fergana valley of Uzbekistan, is a stark fact of life in the Muslim republics that, perhaps, will drain away their energies and resources.[24] Nonetheless, Islam is a growing force, and it does not take much imagination to envision a revived Islamic order stretching from Central Asia to the Bosphorus and, possibly, to Albania's Adriatic coastline, an Islamic common market that will compete with the Orthodox community and the Catholic-Protestant community in western and central Europe. In the long view of history, religion has played both a constructive and destructive role in society. Within states based upon a dominant religion, there is order, but there is also the possibility of intolerance, and there is the clear record of how dogmatic and, in some instances, unscrupulous religious-political leaders have used or manipulated religion to divide people, rather than unite them. Religiously-based orders that adopt an intolerant attitude toward other religions can lead to violence and, perhaps, civil war. On balance, though, religion's positive contribution, particularly in helping to create a social framework of harmony and cooperation by which the commonweal can exist and function, can outweigh and modify its penchant for intolerance. It has been the foundation of order in societies stretching from ancient Israel to Kievan Rus to the United States today. It might very well be the key to the evolution of a stable order on the Eurasian plain. The key is to have leaders who encourage respect and cooperation and who administer justice in accordance with the moral principles that virtually all of the mainline religions embrace.

Notes

1.   William Henry Chamberlain, "Religions Face Common Foe in Russia," March 29, 1935, and "Communism: The Faith Without God," January 10, 1934, in *The Christian Science Monitor.* as reprinted in Richard E. Ralston, ed., intro. by Earl W. Foell, *Communism: Its Rise and Fall in the 20th Century* (Boston, MA: *The Christian Science Monitor*, 1991), pp. 21-28 and 63-66, respectively.

2.   Walter Kolarz, *Religion in the Soviet Union* (London: Macmillan & Co LTD, 1961), p. 14.

3.   *Izvestiia*, April 2, 1937.

4.   Dimitry Pospielovsky, *The Russian Church Under the Soviet Regime, 1917-1982*, 2 vols. (Crestwood, New York: St. Vladimir's Seminary Press, 1904), Vol. 2, pp. 327-471, passim; Michael Bourdeaux, *Patriarchs and Prophets* (London: Macmillan, 1970); Nikita Struve, *Christians in Contemporary Russia* (London: Harvill Press, 1967); Trevor Beeson, *Discretion and Valour* (London: Fontana Books, 1974); Eugene B. Shirley, Jr., and Michael Rowe, eds., *Candle in the Wind* (Washington, D.C.: Ethics and Public Policy Center, 1989), pp. 65-295.

5.   Shirley and Rowe, *Candle.*

6.   Lawrence Uzzell, "The KGB's Agents in Cassocks," in *The Christian Science Monitor*, April 20, 1992, p. 19.

7.   Pospielovsky, Russian Church, Vol. 2, pp. 350-51, 461; Dimitry V. Pospielovsky, *A History of Soviet Atheism in Theory and Practice, and the Believer*, Vol. 1: *Soviet Antireligious Campaigns and Persecutions* (New York: St. Martin's Press, 1988); Dimitry Pospielovsky, "Intelligentisa and Religion," in Dennis J. Dunn, ed., *Religion and Communist Society* (Berkeley , CA: Berkeley Slavic Specialties, 1903), pp. 11- 36.

8.   Dennis J. Dunn, "Religion and Nationalism in Eastern Europe," in Dennis J. Dunn, ed., *Religion and Nationalism in Eastern Europe and the Soviet Union* (Boulder: Lynne Reinner Publishers, 1987), pp. 1-13; Pedro Ramet, *The Politics of Religion in Eastern Europe and the USSR* (Bloomington: Indiana University Press, 1987); Pedro Ramet, *Religion and Nationalism in Soviet and East European Politics* (Durham, North Carolina: Duke University Press, revised and expanded edition, 1989).

9.   See Pedro Ramet, ed., *Catholicism and Politics in Communist Societies* (Durham, North Carolina: Duke University Press, 1990); Janice Broun, *Conscience and Captivity: Religion in Eastern Europe* (Washington, D.C.: Ethics and Public Policy Center, 1988); Marie Broxup, "Islam," in Shirley and Rowe,

Candle, pp. 209-13; Alexandre Bennigsen and Marie Broxup, *The Islamic Threat to the Soviet State* (New York: St. Martin's Press, 1983).

10. Hansjakob Stehle, *Eastern Politics of the Vatican. 1917-1979* (Athens: Ohio University Press, 1981), p. 373; Dennis J. Dunn, *Detente and Papal-Communist Relations, 1962-1978* (Boulder: CO: Westview Press. 1979): pp. 162, 165-66; Dennis J. Dunn, "Global Reach," *The Wilson Quarterly*, Vol. 6, Autumn 1982, p. 116; Broun, *Conscience and Captivity*, p. 12.

11. Pospielovsky, *Russian Church*, Vol. 2, pp. 457-61.

12. Broun, *Conscience and Captivity*, pp. 12, 87-88.

13. To be sure, Gorbachev's policies did lead to dramatic changes in Soviet domestic and foreign policy, especially in regard to censorship, Eastern Europe, and national liberation movements.

14. David E. Powell, "The Revival of Religion," in *Current History*, October 1991, p. 332.

15. *Izvestiia*, July 10, 1991.

16. *The Wall Street Journal*, March 23, 1992.

17. Marshall I. Goldman, "Kapital-ism," *World Monitor*, April 1992, pp. 29-33.

18. Richard Pipes, Speech entitled "Russia in Revolt" on National Public Radio: Commonwealth Club of California: San Francisco, January 29, 1992.

19. Powell, "Revival of Religion," p. 332; Uzzell, "The KGB's Agents," p. 19.

20. Uzzell, "The KGB's Agents," p. 19.

21. Oxana Antic, "Church Reaction to the Coup," *Report on the USSR*, Vol. 3: No. 38, September 20, 1991, RFE/RL Research.

22. Interviews by the author in Moscow, St. Petersburg, Novosibirsk, Irkutsk, Odessa, and Yalta, May 17-31 and July 4-5, 1992.

23. George Mirsky, "Central Asia's Emergence," *Current History* (October 1992), p. 336.

24. Adam Ulam, "Looking at the Past: The Unraveling of the Soviet Union," *Current History* (October 1992), p. 346; Mirksy, "Central Asia's Emergence," p. 336.

2

Church and Society in Russia Today

Vladimir Ivanov

1

Vladimir Soloviev foresaw the coming of an epoch of upheavals and disasters as early as the nineteenth century and, looking closer into the spiritual essence of Russia, posed this question:

"What kind of East do you wish to be—the Russia of Xerxes or Christ?"[1]

To be "the Russia of Xerxes" is to be a country where the totalitarian-atheistic ideology exercises unbridled rule, where the ruling Communist party turns the million-strong people into a powerless herd of slaves, where a bloody socialist experiment is carried out. To be "the Russia of Christ" is to be a country where the people not only confess the Gospel truth and perform particular traditional liturgical actions, but really live with Christ and in Christ, according to His commandment: "Abide in me, and I in you. As the branch cannot bear fruit of itself, except it abide in the vine; no more can ye, except ye abide in me" (John 15:4).

Almost one hundred years have elapsed since Vladimir Soloviev wrote his prophetic verses. During seventy of them, Russia seemed to irretrievably become a country of Xerxes where an anti-Christian state was built by ruthless and brutal means. Fedor Dostoevski's hope that the Russian "God-bearing" people were capable of renewing the world proved an ungrounded utopia.[2] Nevertheless, one cannot escape noticing the fact that the "kingdom of Xerxes" was possible only through a ruthless extermination of sixty million Russian people.

Now, this "kingdom" has collapsed before our own eyes. President

Yeltsin has solemnly declared the end of the "socialist experiment" in Russia.[3] Does it mean that Russia will become a "country of Christ"? What has actually happened—a change in power or the beginning of a new historical period?

Russian history bears a distinct mark of tragic upheavals whenever radical changes are introduced to impose a basically new type of civilization. Thus, the reign of Ivan the Terrible from 1533 to 1584 was marked with unprecedented atrocities and repressions, but all of these bloody excesses happened within the framework of an Orthodox monarchy, though one burdened with Tartar influences. Even the socio-political innovations made by Ivan IV were fully blended with Moscovy's traditional order. Peter I's reforms, however, present a completely different case as they led to a full transformation of Moscovy into a country imitating the Western European type of civilization.

In analyzing the events of 1991-1992, it is appropriate to ask: Which scenario, the first or the second, is being followed by Russia now? It is not clear yet. There is one opinion that what is happening in Russia is a radical modification of the old communist system. On the other hand, the developments can be conceived to be Russia's painful entry into a fundamentally new stage of its historical evolution which can be compared to Peter the Great's reforms. In the first days after the August failed coup, many were inclined to accept the second opinion. But in the course of time a more cautious, even pessimistic, assessment of the situation has begun to prevail.

In point of fact, however, the two tendencies, oddly overlapping, represent real forces in Russian reality and the outcome of their struggle has not yet been determined. If we put aside the variant of a restoration of the communist totalitarian system, even in a new and unexpected wrapping and coloring as well-known and predictable in its consequences for Russia, then it would be interesting to look into a possible development that can be described as a radical change in the type of Soviet civilization.

What alternatives to this civilization are there in today's Russia? Most popular are two of them, with possible modifications. The first vision of a new civilization is pinpointed as "returning to the civilized world." On the legal level at least, it means organizing life in keeping with existing international standards, in other words, establishing a law-governed democratic state. The market economy, as it exists in America and Western Europe, is considered difficult to achieve, but alone the necessary ideal for Russia. The dark side of this alternative is a mechanical transfer of Western patterns to Russian soil without reference to its peculiarities. At the same time there is a grave danger of possible criminalization of this process, as was pointed out by Alexander Solzhenitsyn already in 1991.[4] Another alternative is the creation of a "home" civilization based on returning to the origins of Russian life. In practice it would mean an attempt at the restoration of the Russian Empire as it was before 1917.

What is the attitude of the Russian Orthodox Church towards these alternatives? In the first place it is necessary to point out that we are not speaking here of the Church as the mysterious divine-human Body of Christ, but rather about various opinions of its ministers and members who present a chorus of often contradictory voices. But before describing the major tendencies in Russian theological thought today, it is necessary to have a clear idea of the ecclesio-social context in which these tendencies find nourishment for their development.

2

The first signs of "restructuring" in relations between the Russian Orthodox Church and the state appeared in 1988, with its pattern valid to this day. The Church has been given an opportunity for broadening, though slowly and gradually, the sphere of its work. The return of confiscated churches and monasteries to the Church has begun. With every year this process has gained momentum and become massive of late. It is impossible to give precise statistics since every day brings new information in this respect. In 1992 the Russian-Orthodox Church had over 15,000 churches, whereas before 1988 there were no more than 5,000. There are over 200 churches with communities in Moscow alone. Since most of them have been returned either destroyed or turned into warehouses, it is possible to celebrate only in 123 churches in the capital. Before 1988 there were only forty-five active churches there.

Among other important events in 1988 was the signing of an agreement to give the major churches in the Moscow Kremlin back to the Russian Orthodox Church. Equally impressive has been the reopening of monasteries. If before 1988 there were some twenty monasteries, by the end of 1992 over 160 of them had been reopened. As all new monasteries are returned in extremely miserable condition, even under the most favorable circumstances it will be many years before they are raised from ruins to become well-ordered cloisters. Almost all monasteries have as few as from two to five monks who are too busy with the restoration work to have time and strength for the spiritual and liturgical life.

Ordinary parishes have experienced similar difficulties. The number of clergy is too small for all these reopened and registered parishes. At the same time, growing financial difficulties because of inflation in Russia have rendered the Church too poor to renew the whole system of theological education and training. This system suffered a lethal blow when after the 1917 October revolution all the theological institutions were closed in a short period of time and all forms of religious instruction in school were prohibited by law.

This blow was fatal in its consequences for Russian culture also because development of theological, philosophical, and historical thought, so successfully nourished in the theological academies in St. Petersburg, Moscow, Kiev, and Kazan at the beginning of the twentieth century, was artificially checked. Stalin's permission to reopen a small number of theological educational institutions in 1943 brought about a quickly-developed system aimed at training parish priests, which suffered another heavy blow in the early 1960s under Khrushchev. In 1988 the Russian Orthodox Church had two theological academies, in Moscow/Zagorsk and Leningrad, and three seminaries, in Zagorsk, Leningrad and Odessa. The new situation after 1988 made it possible to open new theological educational institutions. In 1992 there were already three academies, ten seminaries and twenty theological colleges. All of them are threatened with closing now because of the general impoverishment which has also affected the Church.

In a situation of the shortage of food, clothing and medicine, not to speak about religious literature and all the rest that is necessary for the normal process of education, heroic efforts are being made to enable theological schools to survive this seemingly endless period. In this situation of survival when professors receive a salary that is just enough to buy food but not books, when students live under conditions that Western persons can hardly imagine, there are neither resources nor prospects for any fruitful development of the Russian theological tradition. In view of the dramatic shortage of clergy, all efforts are being made to uphold the tradition of theological education, but the situation is extremely unfavorable for preserving even what was available until recently.

The same difficulties are faced by the Church in the area of religious education in the schools. If since 1943 theological schools could at least drag on in some existence, even as they were limited and controlled by the atheistic state, religious education in the general schools was prohibited altogether. Therefore, when the new law on religion in 1990 allowed religious education and the priest became a desirable guest in school, the Church turned out to be practically unprepared for such a radical change, for quite understandable reasons though. To be effective, religious instruction depends on the personal abilities of a particular priest; but in most cases priests lack the necessary education and do not have the necessary textbooks or methodological guides. Recently an opportunity has appeared to establish private schools, including Orthodox gymnasia. The statement of the research department of the Brotherhood of the Radonezh Saints may be cited as typical in its analysis of the problems of Orthodox gymnasia:

> As regards Orthodox spirituality, the experience of the traditional classical education has proved inadequate, for, among other

reasons, it is the Russian intelligentsia's lack of faith that has resulted in the nation's present condition. And if we have realized the importance of creating Orthodox spirituality in a person, probably we should not pin hopes on the past experience.

True, the past has not produced a model which can be made the basis of contemporary religious education. Characteristically, this problem has always been one of the most difficult in Russia. The efforts of the first Kievan Princes to organize schools in the Byzantine fashion after the Baptism of Russia failed. As a result, the first theological schools in Moscovy emerged as late as the end of the seventeenth century. Following Peter the Great, the whole system of education in Russia was organized according to the Western European pattern without taking into account either Orthodox tradition or the Russian mentality. At the same time, among the positive traits in the Russian attitude toward education was distrust of purely rational methods of teaching or relying only on the ability for abstract judgement. The Russian people, often unconsciously, cherished the ideal of holistic knowledge, embracing the whole of man including his spiritual nature.

The Russians, however, have failed to implement this ideal in an accomplished system of education. Clearly, the present period of disintegration and chaos is not favorable for its development, although the need for it is urgent as never before in Russian history.

Of special importance after the disintegration of the USSR is the problem of religious education in the army; it is now possible in theory, but far from being realized in practice. In October 1992, Patriarch Aleksi II of Moscow and All Russia expressed a special concern over "demoralization and criminalization of the army, which is fraught with a terrible tragedy for our country."[5] His answer to the question asked by a correspondent of Krasnaya Zvezda, the army newspaper, on the possibility for the Church to help the crisis-stricken Russian Army spiritually deserves special attention as an expressive description of the situation:

> Before the 1917 revolution, every army unit had its own priest. Today, unfortunately, it is not feasible because of the lack of priests even at parishes.... I believe the time has come for us to think about a provisional system of pastoral service in the army until the permanent institution of army chaplains is established. This system could consist in appointing to each army unit a priest from the nearby parish for him to visit the servicemen, say, once a month.... Such visitations could be also helpful in emergency when there is a danger of clashes in a unit, or hostilities are possible, or a suicide is attempted.... But if spiritual assistance is used to impose par-

ticular convictions, the more so at the commander's order, then it will only lead to a greater lack of spirituality.

This problem also is evident in all other aspects of life in Russia.

It is clear for all those who have preserved a historical memory that the status of the Russian Orthodox Church as the state religion in the Russian Empire was more damaging than beneficial. The forced imposition of Christian ideals and norms of life led in the nineteenth and twentieth centuries to an extremely negative reaction and prepared the way for the explosive wave of militant atheism. Yet for those who are not capable of learning from this tragic experience, a dangerous illusion arises that it is possible to make Orthodoxy again a kind of state religion, to be imposed in an almost forced manner. Caught in the traditional idea of the Church as an obedient servant of the state, many political forces and parties are now trying to use it for their own purposes. This pressure on the Church comes especially tangibly from the so-called right-wing bloc—a wide range of political parties and movements, ranging from communists to extremely Orthodox nationalistic forces with a fascist tinge. Using the difficulties involved in changing from totalitarian socialism to democratic society, they put forward a "save Russia" slogan, implying a monstrous symbiosis of Soviet communism and medieval Orthodoxy.

As far as the democratic movements are concerned, they do not always have the proper understanding not only of church problems but also of Christian values which are often viewed as an impediment to building a market economy. Since the Church as compared to other forces and structures has preserved a certain stability, it is labelled "the last imperial structure" to be destroyed. In this situation the Russian Orthodox leadership has adopted a position expressed briefly by Patriarch Aleksi II as follows: "No political marriage for the Church." As a result the Church is accused of distancing itself from political reality and being unable to make a positive contribution to social development.

3

In addition to political problems, the Church is facing many internal ones resulting from the territorial disintegration of the Soviet empire and the emergence of a number of sovereign states. Many of these states are using nationalistic sentiment as a tool for breaking traditional ties. In this respect, the existence of a single Moscow Patriarchate is considered a serious obstacle. Certain forces, who themselves are alien to any religiosity, would like to have their own national churches under their control. The idea of Orthodoxy as a number of national state churches remains fairly widespread.

Vladimir Lossky, an outstanding Russian theologian, was right in observing in his time that for most of Catholic and Protestant authors who have expressed themselves on the subject, Orthodoxy is a federation of national Churches based on political principles, i.e., the Church of a state. It is only ignorance of the canonical foundations and history of the Church that can make them risk such generalizations. The idea that the unity of a national Church is based on political, ethnic or cultural principles is considered to be heresy in the Orthodox Church.[6]

At the same time, it should be admitted that many things in the life of Orthodox churches do look at first sight as though conditioned by the state and political factors. It is not surprising that this stereotype affects people's attitudes to the Church in a situation when new national states are emerging.

An especially strained situation developed by mid-1992 in the Ukraine, Moldavia, and the Baltic states. By 1993, the most dangerous moment seemed to have passed and the further course of events appears to be more predictable, though the conflicts are far from settled. The conflict in the Ukraine is a good illustration of how explosive political, national, and ecclesiastical interests can be when they overlap. The very logic of the development of this conflict is extremely instructive. As early as the perestroika years, the Ukraine's example showed that the historical Christian traditions alone cannot fill the spiritual and ideological vacuum caused by the collapse of the materialistic ideology which dominated people's consciousness, and even more, they can become a source of new confrontations.

The fact that such problems are not unique for one region is shown by the whole of European history saturated as it is with religious wars and persecutions. It is sufficient to remember that the Thirty Years War was caused by a conflict between Catholics and Protestants and the current confrontations in Ireland and Yugoslavia have been aggravated, unfortunately, by the religious-ecclesiastical factor as well. The danger of such conflicts in the near future was highlighted in a timely way by the Tenth Assembly of the Conference of European Churches (September 1992, Prague).

Before the August failed coup, the primary problem in church life in the Ukraine was confrontations between the Orthodox and the Uniates. The Uniate Church, which emerged in the Ukraine in the late sixteenth century, was among those banned by Stalin in the USSR. In 1946 a Council of the Uniate Church was held and declared, under great pressure from the state, its own incorporation into the Russian Orthodox Church. Nevertheless, the Uniates continued underground. In the perestroika years, the Uniate Church was registered again and officially recognized by the state. Serious and often bloody conflicts began about the division of church property. Having spread to the Western Ukraine, the conflict had a great impact on the ecumenical climate in Europe as a whole.

The conflict has brought relations between the Roman Catholic Church and the Russian Orthodox Church to the brink of rupture, though many steps had been taken in the 1970s toward unity. The Vatican's position in regard to Uniatism not only in the Ukraine but also in other regions resulted in a cooling of its relations with all other Orthodox Churches. After the August failed coup, another problem emerged in the Ukraine, connected with the demand by Metropolitan Filaret of Kiev and Galich that the Ukrainian Orthodox Church secede from the Moscow Patriarchate and be granted full independence, i.e., autocephaly. This demand was voiced in November 1992, at the height of the political friction between Russia and the Ukraine, which was threatening to grow into an armed conflict. To consider this demand, the Holy Synod of the Russian Orthodox Church convened a Bishops' Council (March 31-April 5, 1992) which decided that this problem should be referred to the next Local Council as required by canonical regulations. By that time it had become evident that the episcopate, clergy and laity were actually against immediate autocephaly. Since there are many Russians living in the Ukraine, and in some parts of the eastern Ukraine, they even comprise a majority of the population, any haste in granting autocephaly would provoke another series of divisions and schisms.

Without entering into the details of this conflict, I should mention that several church jurisdictions had been formed in the Ukraine by mid-1992. Metropolitan Filaret established a church of his own, which, especially in the beginning, enjoyed strong support from the state, so much so that the new head of the Ukrainian Church, which remained with the Moscow Patriarchate, could not even enter his residence and cathedral. A whole series of clashes between adherents of different jurisdictions began. At the same time, a positive tendency appeared when most believers refused to see the Church turned into an obedient tool of political forces and, while recognizing the need for Ukrainian ecclesiastical independence, did not want to gain it by force in the interests of certain non-church groups.

The fact that problems of jurisdiction do not necessarily bring schism and confrontation is illustrated by the situation in the Baltic states in 1992. In spite of the fact that they were not members of the CIS, the Orthodox dioceses there did not display any desire to be independent (autocephalous) Churches. At their diocesan meetings, they expressed the wish to stay in the jurisdiction of the Moscow Patriarchate.

Thus, in the situation of prevailing centrifugal tendencies manifested in very diverse spheres of life after the disintegration of the USSR, the Russian Orthodox Church has withstood the attack of forces seeking to plunge it into chaos. This does not at all mean that the future will not bring new trials, but the past year, perhaps for the first time in Russian history, has taught the Church to distinguish the sphere of its own life from the political interests of the state. During the decades of Soviet totalitarianism, the church leadership adhered to a certain strategy in the hope that compromises would ensure a continuation of liturgical and sacramental life. After the August coup, the Church has found itself in a situation where, pressed from all sides by political power groups, it should distance itself from power struggles and not let them draw it into deep chaos. This stance is consistent with the basically apolitical nature of the Russian people's psychology. Millions of people living in a situation of general impoverishment come to the Church not to make it into a sort of a political party club, but to find there strength for their souls.

4

What can the Church, exhausted as it is by the seventy year-long oppression and rendered bloodless by mass repressions and psychological terror, offer them? First of all, it offers that which it has managed to preserve intact against all odds, that is, the liturgical traditions coming from the Middle Ages. From the outset, the Russian Church has been predominantly liturgical in nature. Theological thought has been poorly developed. Independent philosophical search had begun only in the later nineteenth century, and soon it was violently interrupted by the October 1917 revolution. Most representatives of Russian theology and religious philosophy were either executed or exiled.

Today as their tradition no longer exists, we can only start to rediscover and study what was formerly banned or forgotten. This is the reason for the current lack of an intellectual theological potential in the Church which would enable it to overcome its artificially implanted conservative-defensive psychology. The Soviet regime was especially interested in making the Church a liturgical ghetto with worship conducted in a language unintelligible to the people as well as for the canonical norms to remain medieval, out of touch with the real needs and problems of contemporary life. On the other hand, the faithful themselves are accustomed to seeing in power an instrument of oppression and fear to lose what they have. Any reform, therefore, is regarded as an attempt to distort the tradition inherited from their ancestors.

Thus, the influences that come from two opposite sides have artificially imposed upon the Church a static and archaic image. Recently this archaism has become stronger as the people, exhausted as they are by today's reality, come to church to get rid of the pressures of everyday life for at least some hours. They like to hear the Holy Scripture read in Church Slavonic and to enjoy the sound of hymns. This situation causes a special concern. Christianity is the religion of the Logos incarnate. It is not alien to thought, but rather elevates thought to a principally new, inspired level. To deny Christianity a spiritual and cognitive clarity is to bring it to stagnation and provoke dangerous lapses of consciousness into the painful illusions described by the Orthodox ascetics as "enticement". Persons who are scared off by this archaic image of the Russian Church are tempted to break away from the thousand year-old tradition of spiritual life. There emerge sub-cultures devoid of any intrinsic bonds with the Russian tradition. As a result the Russian people, at the end of the twentieth century, find themselves in a very dangerous situation. The future will show whether they are able to withstand the trial which threatens to destroy the very foundations of Russian spiritual life.

Notes

1.   Cf. Vladimir Soloviev, *Le grande controverse et le politique chrétienne (Orient-Occident)*, (Paris: Aubier, 1953), pp. 51-55.

2.   Cf. Nicholas Berdiaev, *Dostoievsky, An Interpretation*, tr. Donald Atwater (London: Sheed & Ward, 1936), p. 160.

3.   John Morrison, *Boris Yeltsin, From Bolshevik to Democrat* (New York: Dutton, 1991), pp. 150, 265.

4.   Aleksander Solzhenitsyn, *Rebuilding Russia* (New York: Farrar Strauss & Giroux, 1991).

5.   Cf. *Glaube in der 2 Welt*, No. 12, 1992, p. 8.

6.   Vladimir Lossky, *The Mystical Theology of the Eastern Church* (London: James Clarke, 1957), pp. 14-15.

3

Ethics and Economic Activity
in Russia

Alexander Zaichenko

It would be a simplification to assert that there is a direct relation between Christianity and the efficiency of an economy. In general, the economic behavior of a people is governed by their ethical standards and their norms of conduct at work and in society. These in turn are justified by morality and the highest spiritual values such as love to God, love to neighbor and obedience to God's commandments. Finally, strong morality derives from personal faith, from intimate relations with one's Creator and Saviour.

As the Bolsheviks destroyed churches and subjugated Christianity in Russia, they took satisfaction in the elimination of their main rival in the struggle for the hearts of the Russian people. The intense struggle of the Soviet power against religion resulted in a rejection of Christian teaching, morals, and ethics on the part of many millions of the population in Russia. Only the dramatic weakening of the social role of the church, of its influence in the society, can account for the relative ease that accompanied the campaign for annihilation of the free peasantry and the passive resistance to the total repression of absolutely innocent people. The church was robbed of its "mottoes" of promising the attainment of happiness and bringing forth a new type of person. The leaders of the church were persecuted, new cults and new centers substituted for the old religious temples; this time they were created in the interests of the Communist party, of the Soviets, of the state.

But there was something that the communists had not foreseen. Time showed that visible success in the de-Christianization of the country was paid for at a very high price, too high for the state, for its people, and humanity at large. Having liberated itself from absolute moral principles, the society which had replaced them with political ideology found itself a prisoner of the false idols of the 1930s-80s. Compassion gave way to a cult of heroism which faded and died in recent decades, despite all official efforts to reverse the process. Mutual trust and confidence were displaced only to let in total suspicion and distrust of those around one! The behest of forgiveness was replaced by the motto "nothing is forgotten." Love, mutual assistance, charity, cordiality, proceeding from traditional values, including Christian ones, gradually gave way to a semi-official code of behavior in the work place. At social centers, in public, the communist code became a means of alienation of each person from everybody else.

Family alone remained a place for preserving general humane values. But it was a passive preservation where spiritual and moral ideas and ethical standards gradually, with every new generation, weakened until they were forgotten or only reproduced on a much narrower scale and scope. This is hardly surprising, as absolute moral values and standards now are dead in the minds of the majority of people while the official idols did not become something living in their hearts and souls. In a few more generations, there would be nothing left to pass down to posterity except the darkness of nihilism, moral looseness, spiritualessness, and relativism. These now are the present standards in people's behavior. All of them hide from view any landmarks pointing the way to a contemporary community of civilized humanity.

At the present time, the norms of economic behavior in Russia reflect several types of ethics which in turn reveal the different kinds of culture still existing in the country. They include traditional, utilitarian, and Christian types of ethics. Traditional ethics embody a remnant of the ancient patriarchal pagan culture which is still alive in some rural areas, as it was partially adopted and conserved by Orthodox Christianity. Utilitarian ethics came with the secularization of society and are based on a set of rules similar to those of the urban industrial and post-industrial societies of the West. Actually, this type is a parasite on traditional and Christian ethics and has no moral foundation; utilitarian standards represent not ethics but etiquette. Christian ethics cannot be said to be based on the Orthodox culture, a culture which gave most attention not to personal but group norms of behavior (obedience to authorities, preference for state versus individual interests). Instead, Christian ethics is seen best in the persecuted (by the state and official Church) Protestant movements which have had a rational and mystical orientation.

All three types of ethical standards have always been weak in Russia and were nearly destroyed altogether in recent decades by the communists as they proclaimed their motto: "Everything is good, that is good for communism." Eventually, the new rulers of Russia became concerned about a lack of ethical values because they needed motivated workers and especially well-motivated soldiers. At the end of the twenties and the beginning of the thirties, they found themselves at a loss when they tried to develop some substitute for the ethics they had destroyed. At last, Stalin found a new Bolshevik method of motivation based on fear, exile, and prison, most of all on the terrifying fear of death. Soviet rulers imposed the death penalty for economic crimes and there was imprisonment for coming late to work by even three minutes. Such notions as moral stimuli and a work ethic ceased to exist among the majority of Russian workers. For decades, the economic activity of the population was enforced by the fear of physical and later economic punishment. To the present, the whole of production remains beyond any sphere of moral incentives both for the workers and managers, devoid of ethical principles.

Later as fear began to disappear, a new phenomenon emerged: moral emptiness. Now after perestroika, within the nation a zone of moral emptiness embraces the majority of the Russian people. Part of that zone is represented by criminal and quasi-criminal elements (due to the mass criminalization of society during the communist rule) — the other part by people who have made the relativistic approach their life pattern.

Criminalization of society is a relatively new phenomenon in modern Russia and has emerged as a result of certain negative factors. First, a growing number of people have become influenced by criminal culture. For many years during the course of communist repression, about ten percent of the adult population was imprisoned or exiled in areas where there was a high concentration of former convicts. In the middle of the 1950s, in the USSR, more than thirty percent of the population was brought into criminal surroundings. Now the proportion has declined, although it remains as high in some areas in Siberia, the Far East, the Far North and Kazakhstan. But to date, Russia retains the world record for the number of citizens spoiled and being spoiled by a dreadful system of prison camps.

Second, before the 1960s, Soviet managers and government officials were servants of the totalitarian power of the Communist party. Eventually, the later evolution of the system allowed them to become the masters of the state. As members of the "nomenclature" class, they derived their incomes through massive corruption; in fact, they were the actual owners of national property. After perestroika, state officials at all levels have tried to undermine the process of privatization in order to preserve their own economic and social status. Formerly they ignored the state laws, introducing their own rules and instructions. Now, the bureaucracy adopts many laws and instructions instead which are both controversial and often openly anti-market. As Professor Jacob Gilinsky of the Institute of Sociology in St. Petersburg declared: "Today in Russia there is no legal business at all."[1]

Third, the Soviet economy for some decades has been running on—not with the help of laws, instructions and rules, but in spite of them. Although the majority of all offenses committed by plant managers were justified by production demands, some were nonetheless of a purely criminal nature. In any case, such practices are still widespread among officials and managers of private enterprise. They grossly undermine any ethical climate in the national economy and provoke a hostility at the grassroots to any market transformation of the economy. There are good reasons to believe that this situation will continue because religion and ethics in the country have been kept down artificially for the past seventy years.

Russian Ethical Enclaves

Historically, Russian religious opposition (sectarianism) has not been as socially passive as the representatives of official atheism have claimed. Rather, it was socially and economically dynamic. Sects in Russia have been oriented toward materializing their teachings—their views on land, property, church, power, relations at work, in society, and the family.

Whether the Old Believers, Sabbatarians, Dukhobors, Molocans, Baptists, Adventists and Mennonites consciously realized it or not, they actually have been the bearers of democratic social precepts and progressive economic relations. In fact they have been noted for their creative ideology, psychology, and especially practical activity. In Russia, sectarian movements often were based on the precept that "man is the house of God." This spiritual and civil concept of humanity stood in opposition to authoritarianism, hierarchy, and the classical rites of Orthodoxy, indeed against the very institution of the Russian Orthodox Church.

On the sectarian view, human beings are sacred because they are the embodiment of the Living God in the form of the Holy Ghost. Facing their own inner world, they renounced both past and present authorities, the royal clothes of the clergy, rituals, and the "holy" Gospel as well as the beauty and godliness of opulent church buildings. Instead, the sectarians turned to the Holy Ghost, following their own principles of spiritual growth. Truth was seen as the lodestar of moral values in everyday behavior at the same time that it determined the transition from a traditional semi-pagan model of society to a social structure governed by respect for human values.

The traditional norms of social conduct for personality (characteristic for Catholicism and Orthodoxy) were based on strict regimentation and customs that have remained unquestioned. The query about why people did this or that had only one answer: "Because our forefathers did it." Such a response makes people socially passive and alike. Powerful layers of this archaic semi-pagan world outlook can still be found today in the behavioral stereotypes of the bureaucratic apparatus and the social inertia of the people (such as obedience and lack of initiative).

By contrast, a social structure based on respect for human values provides not for repetition of a predetermined set of actions but for adherence to specific spiritual and moral principles. Moral landmarks do not just set the limits for personal conduct in specific situations but require an independent and active search for individual solutions.

As in the case of Western European Protestants during the sixteenth and seventeenth centuries, Russian sectarians from the eighteenth to the twentieth centuries shaped their world outlook in terms of respect for the individuality of each person. Their emphasis was on rights and duties to God and to people, and the value of every man or woman as relying on his or her own activity, initiative, diligence, and common sense. Like the Puritans, many members of forbidden Russian sects believed in a "Gospel of renunciation," presupposing asceticism in everyday life, rejection of life's pleasures, and diligence on the one hand, and thrift and the striving for accumulation, on the other. The life of believers in Christ, for example, was based on the following principles: do not drink wine and beer; do not commit adultery; do not attend christening parties, weddings and merry gatherings.

In order to improve their standing in their own eyes and the eyes of surrounding citizens about them, the sectarians professed not their own spiritual holiness but temperance and strict morality, asceticism of life, and cleanliness of body and homes (as God's houses). This kind of self-assertion through the renunciation of a world that did not accept them served as an additional and powerful impetus for social and economic activity in addition to the doctrinal precepts of a view of the social structure governed by respect for human values.

This phenomenon, in which a small religious community not accepted by society but alienated from it at the same time improves itself by accepting many socially positive norms of behavior, is not new. It appeared both in Western Europe in the sixteenth to the eighteenth century and in Russia from the eighteenth to the twentieth century. Today, it can be found in many different parts of the world. Isolated from the mainstream of public life, deprived of the possibility of government jobs or of moving ahead successfully in recognized economic structures, and discriminated against on grounds of religion, such minorities as the Russian sectarians, Jews, Indian Sikhs, Chinese immigrants, etc., have organized isolated societies of mutual support: collective funds, banks and enterprises, which have successfully developed into leading features of the national economy.

In Russia during the nineteenth and twentieth centuries, such enterprises appeared in cities where new economic relations had developed more strongly than in the countryside. They appeared as well in the southern and eastern rural regions of the empire to which the discriminated sects were exiled. There was free land in abundance, while the religious oppression of the Tsar together with the official Russian Orthodox Church was not very strong. For example, sectarian peasants played a major role in the settlement of the southern Ukraine. Resettled religious "dissenters" brought along not money but their system of relations, organization, ideological values, psychological stereotypes, and economic skills. They bred fine-fleeced sheep, laid out gardens, and engaged in a variety of allowed professions as well as produced the bulk of grain for sale in that region. The same phenomenon appeared in the Amur region, the Caucasus, and other areas of Russia.

Often an impoverished Orthodox village had as neighbor a rich village of resettled sectarians. The latter were an example of the economic advantages of active spirituality. One typical case is described by A. Rozen in his "Notes of a Decembrist."[2] A group of Russian sectarians was resettled in Baku Province at a place which the local authorities called "Outskirts". The villagers proved to be very diligent, united, disciplined, and absolutely teetotalling. Indeed, they were busy trying to prove to themselves and their neighbors that they had been chosen by God ("for which they suffered from the godless authorities").

After only a few years, they had rebuilt the village, bought draft animals and cattle, and sold in local markets. In fact, Outskirts became the best possible proof that their belief was true and beneficial. More and more converts flocked to the village. Alarmed by the turn of events, the governor sent more than one worried petition to St. Petersburg and finally received approval for a counter-propaganda strategy. Volunteers chosen from among the best soldiers of the Astrakhan Regiment (all of them Orthodox Christians) were settled ten kilometers from the village of Outskirts. Bringing brides from Russia, they were given subsidies for building houses and buying cattle and machinery. Their new village was called Orthodoxy.

The local authorities gave the new settlers preferential treatment in the form of more favorable taxes and trade benefits. Still the former soldiers drank and fought each other so much as to lead to ruination. After ten years, a new governor sadly reported to the central government that their Orthodox village was as poor as any other village in Russia. The best farmers and their families had moved to Outskirts and accepted its religion. The state propaganda show had failed!

In Russia before the Revolution, the Old Believers were noted for their vigorous accumulation of investment capital. Their rigid religious, moral and ethical precepts had helped them in establishing businesses, in agriculture, commerce and handicrafts (that is, in the trades that they were allowed to take up). In fact, they produced numerous dynasties of successful merchants, bankers and industrialists: the Tretyakova, the Ryabushinskys, the Sytins, the Guchkovs, the Soldatenkovs, etc. Many of these were widely known for their patronage of the arts and charity. By 1911, Old Believers, who constituted only one and seven-tenths of Russia's population, had produced the bulk of Russia's millionaires.

The sectarians' role as generators of economic prosperity continued even after the communist revolution. In the 1920s, they established numerous communes made up of Baptists and other Evangelical Christians ("Bethany" and "Gethsemane") and these flourished. Organizing on the principles of the first Christian churches, the peasants of Gethsemane were unusually successful in cattle breeding and were an example of diligence to the peasants of Tver Province. But Stalin's collectivization campaign crushed their highly productive enterprises. In practically every region of the former USSR, there were (and still are) villages or other separate little settlements inhabited by exiled non-Orthodox Christians of the same confession. In almost all cases, their citizens possessed better family ethics and work morality than the surrounding population. As a result of their productivity, their living standards were notably higher. Their success became a source of local conflicts and even persecution. Among people living in such enclaves were Christians of various nationalities: Russians, Ukrainians, ethnic Germans, Mennonites and others. In the Crimea, for example, there is to be found a village of Molocans, "Novovasilievka"; in Siberia, "Neoudachnoye" of the Mennonites; in Azerbajan," Prishib" of Baptists and Molocans. Such settlements were islands of prosperity and ethical order in an ocean of inefficiency and moral disarray.

Today Protestant and mystic sectarians are distinguished by their teetotalling attitude, diligence, and wealth rather than any isolation. Numerous investigations and studies have shown them to be highly stable socially and very dynamic economically. Oppression and persecution in recent decades dramatically reduced the influx of Russian Protestants (and to a lesser degree of Orthodox Christians) into the higher educational and professional groups of the population. Believers were expelled from universities, were not allowed to take up prestigious professions, and were not given senior posts. None the less, such groups remained the most healthy morally and the most prosperous economically.

In conclusion we must ask: Is there a chance for improvement in the ethical-moral balance in Russia today? The answer is "Yes" — through the radical privatization of state property, by creating a new class of millions of owners and proprietors. The citizens involved will not only form a social base for the market and democratic transformation of Russia, not only constitute the core of strong political democratic parties and movements but will restore the ethical basis of the Russian economy. Among them, the spread of Christian faith and ethics will be visible in the near future. A new understanding of one's own personal rights and responsibility for his or her property will lead the way to acceptance of responsibility before the Owner and Creator of the universe. The slave who has nothing cares for nothing!

Notes

1. *Moscow News,* Number 9, 1994, p. B-1.
2. Baron A. Rozen, *Zapiski dekabrista (Notes of a Decembrist),* (St. Petersburg, 1907). The quotation from Rozen is reprinted from A. I. Klibanov, *Religious Sects in the Past and at the Present Time* (Moscow: 1973), p. 98.

4

The New Religious Press in Russia

Wallace Daniel

1

The collapse of Communism resulted in much more than the breakdown of the party-state apparatus that had governed Russia for more than seventy years. It also led to the end of an official ideology that had, for a large part of this century, defined the system, established its main beliefs, and served as its basis of morality. This ideology gave prominence in Russia to certain key ideas, including the Party's exclusive right to all forms of authority, the notion that Party leaders possessed a superior understanding of history, and faith in the ability of science to transform the world. There existed in Soviet society, writes a recent historian, "a certain confidence that ideas, especially all-embracing systematic ideas, are worthy of respect as such" and needed "no extrinsic justification."[1] The fall of Communism and Russia's efforts to transform itself have produced a profound struggle over the ideas that will serve as the basis for the new order. The battle has deeply involved religion. In this search for identity, a new religious press has emerged, and it has greatly enriched the level of discussion and played a major role in the effort to rebuild Russian society.

Many of the new religious journals originated in the period prior to the final collapse of the Soviet state. The loosening of restrictions on newspapers and journals in late 1987 and 1988 and the simultaneous reforms in editorial policies significantly altered the material that could be published in the Soviet Union. This period marked the beginning of many new religious journals and newspapers; each of them had a particular point of view about the revitalization of Russian society and the policies that needed to be followed. The new publications become an important part of the debate over the present and future of Russian society. As part of a developing perestroika, they appeared during a time when Mikhail Gorbachev called for more openness and democracy; their emergence along with many other publications signalled the beginning struggle for a free press, an essential characteristic of a pluralistic, democratic society.

The precise numbers of new independent newspapers and journals that began during this period are difficult to ascertain. In 1988, when the so-called "boom period" of independent publications began, a Soviet specialist estimated some 286 of them, of which thirteen were religious publications.[2] In 1989, approximately 520 independent Russian-language publishing organs were operating, printing both in large cities and in small towns all over the country. An accurate count is impossible, because some of the publishers were very small, issuing only fifteen to two hundred copies of their materials; other publishers disappeared after a short period, finding it difficult for financial reasons to survive in the new environment.[3] While numbers are unavailable for the present, the lack of paper and sharply rising costs of printing have probably reduced the number of publishers over the last four years.

In contrast to the leading journals and newspapers which focus primarily on politics and economics, the religious publications, according to a recent Russian writer, "represent small fishes in a very wide ocean of information."[4] But, despite their size, they deserve serious attention, because their numbers reveal neither their readership nor their social impact. These publications, even those issued in a few copies, will often be read by many people; it is not unusual for materials issued in ten thousand copies to be read by one hundred thousand people.[5]

Whose views are presented in the new religious journals and newspapers and to whom are they addressed? First, they reveal the perspectives of independent religious groups and organizations — Orthodox, Protestant, Jewish, Muslim, ecumenical, and others — on important issues facing both churches and society. In the late 1980s, such religious groups began openly to express their beliefs. Second, the readership of these publications are young to middle-aged people, who generally have a good education; they are people prepared to ask theological questions and are searching for a new vision of life. Many of them are interested in relating their own specialized training to a larger and more encompassing view of the world. Aspiring to develop the internal life of the church, they want to relate the church to the community. They understand the need to rebuild the ethical foundations of their society and see religious ideals as essential to that process.[6]

Among the most remarkable of the new publications is the journal *Vybor* which describes itself as a "literary-philosophical" journal of Russia. Founded in 1987, the journal had a difficult time in its early days getting permission to publish. Its original organizers, Father Dmitrii Dudko and the publicist and theologian Viktor Aksiuchits, applied to Boris Yeltsin, then Party boss of Moscow, Mikhail Gorbachev, and Alexander Iakovlev for permission to issue the journal. Failing to receive any response, Father Dudko and Aksiuchits asked for help from Father Pitirim, a high-ranking member of the Moscow Patriarchy. Again obtaining no support, they began to issue *Vybor* in typescript as a samizdat publication. The first several issues were published in one hundred copies, but within a year *Vybor* had expanded to one thousand copies, making it the largest samizdat journal in circulation.[7]

In 1989, *Vybor* gained official sanction to publish. From 1987 through the end of 1992, eight issues were published, each running from three hundred to five hundred pages in length. *Vybor* fits into the Russian prerevolutionary tradition of the "thick journal," once a major vehicle for literary and philosophical discussion. It seeks to revive this tradition, linking it to Russia's religious culture, which came under such massive assault in the Soviet period. From the beginning, the journal has aimed to publish authors of various perspectives on current theological and literary subjects. Such a discussion has attracted much interest; in 1991-1992, the circulation of *Vybor* reached thirty thousand copies.

The journal has two editors, Aksiuchits and the poet and literary critic Gleb Anishchenko. Currently the leader of the Christian Democratic Party in Russia, Aksiuchits completed his doctoral dissertation in philosophy at Moscow State University in 1978, writing on Nikolas Berdyaev and Paul Tillich.[8] Anishchenko finished his degree in philosophy at Moscow State University in 1975, spent two years as an administrator in a Moscow museum, and then, after getting in trouble with the KGB, worked as a laborer until 1987: "I made a gradual transition from being a non-believer to a religious person," he told me, "primarily by reading religious-philosophical literature."[9]

The editors are united not as much by their political views as their conviction of the spiritual value of Orthodoxy over any other religious tradition in Russia. *Vybor* contains a great deal of criticism directed at the Moscow Patriarchy for its administrative shortcomings and especially its past compromises with the Soviet government. The journal sees its primary roles as restoring the religious culture of Russia, as raising again for discussion general questions concerning society and religion, and as rediscovering key aspects of Russia's philosophical heritage that have in the twentieth century fallen into obscurity. It accuses the Soviet government, its officials, and its philosophy of "scientific atheism," of destroying the spiritual foundations of the country.

Vybor finds its main source of inspiration in a group of prerevolutionary Russian writers who, in 1909, published a famous collection of essays called *Vekhi (Landmarks).* These writers included some of the most prominent figures in the intellectual history of Russia, such as the political theorist Peter Struve, the economist Sergius Bulgakov, and the philosophers Semen Frank and Nicholas Berdyaev. While these thinkers had earlier sympathized with Marxism, they had become disillusioned with its emergence among the revolutionary intelligentsia in Russia, especially its economic determinism and its totally secular view of history. They severely criticized what they saw as the radical intelligentsia's extreme self-assertion, self-deification, and dogmatic approach to science and religion, which they believed to be dangerous and an ominous sign for the future. Lenin and the Bolsheviks responded scornfully to these writers and, after 1917 until recently, they were the targets of much abuse in the Soviet Union.[10] "We base our journal on the tradition of *Vekhi*," said Anishchenko. "Its emphasis on the spiritual reached into a deeper layer of Russian culture than the Bolsheviks and the radical intelligentsia. We seek to reclaim the discussion that the writers of *Vekhi* held and to underscore its significance for the problems troubling our society at present."[11]

As Anishchenko pointed out, the authors of *Vekhi* predicted a catastrophe in Russia in the twentieth century. They saw the causes of this coming catastrophe in the split consciousness of the revolutionary intelligentsia. Members of the intelligentsia separated the world into the scientific realm, which they identified with progress, and the religious, which they likened to backwardness and which they sought to destroy.[12] The tragedy of this action, Anishchenko maintained, is that Russian culture did not exist apart from its religious moorings; an assault on this framework meant an attack on Russian culture in general.[13] In recreating Russian culture and in restoring its religious-philosophical thought, the editors of *Vybor* argued that the Orthodox Church must take the lead. If the Orthodox Church fails in this task, no one will be able to succeed.

In rebuilding Russia's religious culture, the editors of *Vybor* strongly insist on the separation of church and state. But, in reality, the activity of the journal suggests a definite ambiguity about the journal's involvement in political activity. Creating what Anishchenko calls an "environment for the development of religious consciousness" has led writers for the journal directly into political activity. Anishchenko himself helped to write the "Law on the Freedom of Religion," and Aksiuchits leads the Russian Christian Democratic Party. *Vybor* takes a particularly strong stand against tying Russia too closely to the West, economically and politically, and, in the process, losing its own identity. While the danger of this approach consists of becoming isolationist, its editors insist that they do not want to turn Russia inward. Rather, they fear that the current attractions to Western capitalism and materialism will overwhelm the country's traditional culture, best expressed in its literature, music, and spirituality. In the last several years, *Vybor* has served as a leading vehicle to writers who embrace this belief and who find the authors of *Vekhi* to have immediate relevance to Russia's present condition.

2

A very different approach to current issues may be found in another newly emergent newspaper called *Protestant*. This newspaper, issued twice a month, was founded in Moscow at the end of 1988. It experienced extremely rapid growth, expanding from a printing in its first several months of 15,000 copies to a present circulation of 50,000 copies, a figure that reflects the increasing attractions of Protestant religions among Russia's population. The newspaper identifies itself as evangelical Christian and Baptist, and it reveals a variety of points of view—Methodist, Presbyterian, Lutheran, Baptist, and Seventh-Day Adventist—Protestant groups that have long existed in Russia and have flourished in the urban centers in recent years.

Lacking any close association with the Soviet government and the KGB, these Protestant denominations do not have to resolve many of the difficulties confronting the Orthodox Church; thus, they enter the new period uncontaminated with these burdens. Protestant churches are able to direct their energies to present issues and their newspaper displays such a focus. But *Protestant* does not take a narrow, sectarian approach to religious and social problems. It also deals with matters concerning other religions, such as the recent creation by a group of young scientists of a center of Orthodox culture in Novosibirsk and a conference on "The Spiritual Rebirth of Russia and the Russian Emigration."[14] The newspaper's major concern is the rebuilding of Russia on spiritual foundations, a process in which it wants to play an active part.

Protestant claims its main purpose is evangelical and the application of Biblical principles to everyday life. The newspaper devotes a large amount of attention to one of the greatest problems of recent decades—the plight of children. The number of homeless children has grown spectacularly, now surpassing by far the number following such calamities as the purges and the Second World War.[15] *Protestant* focuses on topics that many see as central issues in Russian society, as the country has moved rapidly from an agricultural to an urban society. The fragmentation and disunity of the community and the disintegration of the family have been constant problems, which recent events and especially financial pressures have exacerbated. *Protestant* tries to address these concerns by emphasizing certain principles that its writers see as fundamental to social stability: respect for authority, regard for individual dignity, compassion and, most important, building relationships on love. As a top priority, the newspaper claims, children "must be taught to adjust to this new life" as well as the principles mentioned above; otherwise, asserted a recent writer, "they will reach the same conclusion as Ivan," in Dostoevski's *The Brothers Karamazov,* that "if God does not exist, then everything is permitted."[16]

Despite disavowing interest in politics, the newspaper does show considerable concern for the structure of the new political order. *Protestant* supports the building of a civil society; it strongly affirms the need for tolerance in the new order and believes that Biblical teachings provide solid support for this need. The newspaper claims that kindness and respect for the individual are essential aspects of a civil society. Yet these features were not stressed by the previous Communist government; its arrogance and its persecution of dissenting views did not allow toleration to develop. Instead, according to *Protestant,* force became a dominant feature of society. The churches must now work toward replacing that violence with a new ethic.

A different emphasis on Russia's primary needs may be found in another journal that began publication in Moscow in 1992. *Moskovskii zhurnal (Moscow Journal),* edited by the historian and archivist A. F. Grushina, appears four times a year. This journal defines its main interests as literary, artistic, historical, and regional topics, focusing especially on the role of the Orthodox Church and major religious leaders in the country's history. All the issues that have appeared so far, each running from sixty to seventy pages, have dealt with this theme.

Moskovskii zhurnal began its first issue of 1992 with a feature story on the architect P. D. Baranovskii, who was born in 1882 and became one of this century's leading restorers of historical monuments in Russia, Ukraine, Belorussia, and the Caucasus.[17] Doing most of his work from 1929 to 1984, Baranovskii succeeded, despite the destructive forces of the twentieth century, in preserving key memorials in the historical and spiritual life of these regions. A central part of his work has been the restoration of monasteries, including the Novodevichi monastery and the Kazan Cathedral in Moscow. According to his own testimony, Baranovskii attempted to see through the eyes of the old craftsmen, whose creations tried to link spiritual elements with the physical. By preserving these monuments, his work kept alive a rich architectural tradition. He accomplished such a task, testified the author of the article, "in extremely difficult years," when the state tried to eradicate memory. Baranovskii "would not allow himself to lose sight of his vision or to be intimidated by the terror." He kept his imagination intact "during a period when no profession was more difficult than that of an architect- preservationist."[18]

Moskovskii zhurnal has attracted a group of writers and scholars who desire to restore monuments of history and culture, recognizing in them key elements in Russia's search for its own identity. The country's recovery of its memory, especially the spiritual aspects of its past, is a feature to which the journal gives much attention. While the role of the Orthodox Church is a central component of this task, the journal conceives its mission as broader than focusing only on that institution. It deals with spiritual themes and their expression in literature and art. It also seeks to protect monuments of local significance, and to revive the traditions that created them, seeing these tasks as essential to the rebuilding of the Russian state.

The authors of the journal often relate creativity to spirituality. In art, for example, the creativity of the painter derives from a connection to the sources of his or her being; in the Soviet period, when nature was not viewed as having a spiritual dimension, it became increasingly difficult for the artist to depict this spiritual quality of nature, to preserve the wholeness and the harmony of the world. Similarly, a recent issue of the journal reprinted the Russian philosopher Ivan Il'in's essay, "Filosofiia kak dukhovnoe delanie" ("Philosophy as a Spiritual Activity").[19] In this essay, which remained unpublished under the Soviet government, the well-known early twentieth century philosopher argued that a fundamental connection existed among the tasks of philosophy, science, and the spiritual world. There are dangers in the approach that the editors of *Moskovskii zhurnal* take. Carried to an extreme, their efforts may promote nationalism and crude forms of patriotism. But the materials they have published thus far are not aggressive and display neither xenophobia nor ethnic exclusiveness. The values they promote consist mainly of cultural awareness and the need to rediscover traditions and thinkers who might contribute to building a humanistic culture in Russia, elements in Russia's search for its own identity.

The journal *Slovo* also deals with similar topics. Issued monthly, *Slovo's* contributors include such well-known writers as the priest Lev Lebedev and a highly educated group of biologists, chemists, and publicists who are close to the Orthodox Church. This circle of writers considers harmful the ideas of "religious dissidents," and they support the positions taken by the Moscow Patriarch, from Tikhon to Pimen, whom they believe protected the church from destruction in the twentieth century. *Slovo* gives considerable attention to preserving the monuments of Russian culture, to protecting them against local organs of government, and to seeking the registration of church parishes. The editorship wants to create a legal service to pursue these goals.

A repeated theme expressed in the pages of *Slovo* is the need to develop and refine the internal strength of the society, and to prevent it from caving in to "pressure from foreign organizations and governments."[20] The journal is highly critical of the "doctrine of scientific atheism," the ideology which guided the country for decades, for "its extreme glorification of man, its attempts to make him lord of nature." Now that the old order has collapsed, the journal wants to create a civil society based on Russia's traditional culture and values. Writers of *Slovo*, like *Moskovskii zhurnal*, see it as their "patriotic obligation" to keep the best features of that culture from being destroyed in the rush to construct everything anew.

3

The most critical treatment of the doctrine of scientific atheism emerged in a journal that had been one of the leading Soviet publications during the last thirty years, *Nauka i religiia (Science and Religion)*. This journal, founded in 1959 at the height of Nikita Khrushchev's campaign against religion, played for nearly thirty years a major role in the government's ideological assault against what it proclaimed "religious superstition." In this period, *Nauka i religiia* repeatedly published articles emphasizing science as the path to ultimate truth; simultaneously, many articles featured in the journal dealt with the social injustices and human suffering which religion had fostered. The journal served as a counterpart to the Museum of Religion and Atheism in Leningrad, where instruments of torture used in the Inquisition and other artifacts were featured, graphically showing the human misery inflicted by the Church. The editors of *Nauka i religiia* aimed, through education, to move Soviet citizens to a higher level of understanding of the world and to wipe out religious beliefs, which they associated with Russia's rural society.[21]

In the late 1980s, however, the journal's policies began to change. Mikhail Gorbachev's call for a reconstruction of the ideological framework of the country and a more open discussion of present problems, including morality, contributed to this transformation. In this journal, commemoration of the millennium of Christianity in Russia in 1988 also led to many articles about the history of the Orthodox Church. This time the treatment was much more positive; it often dealt with the Orthodox Church's contributions to the country, particularly in times of crisis — during the Mongol invasion, the Time of Troubles, and the Great Patriotic War.

An additional reason for this change in the journal's editorial policy concerned several sociological studies that clearly showed the presence of deep-rooted religious beliefs among the Soviet population.[22] In a journal devoted to a scientific exploration of the world, such carefully-constructed, objective data could not be ignored. Moreover, this data, gathered in several different cities and regions of the Soviet Union, yielded further surprising results. They showed religious beliefs to be most prevalent among young and middle-aged people, living in urban settings and often having completed a high school or university education. The data further revealed that the highest rates of atheistic beliefs were found among the older generation, Russian citizens born in the 1920s, 1930s, and 1940s and with less education than their younger counterparts. The studies led to the unwelcome conclusion that educational methods used in the past three decades to eradicate religion had not only failed, but had ironically produced the opposite results from what had been intended. *Nauka i religiia* frankly admitted such a failure.[23]

The causes, according to the editors, lay in the crude methods which schools had employed to criticize Christianity and other religions. In addition, Soviet educators, the editors acknowledged, had misunderstood some of the deeper spiritual needs of human beings, and had not spoken convincingly about them. As the society had become more educated, a large gap had opened between the material presented and the interests of the readers. In an effort to address the gap, the journal called for a wider dialogue between atheists and religious believers.[24]

Beginning in 1988, *Nauka i religiia* carried such a discussion. Recognizing the moral crisis in which the Soviet Union found itself, the journal published a remarkable exchange between representatives of the Church and the Communist party on problems confronting the Soviet Union, especially concerning the spiritual needs of the Soviet people.[25] Responding to Mikhail Gorbachev's call at the Twenty-seventh Party Congress in 1986 for a "fresher, more dynamic, and more creative" discussion of the spiritual and moral problems of Soviet society, the journal's coverage included roundtable discussions, articles about the historical role of the Orthodox Church, and debates between church and party officials on current social issues. The relationship between science and religion lay at the center of this discussion. The educational approaches offered by both the Party and the Church to science and to solving social problems received a great deal of coverage.

In subsequent years, *Nauka i religiia* mirrored the changes taking place in Russia and the Soviet Union. It began to focus more on the revival of the Orthodox Church and the contributions it had made to Russia's identity in the past. The journal also published important materials from earlier periods about key religious figures, writers, and scholars who had heretofore received little attention in the schools and, consequently, were not widely known. An extremely significant inclusion was the publication of writers who had contributed to *Vekhi* in 1909.[26] Their criticisms of "scientific atheism" were given considerable coverage. The impression one gets from these materials is that the editors of *Nauka i religiia* were not only trying to reclaim a forgotten religious heritage, but were also seeking to discover elements in the past that could speak profoundly to Russia's present condition.

An additional aspect of this search also included the journal's attempt to reach beyond Russia's borders to the East and West. *Nauka i religiia* has had a distinctively ecumenical point of view; its editors have seen many problems not only as Russian but as global issues. For example, it conducted an interview with Harvard theologian Harvey Cox on sustaining religious faith in the large contemporary city, in which Cox raised many questions about the church's cultural role in secularism. *Nauka i religiia* published a discussion with the United States' ambassador to the Soviet Union, John Matlock, on the relationship between religion and ecology. The journal printed an interview with the Metropolitan of Northern India and Delhi, Paulos Mar Gregorios, on global warming, the threat of nuclear catastrophe, and their connection with industrial society.[27]

Repeatedly, in dealing with such problems, writers for *Nauka i religiia* have seen them as moral issues. These authors have pointed to the relationship between the dogmatic, arrogant approach to nature and to humankind, which they believe characterized much of Soviet thought, and many of the problems currently threatening civilization. The journal, whose printing in early 1993 amounted to over 130,000 copies, continues to enjoy a large audience. In its approach to both science and religion, *Nauka i religiia* has undergone a complete transformation.

4

The newspapers and journals included in this discussion present diverse religious views, in part shaped by their different theological assumptions and the social problems they see as preeminent. These publications have made available a sustained critique of communism, and have provided different ways of looking at the world than the official ideology that long dominated public discussion of social and religious issues in the Soviet Union. While these publications take diverse approaches, several common themes run through their treatments of contemporary needs.

Religion and Art

As a large part of the population showed increasing interest in religion, the connections between religion, creativity, and values evoked an especially sharp analysis. Explored in contemporary works of art, literature, and film, these relationships received much attention in the new religious publications. In part, interest in such issues appeared as a reaction to the seventy-year assault on the religious world view. But, in addition, many writers were responding to the narrow, specialized vision of the world which state education had presented to them and which they now found inadequate. These writers reexamined scientific and artistic geniuses in the past who had not seen science, art, and religion as separate fields, but rather had drawn on all of these disciplines to produce some of the greatest works of civilization. Such creative geniuses as Leonardo da Vinci and Johann Wolfgang Goethe were presented as model figures who had successfully bridged the division between religion, science, and art. Rather than seeing science and poetry as presenting opposite approaches, they ought to be viewed as complementary in their nourishment of creative thinking.[28]

In a thought provoking article in *Nauka i religiia*, the Kirghiz writer Chinghiz Aitmatov explored the relationship between religion and culture.[29] One of the main characters in his article, which consisted of a dialogue among three people, maintained that the most creative works of Russian literature essentially dealt with religious problems and themes; the church had also inspired many of the greatest monuments of art and architecture. Religion had contributed to the greatest memorials of Russian culture, while atheism had destroyed them. But another of Aitmatov's characters in the dialogue was aware that religion, too, had given rise to destructive impulses in Russian and Soviet society: the cult of personality essentially had a religious foundation; the church in the past had promoted or remained silent about acts of extreme cruelty, and it had supported the autocratic state. In the present, Aitmatov observed, a primary purpose of religion in the former Soviet Union is to serve as a humanizing influence, to provide a source of beauty, and to hold up such ideals as kindness and love of one's neighbor. While these elements might not influence art directly, he claimed that they provided the framework that nourished and sustained human creativity.

In emphasizing the role of art as an act of moral imagination, such writers as Aitmatov stand in a long line of earlier Russian thinkers from Chaadaev to Dostoevski, Tolstoy, and Chekhov. They also recall the writers of *Vekhi* and their challenge to the rationalism and materialism of Marxism-Leninism. In dealing with the purpose of art, Aitmatov and other contemporary writers often refer to M. M. Bulgakov's *The Master and Margarita*, among the most popular recent novels in Russia.[30] Bulgakov offers to the present generation of Russians a bridge to cultural traditions that were nearly lost; he also offers a vision of the artist as one who must provoke men and women to think about what it means to be human, and as one who must pursue this task wherever it may lead.[31]

Religion and Memory

Closely related to the theme of religion and art is another crucial component of personality, the recovery of memory. Describing the role of memory, Simone Weil has written that "the future brings us nothing, gives us nothing; it is we who in order to build it have to give it everything, our very life. We possess no other life, no other living sap, than the treasures stored up from the past and digested, assimilated and created afresh by us."[32] In Russia since the 1917 Revolution, events have repeatedly attempted to erase connections with time, place, and memory. The Civil War, foreign invasion, the purges, the deliberate attempts to suppress remnants of the past have had a devastating effect on the remembrance of times past, ranging from family archives to local historical traditions. The journals discussed above are all part of the effort to recover past traditions and to accomplish what Weil referred to as "creating them afresh."

In his recent book on history and memory, David Lowenthal refers to the past as a "foreign country." It is not dead, he says, "it is not even sleeping. A mass of memories and records, of relics and replicas, of monuments and memorabilia, lives at the core of our being."[33] In Russia this intertwining of the present with the past, this attempt to revivify the memory, lends powerful testimony to Lowenthal's statement. The editors of *Vybor's* emphasis on the religious culture of prerevolutionary Russia and especially their attention to the writers of *Vekhi* are aimed at restoring these elements of the past and at moving them to the center of the present quest for identity. Similarly, *Moskovskii zhurnal's* descriptions of Russia's cultural monuments convey also the values associated with the building of these monuments — the appreciation of beauty, the sense of humility, and the striving for harmony with nature — qualities the editors seek to reaffirm.

In the attempt to reacquaint Russians with their spiritual heritage, these journals have devoted attention to two figures whose lives are particularly significant to this quest: Archpriest Avvakum and Grigorii Skovoroda.[34] Archpriest Avvakum, the seventeenth-century Old Believer, is a prime example of the "passive sufferer" whose defiant stand against the state led to many years of exile and prison and eventually to his burning at the stake. Skovoroda, the eighteenth-century philosopher, was a major critic of the European Enlightenment's emphasis on rationalism. Taking to the road and traveling widely, he wrote some of the most hauntingly beautiful passages in the Russian language about identity and consciousness. Both figures were lonely seekers of truth, outcasts from their societies, who left brilliant literary testimonials of their struggles. In the rediscovery of the memory, a large question will be whose past will be re-created. The attention given to such people as Avvakum and Skovoroda is a solid reminder of the diversity and richness of Russia's spiritual tradition, testimony also that some of its most creative religious thinkers existed outside the Orthodox Church.

Religion and Community

A major theme that runs through the new religious journals concerns the need to rebuild the foundations of the community. The authoritarian government under which Russians lived for most of this century imposed a particular kind of order on society; it sought to confine individual activities to the narrowest possible limits. The historic transformation of recent years has shattered this order and has freed society from its former restraints. Yet the rebuilding of the social order, a process which will take many years, has barely begun. In the meantime, every conceivable kind of social vice has come explosively to the surface. President Václav Havel of the Czech republic has eloquently described such a state of affairs for Eastern Europe in words that might apply equally to Russia: "And thus we are witnesses to a bizarre state of affairs: society has freed itself, true, but in some ways it behaves worse than when it was in chains."[35] Havel points to the rapid growth of criminality, the hatred among ethnic groups, the intrigue, demagoguery, and hunger for power, the rabid pursuit of particular interests and, underlying all of these elements, a wholesale lack of tolerance, moderation, understanding, and reason. In addition, a new attraction to ideologies has emerged, as if the collapse of Marxism-Leninism "left behind it a great, unsettling void that had to be filled at any cost."

The discussion of community strongly recalls the question about Russia's identity, posed more than 150 years ago by the nobleman and writer, Peter Chaadaev. In a famous letter published in 1837, Chaadaev asserted that Russia remained a void in human history:

> In our houses we are like campers; in our families we are like strangers; in our cities we are like nomads.... Alone in the world we have given nothing to the world, taken nothing from the world, bestowed not even a single idea upon the fund of human ideas, contributed nothing to the progress of the human spirit.[36]

Chaadaev essentially referred to the drabness of Russia's imperial culture, and Nicholas I dismissed his accusation by declaring Chaadaev a "madman." But his assertions continued to haunt Russians for several generations. Presently, the question Chaadaev asked about Russian culture and society has come back again. Russia once more has before it this provocative question, observed a recent writer, "similar to the one posed in Chaadaev's time," about its identity, the nature of its community, and its relationship to the West.[37]

While a society based on law and legal contracts is repeatedly seen as a fundamental goal, education is viewed as the key to rebuilding the foundations of the community. The new educational institutions, in the religious journals, are perceived as essential for teaching about the dignity of the individual, toleration, and responsibility. But in addition, some of the writings about reconstructing the community contain aspects of the

Slavophiles, nineteenth-century thinkers who argued that Russian culture had some distinctive and valuable features to offer, which they believed were lost long ago in the West. Such elements included mutual aid, a balance between individual and collective interests and the concept of *sobornost'* or brotherhood. These qualities are once again depicted as under assault from the economic pressure of the West, and they need to be preserved or shielded from efforts to replace them with the values of Friedrich Hayek and Milton Friedman.[38]

The new religious publications that have emerged in Russia in the last four years exhibit a variety of views on issues facing the country. As a Russian writer has recently argued, what the present needs most is not greater fragmentation but efforts to seek common ground. These attempts will involve creating a new general language of culture; they will also require an original synthesis that draws together the spiritual and such diverse fields as science, economics, communications, and history. Most of all, he writes, Russia needs a deeper understanding of its own culture, and especially the role of religion in that culture.[39] The publications examined in this essay serve as a focus for members of the intelligentsia to bring their knowledge and experience directly to bear on political and social questions. These publications provide a basis for an extremely useful dialogue as Russia seeks to rediscover its spiritual culture and redefine its identity.

Notes

1. Geoffrey Hosking, *The Awakening of the Soviet Union* (Cambridge, Mass.: Harvard University Press, 1990), pp. 11-12.

2. A. I. Suetnov, "Samizdat: Novyi istochnik bibliografirovaniia," *Sovetskaia bibliografiia* (1989), No. 2, p. 28, and No. 5, p. 18.

3. S. Ivanenko, "Novaia religioznaia pressa," *Nauka i religiia*, No. 5, May 1990, p. 28.

4. Ibid.

5. Ibid.; see also the excellent bibliographical guide to published materials on religion in the former Soviet state, *Ministerstvo kyl'tury RSFSR, Akademiia nauk SSSR, Gosudarstvennaia publichnaia biblioteka, Sovetskoe gosudarstvo i russkaia pravoslavnaia tserkov': K istorii vzaimootnoshenii (Metodiko-bibliograficheskie materialy v pomoshch' rabote bibliotek-metodicheskikh tsentrov)* (Moscow: Gosudarstvennaia publichnaia istoricheskaia biblioteka RSFSR, 1990).

6. This paragraph relies heavily on *Ivanenko*, "Novaia religioznaia pressa," p. 28.

7. Gleb Anishchenko, interview by author, Moscow, June 1, 1992.

8. *Viktor Aksiuchits*, interview by author, Moscow, May 29, 1991.

9. *Gleb Anishchenko*, interview by author, Moscow, June 1, 1992.

10. William Van Den Bercken, "Postcommunism avant la lettre: Russia's Religious Thinkers on Communism in 1918," *Religion State and Society*, Vol. 20, Nos. 3-4, 1992, p. 246.

11. *Gleb Anishchenko*, interview by author, Moscow, June 1, 1992.

12. Ibid.

13. Ibid.

14. Iurii Mochulin, "Miloserdie i politika," *Protestant*, May 1991, p. 11.

15. On the problem of children, see Francine du Plessix Gray, *Soviet Women: Walking the Tightrope* (New York: Doubleday, 1989), pp. 186-87.

16. A. Terent'ev, "Taiashchiisia v rebenke svet," *Protestant*, May 1991, p. 8; see also Valentin Nikol'skii, "Podarish' istorku tepla," *Protestant*, January 1993, p. 6; Alla Berezhkova, "Vozliubi samogo sebia," *Protestant*, January 1993, p. 7, and "Dolia sirotskaia," *Protestant*, March 1993, p. 7; Valentin Tregub, "Na chem zemlia derzhitsia," *Protestant*, March 1993, p. 5.

17. Iurii Bychkov, "Tverzhe kamnia: K 100-letiiu so dnia rozhdeniia P. D. Baranovskogo," *Moskovskii zhurnal*, No. 1, 1992, pp. 4-12.

18. Ibid., p. 4.

19. Ivan Il'in, "Filosofiia kak dukhovhoe delanie," *Moskovskii zhurnal*, No. 2, 1992, pp. 33-40.

20. *Ivanenko*, "Novaia religioznaia pressa," p. 29.

21. Rudol'f Balandin, "Otdelit' ateizm ot gosudarstva," *Slovo*, No. 2, February 1989, pp. 10-11; see also Eduard Machul'skii, "Kazalos' by, ves izmanilos'," *Slovo*, No. 7, July 1989, p. 9.

22. E. Kublitskaia, "Obshchestvo massovogo ateizma glazami sotsiologa," *Nauka i religiia*, No. 1, January 1990, pp. 34-35.

23. Ibid., p. 35.

24. A. Onishchenko, "Novye argumenty v starom spore," *Nauka i religiia*, No. 5, May 1988, pp. 6-8.

25. V. Pazlova, "Dialog? Poka tol'ko znakomstvo," *Nauka i religiia*, No. 6, June 1988, pp. 30-31.

26. See Wallace Daniel, "Religion and Science: The Evolution of Soviet Debate," *The Christian Century*, Vol. 109, No. 4, January 29, 1992, pp. 98-100.

27. Budet li Bog v budushchem?," *Nauka li religiia*, No. 7, July 1988, pp. 16-19; "Gumanna ili nauka?," *Nauka i religiia*, No. 1, January 1990, pp. 22-23; "Religioznoe vozrozhdenie iii nravstvennye iskaniia?," *Nauka i religiia*, No. 7, July 1989, pp. 15-16; "Spacti zhizn' na zemle," *Nauka i religiia*, No. 1, January 1990, p. 13.

28. B. Raushenbakh, "Religiia i nravstvennost'," *Znamia* No. 1, January 1991, p. 215.

29. Leonid Stolovich, "Razgovor ob iskusstve i religii," Nauka i religii, No. 7, July 1989, pp. 5-8.

30. See, for example, ibid.

31. Andrew Barrett, *Between Two Worlds: A Critical Introduction to the*

"Master and Margarita" (Oxford: Clarendon Press, 1987), p. 327.

32. Simone Weil, *The Need for Roots: Prelude to a Declaration of Duties Toward Mankind*, trans. Arthur Wills, with a preface by T. S. Eliot (Boston: The Beacon Press, 1952), p. 51; the attempt to rediscover the historical memory is examined in my article, "The Vanished Past: Russia's Search for Identity," *The Christian Century*, Vol. 110, No. 9, March 17, 1993, pp. 293-96.

33. David Lowenthal, *The Past is a Foreign Country* (Cambridge: Cambridge University Press, 1985), p. xxv.

34. A. Timofeev, "Kolokol Pustozerska," *Slovo*, No. 2, February 1990, pp. 30-32; Iurii Barabash, "Grigorii Skovoroda—bogoslov, mistik, ateist?," *Nauka i religiia*, No. 2, February 1988, pp. 43-45.

35. Václav Havel, "Paradise Lost," *The New York Review of Books*, April 9, 1992, p. 6.

36. Peter Chaadaev, quoted by G. A. Hosking, *Empire and Nation in Russian History*, Charles Edmondson Historical Lectures, No. 14, Baylor University, February 3-4, 1992 (Waco, Texas: Baylor University Press, 1993), p. 30.

37. B. Grois, "Poisk russkoi natsional'nyi identichnosti," *Voprosy filosofii*, No. 1, January 1992, p. 59.

38. See, for example, Viktor Aksiuchits, "V plenu novykh illiuzii," *Nezavisimaia gazeta*, October 23, 1992.

39. G. Pomerants, "Dolgaia doroga istorii," *Znamia*, No. 11, November 1991, p. 183.

5

Christian Democrats in Russia, 1989 - 1993

Paul D. Steeves

When the television camera pans across the chamber of the Russian parliament, black robes of priests stand out amidst the sea of gray suits. They are a small but significant evidence of recent change. They are a symbol that the gates into the political arena have been opened to religiously based political action. In particular, they represent the entry into that arena of a new political force, one which advertises itself as explicitly Christian.

The two priests in the Russian Congress of People's Deputies, along with a layman in the parliament, were the principal founders of a political party called the Russian Christian Democratic Movement in April 1990. They represent, although they do not define exhaustively, a significant element of Russian political life of the recent past, which may be treated together under the label Christian democracy. In this paper, I trace the diverse manifestations of the politics of Christian democracy in Russia since 1989.

Christian democracy does not represent a unitary movement in Russia, although it is a perceptible phenomenon. Christian democracy in Russia comprises a broad diversity of people, organizations, and ideas. Its wide organizational variety is expressed in the separate groups that have appropriated the label of Christian democracy. There is the Christian Democratic Union created by Alexander Ogorodnikov, which refuses to enter election contests; there is the Christian Democratic Party of Russia created by Alexander Chuev; and there is the Russian Christian Democratic Movement, a self-proclaimed parliamentary party, founded by fathers Gleb

Yakunin and Viacheslav Polosin and a religious journalist, Viktor Aksiuchits, all of whom were elected people's deputies in March 1990. And there is another Christian Democratic Union that appeared because just over a year ago a deep and probably irreconcilable schism opened between Father Yakunin and Aksiuchits which prompted Yakunin to create a new organization which commandeered the name of Ogorodnikov's original organization.

Besides the organizations which define Christian democracy, there are its leading individuals. I have just named several men who have figured prominently in the emergence of Christian democracy in Russia. Three of them define discrete streams of Christian democracy that I will identify in this paper. These three are the priest Yakunin, the journalist Aksiuchits, and the artist Ogorodnikov. Yakunin has established himself as clearly the most liberal of the three, while Aksiuchits advocates the most overt form of Russian nationalism among them.

Alexander Ogorodnikov deserves pride of place as initiator of Christian democratic activity in Russia. Born in 1950, he served ten years in labor camps for dissident activity in the leadership of the Christian seminar activity of the 1970s. He was amnestied in 1987.[1] In August 1989, he organized the Christian Democratic Union in Moscow. His organization was admitted immediately into the Christian Democracy International based in Brussels, which comprises parties in over fifty countries.[2]

The Democratic Union encompassed groups in several cities and regions of the USSR. It published a journal named the *Herald (Vestnik) of the Christian Democratic Union*. Ogorodnikov said that the purpose of the Christian Democratic Union was not to entangle the church in politics but to work out a political program on the basis of the church's teachings. Russia, he said, had a distinctive opportunity for working out a Christian political strategy because "it would be difficult to find another country in the world which has been so closely bound to Christianity as Russia has been."[3] These first stirrings of Christian democracy in Russia expressed an early recognition that the gathering collapse of the Soviet totalitarian and atheistic system should elicit a response from those who believe that the Gospel has certain knowledge that must serve as the foundation for building a renewed society. The fundamental element of the Gospel's message to which the Christian democrats pointed was the recognition of the human as the image of God.

Dissension within the union erupted almost immediately. At the time of the elections to the Russian parliament in March 1990, the Moscow affiliate, led by Viktor Rott and Alexander Chuev, publicly opposed Ogorodnikov's candidacy for a seat from Moscow. They accused him of embezzling five million rubles. Ogorodnikov's supporters circulated a brochure charging Chuev with cooperating with the KGB in infiltrating and trying to destroy the union.[4] By the time the elections were over, Christian democracy in Russia had splintered. But its several resulting fractions survived to become politically active and to draw considerable attention to themselves in the media.

In April 1990, the press agency TASS and Moscow Television News Service provided reports of the formation of what was to become the most well known representative of Russian Christian democracy. On April 8, three successful candidates for the Russian congress, who earlier had worked with Ogorodnikov, formed a parliamentary party. They were Gleb Yakunin, Archpriest Viacheslav Polosin, and Viktor Aksiuchits. They called their party the Russian Christian Democratic Movement (RKhDD).

Yakunin, born in 1935, is an Orthodox priest who was sentenced to labor camp in 1979 on the charge of anti-Soviet agitation. He was amnestied in 1987. Polosin was born in 1956 and became a priest in 1983 upon graduation from the Moscow seminary. Aksiuchits was born in 1949 and received a degree in philosophy from Moscow State University in 1978. He was a Communist party member from 1971 to 1979.[5] The biographical details of these three provide sufficient basis to understand that the relations between Christian democrats and the patriarchal church would not likely be close or cordial, and they have not been.

The organizing congress of the Democratic Movement, attended by 300 delegates, elected a fifteen members policy committee called a "duma." Its membership held widely divergent political views, from the liberalism of Yakunin to the monarchism of Vladimir Karpets. Karpets tried to have the word "democratic" removed from the organization's name. (Other members of the duma were Gleb Anishchenko, Artem Artemov, Boris Bychevskii, Oleg Denisenko, Alexander Kazakov, Oleg Kostetskii, Evgenii Poliakov, Vitalii Savitskii, Valerii Senderov, Aleksei Chubisov, and Anatolii Shut'ko.) The absence of Alexander Ogorodnikov from the new party was conspicuous. He condemned its formation as "completely unethical" because the deputies had been elected by their constituencies as independents and only after they took their seats did they declare their affiliation.[6]

Aksiuchits was distinguished among the leaders as an aggressive political organizer who aspired to create a mass party that would attract supporters from all religions and even nonbelievers. In the summer of 1990, he told a journalist about his hopes for the movement becoming Russia's ruling party.[7] Polosin, by way of contrast, played down Aksiuchits' goal. For him it was more important for the movement to influence society, through argument and legislation, in favor of Christian ideals.

The program of the movement advocated the convocation of an Assembly of the Land (Zemskii sobor), whose purpose would be to decide on the state system for Russia, which might be either a republic or constitutional monarchy. Before the meeting of the assembly, the movement proposed that Russia have a government led by a president elected by the whole country. Christian democrats pledged themselves to cooperate in the promotion of parliamentary politics in Russia and to insure the protection of basic civil rights. In particular, they stated their intention to work for a law introducing full religious freedom in Soviet Russia and for a decree making Christmas a national holiday. They called their ideology "enlightened patriotism" and recognized that their principles would place them, among western European political movements, to the right of center.[8] For Aksiuchits, "enlightened patriotism" meant that the premises upon which reform of Russia should be based were the values of the thousand-year-old Orthodox culture. He explicitly rejected the "nationalistic arrogance" and "chauvinistic aggression" of such organizations as Memory (Pamyat') who, he claimed, had no real understanding of the Orthodox Christian foundation of Russian history.[9] Anishchenko, who throughout the numerous subsequent disputes among Christian democrats remained closest to Aksiuchits, summarized his understanding of "enlightened patriotism" in a way that left no doubt about the movement's adherence to a politics informed by Orthodox tradition: "The Russian nation and Russia in general are inconceivable without Christianity."[10]

The platform of the party contained strident anticommunist rhetoric. Marxist ideology, it declared, was a "demonic force" that was responsible for all that was bad in Russia. As the "most radical theomachistic doctrine and force in world history," Marxism's ultimate success would mean the "establishment of the kingdom of evil on earth."[11] The evident practical political goal of the Christian Democratic Movement was the removal of the Communist party from the government of Russia. Little perspicacity is required to conclude that differences of opinion among the leaders of the party would tear it apart if that single goal that united them were to be achieved.

From the start, Father Gleb Yakunin's role in the organization was marginal. He did not accept the post of one of the three co-presidents of the party that called itself the Russian Christian Democratic Movement. Aksiuchits was the dominating figure. The other two presidents with him were Polosin and Gleb Anishchenko. Anishchenko edited the Christian democratic newspaper, *The Way (Put')*, and journal, *Choice (Vybor)*.

A month after the RKhDD organized itself, the other fractions of Christian democracy took similar action. On May 2, Ogorodnikov convened in Moscow a conference of his remaining supporters. They condemned the "schismatics" (raskol'niki) and insisted on their right to continue as the Christian Democratic Union.[12] On May 12, 1990, Chuev transformed his Moscow organization into the Russian Christian Democratic Party.[13]

The Christian Democratic Movement proved itself the most effective political force of the Christian democratic groups. In the early stages of the organization of the Russian Congress of People's Deputies, Aksiuchits was nominated for chairman, the post that Boris Yeltsin eventually won.[14] Polosin took up an important office by becoming chairman of the Committee for Freedom of Conscience, Religion, Philanthropy, and Charity. The other two co-presidents of RKhDD became members of this committee.[15] This committee drafted the law on Freedom of Religion that the congress passed in October 1990. This law achieved the Christian democrats' goals of over-turning the Stalinist restrictions that had hemmed in religious activity for sixty-one years. It gave to religious organizations all they desired by way of opportunities to proselyte in public, conduct charitable work, and en-gage in economic activity. Of special importance in the light of Soviet his-tory, the law forbade the creation of any department of the Russian state whose responsibility was the oversight of religious organizations such as had been the hated Council on Religious Affairs of the USSR.[16]

The second conference of the RKhDD met at the end of October 1990 (October 27 and 28). At that time, Aksiuchits claimed that the party had 15,000 individual members and organizations in all parts of the Russian Federation. He expressed his aspiration to draw together into a working alliance various parties and groups whose aim was to revive traditional political values in Russia. The groups that appeared to have the closest affinity with Christian democrats were the Constitutional Democrats and the People's Labor Union which were nonextremist patriotic organizations that opposed the Communist party.[17]

Consistent with its anticommunism, the Christian Democratic Move-ment decided to join the political movement known as Democratic Russia, which the conference identified as a coalition aimed at overcoming the political monopoly of communist ideology. At its first congress a bit earlier in October 1990, Democratic Russia had declared its goal of deposing the Communist party from state power. This alliance encompassed sufficient delegates in the Russian congress to elect Yeltsin chairman of the congress and, eventually, president of Russia in June 1991.

Just as the issue of the union treaty worked out by President Gorbachev for signing in August 1991 began the disintegration of Democratic Russia, that issue soon undermined the cohesion of the Christian Democratic move-ment. One day before the August coup, the Christian democrats gathered in a congress in Moscow that led to Father Yakunin's withdrawal from the movement. The problem had to do with the topic that became the defining issue for Aksiuchits' political stance, the preservation of a unitary state. In the period before the coup, the unitary state he hoped to maintain was the Soviet Union; later it became the Russian Federation.[18]

Democratic Russia convened its second congress on November 10, 1991. That meeting coincided with the state of emergency Yeltsin had declared in Chechnia. Yeltsin's decree provided the catalyst for a schism in Democratic Russia which also confirmed the break between Yakunin and Aksiuchits. The Christian Democratic Movement joined two other Democratic Russia members, the Democratic Party of Russia, led by Nikolai Travkin, and the Constitutional Democrats, led by Mikhail Astafiev, in a bloc which took the name "National Accord" (Narodnoe soglasie). Democratic Russia called for the abrogation of Yeltsin's decree because they viewed it as a form of Russian imperialism. National Accord supported the decree because they saw it as directed to preserving the unitary Russian state. After acrimonious debate, National Accord walked out of the congress and the three parties terminated their membership in Democratic Russia, renouncing Democratic Russia's support for the right of the autonomous republics of the Russian Federation to declare independence. National Accord affirmed its belief that Russia should remain "united and indivisible."[19]

By the end of 1991, the RKhDD calculated that it comprised affiliated organizations in 153 Russian cities and in another thirty cities in other republics, most of the latter in the Ukraine. Fifteen of their members were deputies in the Russian congress; many others sat on local soviets, and RKhDD members were appointed chief executives in Nizhny Novgorod and Tula. The movement claimed over 17,000 registered members.[20]

With his separation from Democratic Russia and Yakunin, Aksiuchits embarked upon a political course that carried him progressively into closer affinity with right-wing nationalist and communist groups while he attempted to avoid the appearance of sharing their extremism. He declared that his chief opponents had become Democratic Russia and "left extremists," but he also rejected the Bolshevism of Nina Andreeva and the rightist radicalism of Memory's Vasilev. From November 1991 onward, Aksiuchits tried to ally with Vice President Alexander Rutskoi, whose occasional outbursts of criticism of Yeltsin and evocation of the vision of "Great Russia" accorded with Aksiuchits views.

The specific points on which Aksiuchits agreed with Rutskoi were the following. He objected to Yeltsin's decision to free prices in January 1992 before privatization had been completed in order to end monopolistic conditions in the economy. He wanted to have a market economy instituted, but he worried that what was actually happening was placing Russia at the mercy of foreign entrepreneurs and turning it into a raw material supplier for industrial powers. He was alarmed by the breakup of the unitary Soviet state and by the signs of progressing disintegration of the Russian Federation. He argued that the boundaries defining the Russian state and demarcating it from neighboring republics were arbitrary products of the Soviet system and should be subject to revision by peaceful means, preferably by referenda. This meant in particular that Aksiuchits, like Rutskoi, raised the issue of the civil rights of the twenty-five million ethnic Russians who were cut off from Russia by these borders.[21]

On February 8-9, 1992, the Christian Democrat Aksiuchits and the Constitutional Democrat Astafiev organized a Congress of Civilian Patriotic Forces. They invited Rutskoi to address the gathering in hopes that he would become the leader of their drive to remove Yeltsin from the presidency and to encourage more assertive Russian measures to preserve the federation and protect the interests of the twenty-five million Russian nationals living in neighboring republics.[22] Rutskoi delivered a keynote speech but then left the congress as extreme rightist groups created an inhospitable atmosphere for him. Despite Aksiuchits' wish to prevent Dmitry Vasilev from even attending the congress, the Memory leader managed to win the right to address the gathering.[23]

At the end of the patriotic congress, Gleb Yakunin held a press conference in the building of the Moscow city soviet in order to denounce Aksiuchits. He was joined by Vitalii Savitsky and Valerii Borshchev, who announced that they were becoming the co-chairmen of a new Russian Christian Democratic Union which had been organized on January 25-26 in St. Petersburg. They accused Aksiuchits of advocating the revival of the Soviet empire by collaborating with "national Bolsheviks." In doing so, they asserted, Aksiuchits had discredited Christian democracy in the eyes of supporters of democratic reform. Consequently, they declared that the political line of the Christian Democratic Movement had "nothing in common with the goals and tasks of Christian democracy."[24] At the same time the new Christian Democratic Union declared its intention to join the political movement calling itself "Democratic Russia," a liberal reformist alliance in which Yakunin occupies a prominent position.

The Christian Democratic International embraced Yakunin's group, declaring it a full member of the world organization, while according to Ogorodnikov's union a subsidiary association. Echoing the hyperbolic Russian political rhetoric, the international organization harshly criticized Aksiuchits for what it charged was his support for totalitarianism and consequent rejection of democratic principles.[25] The objections against Aksiuchits from both Russian and international Christian democrats are exaggerations that interpret expressions of anti-western nationalism as necessarily illiberal, although it seems that Aksiuchits is not as radical a reformist as Yakunin.

In contrast to Aksiuchits, Father Yakunin has consistently supported President Yeltsin. He frequently appears alongside the president in political situations and remains prominent in the minority in the Russian parliament that supports him. Yakunin also played the lead role in publishing information from the KGB's archives that purported to identify specific Orthodox bishops who worked as agents for the secret police before the breakup of the Soviet Union. Father Polosin acquired the documents through his chairmanship of the Supreme Soviet's committee on religious matters. In early 1992, Yakunin and Polosin produced articles for several newspapers that exposed the intentions and mechanisms of the KGB for exploiting the Orthodox church both domestically and in ecumenical church activities.[26] What appears to have been a serious threat by the Russian procuracy to pursue criminal prosecution against Yakunin for security violations finally was stopped by Yeltsin's intervention on his behalf.[27]

Alexander Ogorodnikov, representing the original Christian Democratic Union, did not support Yakunin and Polosin in their exposure of the KGB links in the church. Such revelations damaged the church, he said. It would be better for the compromised hierarchs to express their repentance themselves. He also expressed his distaste for the cynical alliance he saw emerging between the current leaders of the church and politicians who only recently were their persecutors. Continuing to refuse on principle to engage his Christian Democratic Union in the electoral process, Ogorodnikov declared that its purpose was to demonstrate "what Christian democracy really means." As an example of this, he cited the charitable activities like soup kitchens and shelters for homeless and runaways which the union operates in Moscow. The union also tries to work through members of parliament to achieve its political goals which include privatization of means of production and advocacy of human rights. Ogorodnikov specified the protection of the ethnic Russians living in the Baltic states as among the civil rights causes that the Christian Democratic Union promotes.[28]

Other Christian democrats who had been more closely associated with Aksiuchits in leading the Christian democratic movement also distanced themselves from him. Several members of the duma of RKhDD criticized his willingness to carry his opposition to Yeltsin so far as to cooperate with the so-called "Red-Brown opposition," meaning the Russian nationalists and Communists.[29] Aksiuchits retaliated against this mutiny by removing five members from the steering body. Father Polosin, who had been co-president with Aksiuchits, denounced his compromise in strong language: "It is as if the Orthodox, in order to combat the Catholics, allied themselves with sodomites."[30]

By the summer of 1992, Aksiuchits found himself isolated from other important elements of Christian democracy, although he retained the support of several of the original duma members, including co-president Anishchenko, Artem Artemov, and Ilia Konstantinov. On June 20, the RKhDD held a congress in Moscow with 240 delegates representing forty-eight Russian cities and regions. The congress elected Aksiuchits party chairman.[31] Aksiuchits continued to claim that he was the leader of Russian Christian Democracy, a role that the media seemed willing to recognize. In August, *Moscow News* published an interview with him in which he called for the Russian Congress of People's Deputies to remove Yeltsin from office and create an extraordinary administration, a "type of government of national accord and committee of national salvation." He announced his intention to run for president of Russia when the extraordinary administration finally declared elections after having restored stability to the country.[32] While in his political statements he appeared largely in agreement with Vice President Rutskoi and the opposition group Civic Accord that united Travkin's, Rutskoi's, and Volsky's political groups, Aksiuchits failed to establish an effective way to work with them. Civic Accord rebuffed his overtures for cooperation, a response which he criticized as their unwise wish to compromise with Yeltsin and keep him in office. Aksiuchits declared unequivocally that Yeltsin must leave the presidency because his policies were leading to disaster for Russia.[33]

In late 1992, Aksiuchits had to stake out his own political position. One distinctive situation, he declared, defined this position: the Christian Democratic Movement alone among political parties had no direct links to nor descent from the old Communist party apparatus. Consequently the movement was free from the inescapable authoritarian habits of the past. Aksiuchits charged that the Yeltsin government, despite its democratic rhetoric, constituted a restoration of totalitarian politics that "under the flag of democracy is establishing a regime of liberal communism." By way of contrast, Aksiuchits declared that the Christian democrats offered a Russian national rebirth based on a one-thousand-year-old culture whose "enlightened patriotism" seemed incomprehensible to the contemporary press, regardless of whether it professed to be leftist liberal or rightist Communist.[34]

Aksiuchits criticized the Yeltsin-Gaidar government for its adherence to a policy he identified as the free market neoliberalism of Friedrich Hayek and Milton Friedman that removed the state's intrusion into the economy by simply abandoning control over prices. As an alternative, Aksiuchits pointed to the Christian Democratic tradition of Germany that promoted a "social market economy" with the state influencing distribution while it was disengaged from production. The Russia that emerged from the old Communist system presented the opposite situation of continued state monopoly of production with an unsupervised market establishing prices. This situation resulted from the liberalization of prices at the beginning of 1992 before privatization of production had been accomplished. Aksiuchits recalled that the Christian Democratic program in Germany had first carried out monetary reform, then privatized production, and, in the end, freed prices.

Because Yeltsin's neoliberalism had begun with liberalization of prices, Russia had fallen into economic ruins. The greater part of the population had been reduced to poverty. Aksiuchits feared most that desperation would drive people to embrace a dictator who promised economic security. He predicted that Boris Yeltsin constituted the image of that demagogic figure.

Aksiuchits calculated that there was as much disaster lying in wait for Russia in the radicalism of western Reaganism, which is what he understood Yeltsin's program to be, as there had been in Lenin's Bolshevism. Indeed, he asserted that there was an essential equality between the two in the practical implementation in Russia. Instead of each of these secularized systems, Aksiuchits offered an indigenous Russian Orthodox alternative.

The number of Russian Christian democrats is small. They constitute a tiny group that currently wields little effective political power. Their potential for effect is reduced even more by the intensity of their disputes among themselves, an inclination toward suspicion and extremism which is a legacy of Russia's political past.

But the Christian democrats are significant nevertheless because they illustrate important patterns and struggles found within the Russian nation. They are searching for a usable past, one which will provide a system of values and beliefs to define the nation's identify and to hold the society together and give it direction. They proceed from the important premise that Russia's history is a history of Christian Orthodoxy and they take seriously what it means for a nation to find and know itself.

It is easy to be skeptical about the prospects of a religiously grounded politics in a supposedly secularized age. That skepticism may be quite justified. But the Christian democrats themselves draw hopeful conclusions from evidence of the effectiveness of Christians democrats in multiparty systems of Europe. They are encouraged by the evident sympathetic treatment accorded Russia's Orthodox tradition in the print and broadcast media. Their optimism may prove to be justified if their message, which seems so out of tune with western secularism, turns out to be quite in harmony with the yearnings of a Russian society in chaos.

Notes

1. Akademiia obshchestvennykh nauk pri TsK KPSS [Hereafter AON], *Khristianskie partii i samodeiatel'nye ob" edineniia. Sbornik materialov i dokumentov* (Christian parties and independent associations. Collection of materials and documents) Moscow, 1990, p. 48.

2. Foreign Broadcast Information Service [Hereafter FBIS], *Daily Report. Soviet Union,* August 29, 1989, p. 80.

3. Igor' Zotov, "Aleksandr Ogorodnikov: Nashe vremia pridet goda cherez tri" (Our time will come in three years), *Nezavisimaia gazeta,* October 29, 1992, p. 2.

4. AON, *Khristianskie partii,* pp. 48, 90-92.

5. AON, *Khristianskie partii*, pp. 131-137.

6. Zotov, "Aleksandr Ogorodnikov," p. 2.

7. Nataliia Iziumova, "Russia's Christian Democrats," *Moscow News*, No. 21, June 3-10, 1990, p. 6.

8. Osnovnye polozheniia politicheskoi programmy rossiiskogo khristianskogo democraticheskogo dvizhennia" (Fundamental principles of the political program of the Russian Christian Democratic Movement), AON, *Khristianskie partii*, pp. 102-114, English translation in *Religion, State and Society*, Vol. 20, No. 3-4, 1992, pp. 179-187.

9. *Iziumova*, "Russia's Christian Democrats," p. 6.

10. Put' k istine, ili za chto ratuiut khristianskie demokraty," (The Path to the Truth, or What Do Christian Democrats Stand For?), *Pravda*, January 7, 1992, p. 2.

11. "Deklaratsiia uchreditel'nogo sobraniia Rossiiskogo Khristianskogo Demokraticheskogo Dvizheniia" (Declaration of the Founding Meeting of the Russian Christian Democratic Movement), AON, *Khristianskie partii*, pp. 118-120.

12. AON, *Khristianskie partii*, p. 47.

13. S. Filippov, "KhDS: Zhit' ne po zlu" (Not to live by evil), *Dialog*, No. 10, July 1990, pp. 31-33.

14. *Krasnaia zvezda*, August 30, 1990, p. 4.

15. Interview with Viktor Aksiuchits, reprinted in *Christian Democracy*, No. 13, May-June 1991, p. 22.

16. Text of the law was printed in *Sovetskaia rossiia*, November 10, 1990, p. 5.

17. Boris Zverev, "Russian Christian Democratic Conference Concludes," *TASS*, October 28, 1990, FBIS, Daily Report, Soviet Union, October 30, 1990, p. 68.

18. *Pravda*, January 7, 1992, p. 2; Natalia Babasian, "New Faces of CDMR," *Ekspres khronika*, No. 13, March 24-30, 1992.

19. I. Zaramenskii, "Ob"edinenie demokratov-patriotov" (Association of Democrats and Patriots), *Kul'tura*, No. 10, 1992, p. 2.

20. "Politicheskii avtoportret. Rossiiskoe khristianskoe demokraticheskoe dvizhenie" (A Political Self-portrait. The Russian Christian Democratic Movement), *Rossiiskaia gazeta*, January 10, 1992, p. 2; Pravda, January 7, 1992, p. 2.

21. Interview with Viktor Aksiuchits, Interfax, FBIS, Daily Report, *Central Eurasia*, February 14, 1992, p. 43; Viktor Aksiuchits, speech on Russian Television Network, February 6, 1992, FBIS, *Daily Report. Central Eurasia*, February 12, 1992, pp. 47-48; V. Aksiuchits, "My vse obmanuty" (We All Were Deceived), *Pravda*, January 21, 1992, p. 4; RFE/RL *Daily Report*, No. 3, January 7, 1992; Aleksandr Rutskoi, "Sil'naia vlast'—dlia demokratii," *Nezavisimaia gazeta*, February 13, 1992, p. 2; Igor Potapov, "The Russian

Christian-Democratic Union: Its Positions and Prospects," *Christian Democracy*, No. 20, July-August 1992, pp. 25-26.

22. Moskovskii komsomolets, January 18, 1992, cited in RFE/RL Daily Report, No. 20, January 30, 1992.

23. Marina Perevozkina, "Who Is Lame in the Left Leg?," *Ekspres khronika*, No. 6, February 1992; A. Shchipkov, "Reds? Brownshirts? Or Whites after all?" *Christian Democracy*, No. 18, March-April 1992, pp. 13-14.

24. Natalia Babasian, "New Party of Christian Democrats," *Ekspres khronika*, No. 6 (February 1992)

25. Anthony de Meeus, "Update on Russian Christian Democracy," *Christian Democracy*, No. 18, March-April 1992, p. 10.

26. John B. Dunlop, "KGB Subversion of Russian Orthodox Church," RFE/RL *Research Report*, Vol. 1, No. 12, March 20, 1992, pp. 51-53.

27. "Father Gleb Yakunin Threatened with Criminal Charges," *Christian Democracy*, No. 19, May-June 1992, pp. 3-4; see also RFE/RL Daily Report, No. 144, July 30, 1992.

28. Zotov, "Aleksandr Ogorodnikov," p. 2.

29. Natalia Babasian, "New Faces of CDMR," *Ekspres khronika*, No. 13, March 24-30, 1992.

30. Igor' Surikov, "Aksiuchits i Astaf'ev teriaiut storonikov?" (Are Aksiuchits and Astafiev losing their supporters?), *Nezavisimaia gazeta*, June 3, 1992, p. 2.

31. FBIS, Daily Report, Central Eurasia, June 22, 1992, pp. 44-45; RFE/RL *Daily Report*, No. 172 (September 8, 1992); No. 182, September 25, 1992.

32. Tat'iana Mikhal'skaia, "Viktor Aksiuchits," *Moskovskie novosti*, No. 33, August 16, 1992, p. 11; cf., V. Aksiuchits, "Gospoda nedavnie tovarishchi" (Recent Comrades of the Lord), *Delovoi mir*, August 25, 1992), p. 10.

33. V. Aksiuchits, "Esli vam doroga Rossiia—uidite v otstavku" (If Russia Is Dear to You, Retire), *Pravda*, October 21, 1992, p. 3.

34. Viktor Aksiuchits, "V plenu novykh utopii" (Captive of New Utopias), *Nezavisimaia gazeta*, October 23, 1992, p. 2; cf., idem, "Ispytanie russkoi idei" (An Examination of the Russian Idea), *Pravda*, October 15, 1992, p. 2.

6

Sociological Models of Religion in Post-Communist Societies

Jerry G. Pankhurst

In early 1991, James Billington wrote a famous article, first circulated among the Washington and Moscow political and ideological intelligentsia, then published in August of that year, describing the difficult situation in the USSR as similar to the problems that a person with a severe fever goes through. The experience is not pleasant, but it is the organism's means of fighting the infection that, if not overcome, would more severely damage or even destroy the person. Billington said, "We are at the fever break in the body politic of Soviet totalitarianism.... The totalitarian fever must break so the patient can stop dying and start sweating, stop lying down and start getting up."[1] Billington went on to portray the Soviet Union as "traumatically enduring the end of [the historic global phase of the victory of freedom] and the beginning of [the phase of the search for authority."][2]

The dramatic medical analogy led some of us to question whether or not the fever had already, perhaps, damaged the organism so much that the patient might not survive. We know now that the Soviet Union did not survive the illness. The question still hangs in the balance for Russia itself.

For each of the numerous times for several years that I have met with public or scholarly groups to discuss the situation of Russia or East-Central Europe and Eurasia, there have always been some portentous events afoot at the time, so maybe we should not inflate those goings on at the moment. We are in a season of portent, a very long season. Billington's "search for authority" phase of history is turning out to be a very dangerous, often bloody, phase. We all hope and pray that ways will be found to stanch the flow of blood and get on with healthy progress.

But what of Billington's optimistic orientation, which asserts the hopeful outcome of a cure after the fever breaks?

First, it appears that certain organic improvements are certifiable. Russia has moved to a stage of post-totalitarian development, even though there are threats of a return to the old ways—or perhaps worse, a move to new, cunningly adapted forms of totalitarianism combining many of the negative potentials of modern civilization. But for now—and I believe for the longer term—Russia has abjured Stalinism and its variants.

Second, the economy, whatever its travails, has turned a corner toward marketization, putting its back to centralized control. I am certain that a less centralized economy will be able to serve the Russian people better than the ossified, mismanaged, and distorted centralized bureaucratic system of the recent past.

Third, respect for human rights has been quite deeply institutionalized in Russia. There remain some problems; indeed, they take on new forms with the other changes afoot. But the foundation of the situation is profoundly different than just a few years ago.

A central part of the new respect for universal human rights is the provision, now reasonably solidly in place, for freedom of conscience and belief. It is in this sphere where this volume wants to focus. There are two basic questions, I think: Can the fever in Russia be healed in part by spiritual renewal? and Can the institutions of spiritual renewal, the churches, and other religious groups, revive themselves and recover from the long siege of illness to reach a stage of health for themselves?

In short, crises of overcoming totalitarianism have transformed into crises of finding stability, order, integration, within the new potentialities of freedom. If we can say that Russia has achieved the basic elements of freedom of a variety of important things — speech, conscience, assembly, etc. — then, we must ask, freedom for what? Religiously sensitive observers and religious actors in Russia itself have various views on what is to be done. Here are a few considerations about what is going on that are meant to facilitate answering the very important question, freedom for what?

Before proceeding — a disclaimer. My comments so far have focused on the Soviet and Russian situation. They may fairly directly apply to the Baltic societies, Belorussia and Ukraine. Beyond these societies, various qualifications must be made; I think the qualifications will fall into place at the appropriate time.

Now, I will turn to a more analytical approach to some of these issues. I am reminded of a frustrated sociology major who, not finding adequate theoretical basis for her research on college admissions patterns, resorted to recounting the so-called "garbage can model" as an explanation — throw it all in the garbage can, because there are too many factors that have an influence on the choice of a college. Similarly, one of my favorite theoretical approaches to social and cultural change is that of anthropologists Godfrey and Monica Wilson. They say that less developed societies always experience a great deal of "muddle" as they change.[3] Can we elevate "muddle" to the level of a theoretical concept here, because there sure is a lot of it in various places, high and low in Russia and Eurasia—not to mention here in the USA![4] Even though the garbage can, or muddle, may provide a more appropriate technique of theoretical analysis, I will nevertheless try to be a bit more concrete and explicit in my theoretical descriptions of what is happening.

Seven Master Processes

There are seven "master processes" that I see at work in the developments in religion in the societies of the territory of the former Soviet Union. These processes are also at work in the former East-Central European societies that had experienced Soviet domination. We have tended to think that religion is some kind of pure essence that was suppressed by the authoritarian governments of the Communists. Now that some of the religious phenomena have poked out through the rubble of the Soviet and post-communist regimes of the region, it is apparent that what was suppressed was religion as it is in real life, not in our dreams. It is religion with roots in a history and its own profoundly important traditions and "habits of the heart" (to quote the title of a famous book about the religious substrate of American culture and society).[5] Many of the traditions and habits of the heart have pre-Soviet roots that were not extirpated by the Communists; some of them should have been, others of them are treasures to preserve. The vital juices coming to the body from those roots, freely nurturing the society and culture for the first time in many years, have their own special impact and unique character.

For each of my seven master processes, I will try to identify a good "marker" or indicator as an example of what I mean.

1. De-Sovietization, including De-Atheization
    Marker: Low religious knowledge and experience

One of the unquestioned consequences of the Soviet period of state atheism was the gradual loss of acquaintance with religious dogma, general information about religion, and with first-hand religious experience. The era was one of enforced reduction of religious knowledge and declining connections with the family or community background in religion that may have been in place. The atheist program built upon a culture that was largely unversed in religious matters in any event, since Russian Orthodoxy stressed liturgical compliance but not theological or intellectual orientations to faith on the part of the populace. Consequently, the post-Soviet population in Slavic areas where Orthodoxy predominates emerged from the Soviet era nearly illiterate regarding religion. What was known about religion was mostly that which could be learned from a few trips to church plus a bit of informal instruction from family members, especially from the inimitable babushka. For all intents and purposes, Russians know almost nothing of the intellectual or philosophical aspects of their faith, and they know virtually nothing about other faiths. The moderate knowledge of religion found in the Tsarist population has declined during the Soviet period to a lower level of knowledge. Only now, with the creation of freer conditions, has it become possible to seek out and obtain knowledge of this important area of life.

2.   Renewal and Revitalization
Marker: Number of churches, religious activity, worshippers

Following the collapse of the ideology of Marxism-Leninism, which was apparently accomplished by the end of the 1970s, at the latest, there was a spiritual vacuum in Russian society. There may have been such a vacuum earlier in non-Soviet societies. The churches have rushed in, and when they attained essential freedoms, they virtually exploded. Two examples from Orthodoxy:

According to the Archbishop of Kaluga, Kliment, in 1988 there were some twenty-five churches in the diocese; when he came to head the eparchy in August 1990, there were thirty-six parishes; when I interviewed him in June 1991, there were seventy-five parishes. Similarly, Metropolitan Filaret of Minsk, now head of the Belorussian Orthodox Church which is tied to Moscow but canonically autonomous, said that in 1988, there were 360 parishes in his church; by August 1992, when I interviewed him, there were 760.

These are truly astounding increases, and they can be matched in several other post-Communist confessions and societies. However, such growth has not come without problems. First, it has occurred in a time of great price inflation; thus, not only must the churches find money to establish new parishes, but the costs are greater than they would have been earlier. These are essentially "brick and mortar" costs, since the parishes have usually been self-generated. However, typically, in the former Soviet Union, new parishes are given old churches, many of which have been left in disuse, or have been grossly misused during much of the Soviet period. The costs of renovation of such structures in normal times are high; in times of inflation, they are horrendous. In my interview with Archbishop

Kliment, he noted with despair that all the new churches were "ruins" and he did not have the funds to repair them nearly adequately. Being a free actor in the market itself causes new strains for the churches.

3.   Pluralization/"Freedomization"/Institutional Differentiation (A combination of an economic model and human rights theory)
    Marker: Number of different churches and denominations

When the disciplining power of the Soviet Party-State was broken, it naturally loosed tendencies for theological sectarianism that precede institutional differentiation. My "hyperbolic principle" of religious group differentiation, which I first published in my dissertation in 1978, argues for this outcome.[6]

The human rights theorist would argue that the propensity for group differentiation has been suppressed, and the condition of freedom has simply released this natural condition to run its own course.

The economic model would argue that there is a pattern of natural product differentiation in the religious market, new groups both appealing to preexisting desires and also creating the desire for their product where it did not previously exist. From the economic point of view, for example, last October's Billy Graham Crusade in Moscow was as much to create a spiritual yearning among the Russians as to satisfy that which preexisted. Having differentiated the Protestant product from the Orthodox or Catholic, the consequence of the Crusade should be a growth in the number of Protestants in Russia. The intentionality of this is not a mystery; the Graham organization is said to have collated the best list of all Protestant churches in the CIS that is available, and they organized a system to get Protestants to "flood" the Moscow market with their witness, recruiting new Protestants as part of the fulfillment of The Great Commission. Billy Graham has said he does not want to harm nor compete with Orthodoxy, but it seems clear that he views the unchurched as fair game for his product appeal.

4.   Nationalization/(Re-)Monopolization/"Establishmentization" (Argued on the basis of an economic model of religion)
    Marker: The organizational impasse of the wannabee religious monopolies; the defensive morale of the establishments; the laziness of the favored monopolies

If the religious monopolies or aspiring monopolies are lazy, they are risking their hard-earned investment in themselves, but laziness and presumptuousness are common among monopolies and wannabee monopolies who do not understand that they really are not monopolies like they used to be. Examples of this condition include the Polish Roman Catholic Church and the Russian Orthodox Church, in both of which the needs for reform are going largely unheeded while the churches pursue an agenda based in nationalist ambitions (for both) or maladaptive defensive resistance to adapting to new conditions (especially for the Russian Orthodox).

Some would argue that a religious monopoly is never fully possible. It would always generate its heretics and sectarians. Thus, I use the term "wannabee" monopoly.

It should be noted that processes three and four have contradictory outcomes for former establishments like the Russian Orthodox Church if the real religious market conditions are put in place by political authority. This qualification of market conditions is important and excludes the Polish case here, for Poland's overwhelming Roman Catholic context does not approach an open market. Because the political authorities in most of the newly independent states on the post-Soviet territory have established religious freedom with little confessional preference in law, religious entrepreneurial groups have jumped in with great vigor to gain market share. While this has caused the defensiveness of a wannabee monopoly, there are also voices within Orthodoxy trying to move the faith to a better competitive position. In some statements, even Patriarch Aleksi II sees the need not just to criticize and fight with newer or more sectarian groups, but to address the market needs or potential product preferences of the people more creatively and adaptively. The result is the interesting discussion of Orthodox spirituality, the quest to rediscover the old pre-Revolutionary theologians and philosophers, the desire to develop a stronger Orthodox social ethic and to get involved in "charity work" (loosely, "social ministry"). Thus, there are both closing down and opening up tendencies.

5.   Secularization/Rationalization
     Marker: Low attendance; apathy toward religion and churches

The great sociologist, Max Weber, thought that modernity necessarily meant the "disenchantment" of the world through ultra-rationalization of life in all spheres.[7] For too long, sociologists have taken this position for granted. However, even as we have now come to criticize it, there are certain aspects of the position which seem to retain validity. Especially in the formally secularized, "de-spiritized" Soviet circumstances—where children were taught disdain for religion and other nonscientific qualities— many people just are not concerned with religion, and it is not important in their lives. They believe that science or other forms of knowledge are all that is needed.

In the mid-1970s, the British sociologist Christel Lane noted that patterns of piety in Russia were quite similar to those in established church societies like Great Britain or Sweden.[8] Almost everyone claims a sort of affiliation, but it seems to mean nothing in their everyday lives.

Though the Russian Church still scores fairly high in measures of prestige among the people, its relative advantage over other institutions has clearly declined.[9] Similarly, the enamorment with the church on the part of some youth, intellectuals, and city folk has begun to wear thin, according to many accounts. There is the tendency to take the church for granted, to return to what would be "normal" patterns for an established church like the Anglican or Swedish Lutheran. Researchers at the Jagellonian University have found that in Poland, while the Catholic Church may have more political power than ever before, public avowals of faith are declining, and mass attendance is also considerably less than under the Communist and early post-Communist regimes.[10] There are some clear political reasons for this pattern; nevertheless, its appearance has still puzzled some.

6. Globalization/Fundamentalization/Sectarianization
    Marker: Sectarian, "fundamentalist" and "cultic" activity

There is a great deal of activity by numerous sectarian and cultic groups in Russia today. This reflects a globalization of the situation in that options from elsewhere have been imported into formerly closed circumstances; in addition, some theorists of globality contend that it stimulates a characteristic form of global, perhaps ecological, consciousness that is represented in some of these new groups. I am talking about the Hare Krishnas, the Unificationists, and a large number of even native shamanist, naturist and similar groups, not to mention the psychics and astrologers, that have become so much a part of the scene. Another response to globality, according to Robertson and other theorists, is the strengthening of the sense of locality. This ironic combination of stimuli led Roland Robertson to coin the term "glocality," that is, a local initiative, a sense of "community," if you will, that reflects the global consciousness of those involved.[11]

7. Privatization/Individualization
    Marker: Change in patterns of piety to more individualized forms; less attachment to the churches, but renewed claims of being religious on a personal basis

This pattern may be an extension of the influence of globalization, or it may reflect secularization on an individual basis; or it may reflect the spiritual response of people who have had no nurture in a church or religious community; or it may reflect an attempt to overcome the religious anomie occasioned by overwhelming new vistas in the religious boutiques that come with pluralization—a seemingly endless selection of religious products is proffered, and one may buy a little from each boutique, but thereby purchase into no one church or faith.

These processes all take place in the context of societies that are changing from ones in which the political/ideological institutional system dominated to ones in which the economic institutional system dominates. In fact, it is this very economic logic—the quest for productivity and efficiency, that quest which dominates the global society itself above all else—that has allowed the new freedoms for religion. If a religion does not play an economic role, it will endanger itself. Rather, those churches and parachurch organizations that do not play a successful economic role—running themselves like businesses in some sense, but more deeply promoting the values and self- conceptions that facilitate economic development—those that do not will decline, and those churches that do, and there will be some that do, will grow and come to dominate the culture in the future.

In the end, then, religious development in the post-Communist or post-Soviet period is, in my estimation, intimately tied up with the general social changes in society.

Recently Blair Ruble, the director of the Kennan Institute for Advanced Russian Studies at the Wilson Center in Washington, D.C., assessed the prospects for the future of Russia and quoted a couple of Russian observers:

> Scornful of Western materialism, Russians have, to quote the author Tatyana Tolstaya, "mocked the English with their machines, the Germans with their order and precision, the French with their logic, and finally the Americans with their love of money. As a result, in Russia we have neither machines, nor order, nor logic, nor money."[12]

Ruble continues:

> Boris Grushin, a leading Russian public opinion specialist, recently told a Wilson Center audience that he can identify five clusters of public opinion in his country ranging from the most retrograde fascism to libertarian democracy. Because these clusters of opinion are in pitched battle with one another, Russia's future remains very much in doubt. None of the five groupings can be readily identified with any particular social faction, Grushin

concluded, because each exists to a greater or lesser degree within
EACH AND EVERY RUSSIAN....[13]

So maybe we should just forget my master processes. Muddle it is!

Notes

The author gratefully acknowledges grant support from the International Research and Exchanges Board and the Faculty Research Fund of Wittenberg University for research travel to Russia during 1990-93. Materials gathered during these and other recent trips formed the basis of this paper.

1.   James M. Billington, "Russia's Fever Break," *The Wilson Quarterly,* Vol. 15, Autumn 1991, pp. 58-65. The quote is from pp. 60 and 64.

2.   Ibid., p. 60.

3.   Godfrey Wilson and Monica Wilson, *The Analysis of Social Change* (Cambridge: Cambridge University Press, 1968).

4. The notion of muddle is not being used for the first time in reference to changes in Russia. Blair Ruble used it several years ago to describe the circumstances in the late pre-Gorbachev era, asserting that the Soviet Union would "muddle through." See Blair Ruble, *The Wilson Quarterly,* Autumn 1985.

5.   Robert N. Bellah, Richard Marsden, William M. Sullivan, Ann Swidler and Steven M. Tipton, *Habits of the Heart: Individualism and Commitment in American Life* (Berkeley: University of California Press, 1985). The phrase of the title, as the authors acknowledge, originated from Alexis de Toqueville's famous treatise on Democracy in America.

6.   Jerry G. Pankhurst, *The Orthodox and the Baptists in the USSR: Resources for the Survival of Ideologically Defined Deviance* (Ph.D. dissertation, University of Michigan, 1978). Further development of the notion is found in Jerry G. Pankhurst, "The Sacred and the Secular in the USSR," in *Understanding Soviet Society,* ed. Michael Paul Sacks and Jerry G. Pankhurst (Boston: Allen and Unwin, 1988), pp. 167-192.

7.   Max Weber, "The Social Psychology of the World Religions," *From Max Weber,* ed. H. H. Gerth and C. Wright Mills (New York: Oxford University Press, 1958), pp. 267-301.

8.   Christel Lane, "Religious Piety among Contemporary Russian Orthodox," *Journal for the Scientific Study of Religion,* Vol. 14, 1975, pp. 139-158.

9.   Recent unpublished data demonstrate this process according to private communication from Iurii Levada, Director of the Center for Public Opinion Research, Moscow.

10. Halina Grzymala-Moszczynska, "Factors Affecting Unconditional Acceptance of the Institution of the Church in Poland;" also Irena Borovik, "Poland: Global Declarations of Faith in the Post-War Period." Both were papers read at the annual meeting of the Society for the Scientific Study of Religion, Washington, D.C., November 6-8, 1992.

11. See, for example, Roland Robertson, "The Sacred and the World System," *The Sacred in a Secular Age: Toward Revision in the Scientific Study of Religion*, ed. Phillipp E. Hammond (Berkeley: University of California Press, 1985), pp. 347-358; Roland Robertson and JoAnn Chirico, "Humanity, Globalization, and Worldwide Religious Resurgence: A Theoretical Exploration," *Sociological Analysis*, Vol. 46 (1985), pp. 219-242; also his paper presented at the international conference on Globalization and Religion, Washington D.C., November 8-10, 1992

12. Blair Ruble, "From the Center," *The Wilson Quarterly*, Vol. 17 (Spring 1993), p. 6.

13. Ibid.

7

Current Developments in Russia and the Response of the Russian Orthodox

Philip Walters

At the start of the 1990s, the Russian Orthodox Church finds itself in a paradoxical position, at once triumphant and defensive. It is claiming the fruits of freedom as its just reward for surviving decades of militant atheism, while at the same time suffering disorientation from challenges it has not had to face for more than seventy years. I will be arguing that neither triumphalism nor protectionism represents a response likely to lead to a fruitful role for the church in Russian society: what is needed is a sober assessment by the church of where the green shoots of growth are actually to be found, followed by a long period during which it patiently nurtures them.

Problems Facing the Church

A Marketplace of Faiths

Totalitarianism produced a strange kind of human being: the gullible cynic. By the 1970s, the Soviet population was starting to understand that despite its claims, Marxism-Leninism answered none of the fundamental questions about the meaning of life; at the same time, there was no possibility of finding out about alternative belief systems. Post-Soviet man therefore combines corrosive cynicism about the official ideology with a readiness to lend credence to almost anything else. As a Leningrad Christian recently wrote, observing the influx of all kinds of new faiths and sects, "There are no irreconcilable ideas for the average Soviet man. He has no religious hierarchy, no taboos, no religious discernment — only the hated

Soviet ideology and the rest."[1]

Such a person has no way of distinguishing true from false, good from evil. Western organizations are flooding into Russia; most have plenty of money and marketing skills; some are good and beneficial, while others are evil and harmful. Russian Orthodoxy is caught up in the maelstrom. Its clergy denounce or more soberly seek to assess the new creeds; at the same time Orthodoxy itself is being taken in vain. By early 1991, says historian Yevgeni Polyakov, "The Russian Orthodox Church was becoming ideological small change in the dispute over ways of saving the fatherland." Political groups of all colors from fascists to Christian Democrats are claiming to be grounded in Orthodoxy. Polyakov describes a "religious boom," but points out that "it would be a great mistake to confuse this with a national revival of Russian spirituality."[2]

Church Jurisdiction

The challenge from outside coincides with fundamental problems within the church. Foremost among these is the question of church jurisdiction. The Russian Orthodox Church in Exile is winning Russian parishes from the Moscow Patriarchate: various "catacomb" and "true" Orthodox churches are emerging from underground and challenging the Moscow Patriarchate for legitimacy; in Ukraine the reemergence of the Ukrainian Catholic Church, illegal from 1946 to 1989, has meant the loss to the Russian Orthodox Church of hundreds of clergy and churches; at the same time there is a complex schism in the Ukraine which began with a split between the Patriarchal Church and the "Russian Orthodox Church" (Kiev Patriarchate) led by defrocked Metropolitan Filaret, and a simultaneous challenge from the revived Ukrainian Autocephalous Orthodox Church.

Interdenominational Problems

An immediate consequence of the two problem areas outlined above has been a sharp deterioration in ecumenical relations, particularly between the Russian Orthodox and Roman Catholic churches. Already sensitive about Catholic intentions after the sudden legalization of the Ukrainian Catholic Church in 1989, the Moscow Patriarchate was further scandalized when in 1991 the Vatican appointed a number of bishops to the USSR as apostolic administrators, including bishop Tadeusz Kondrusiewicz as the first Roman Catholic bishop in Moscow since the 1930s. Patriarch Aleksi II has a long history of international ecumenical work, most recently as President of the Conference of European Churches; but it was on an ecumenical visit to Britain in autumn 1991, at a reception hosted in Lambeth Palace by the Archbishop of Canterbury, that he chose to denounce what he saw as the proselytizing intentions of the Catholic Church. In late 1992, it became known that the Patriarchate had been pressing the Russian government to introduce stricter legislation on the activity of foreign religious organizations on Russian territory.

The Legacy of Collaboration

"The Ukrainian state has achieved its independence," writes Yevgeni Polyakov, "but the Russian Orthodox Church has not achieved its independence yet."[3] Here Polyakov points to another problem which is preventing the church from responding coherently to the challenges of freedom. This is the question of collaboration between members of the church hierarchy and the communist security apparatus. After the August 1991 coup, Father Gleb Yakunin and Lev Ponomarev of the Russian government's Committee on Freedom of Conscience were able to work in the KGB's archives on religion. They published information on close cooperation with the KGB on the part of Metropolitans Yuvenali, Pitirim, and Filaret of Kiev, thus confirming the long-suspected existence of what one critic has dubbed a "Metropolitburo" in the church. In late 1991, the journalist Alexander Nezhny reported that he had recently interviewed Vadim Bakatin, head of the Ministry of Security (the successor body to the KGB), and his deputy, Oleinikov, and that the latter had told him that only fifteen to twenty percent of the Orthodox clergy had refused to cooperate with the KGB.[4]

Four months after Yakunin and Polyakov started work, the archives were closed again. A private prosecution was then brought against the two men by a former KGB general on the grounds that in publishing the material they had betrayed state secrets to the USA. The Orthodox Church has not subsequently requested that any of the archives of the KGB or the Council for Religious Affairs be made public; and Yevgeni Polyakov says that he has evidence that secret commissions, including specialists from the Patriarchate, have been working on the archives and that discussions have been going on about transferring material on religious persecution to the Patriarchate's own archives.[5]

It is clear, of course, that "cooperation with the KGB" can involve many different degrees of compromise. The priest Father Georgi Edel'shtein is one of those who firmly resisted any dealings with the authorities and who suffered at their hands in consequence. He is now uncompromisingly critical of those who did cooperate. Father Georgi was ordained a priest by Archbishop Khrizostom, who was prepared to do so even though twenty-two other bishops had refused. Khrizostom has a high reputation for integrity and spirituality. In 1990 he was appointed Archbishop of Vilnius and Lithuania, where he spoke out in favor of Lithuanian independence.

It now turns out that he was among those bishops who supplied information to the KGB. He claims he never told them anything important, however, and makes a clear distinction between himself and bishops like Metropolitan Mefodi (Nemtsov) of Voronezh and Lipetsk who made their career in the church but were in fact full KGB officers and even atheists.[6]

The option of "discretion" rather than "valor" in the face of militant state atheism has always been open to men of conscience as well as to weak or compromised individuals. In today's Russia, however — in the church as much as in the realms of politics and the economy — the task of mutual understanding and reconciliation has hardly begun. The climate is rather one of mutual suspicion and recrimination. As one participant observed from the floor at a conference in Moscow in February 1993 on the theme of "The KGB Yesterday, Today and Tomorrow," the biggest problem facing Russia today is not economic or political; it is spiritual. Russia is in the grip of a profound "spiritual sickness" ("dukhovnaya bolezh").

Tensions in the Church Leadership

All of the problems described above combine to sap the energies of the church at all levels — leadership, clergy and laity. Another phenomenon producing a degree of paralysis at leadership level is the fact that the sudden arrival of freedom in Russia has brought to the surface natural tensions between conservatives and progressives within the Holy Synod and in the episcopate as a whole. The Russian Orthodox Church ideally proceeds on the basis of unanimity; and at the moment this is hard to achieve. Patriarch Aleksi himself seems to adopt a centralist position; but as we have seen, despite his own ecumenical record, he has felt constrained to speak out against the perceived intentions of the Roman Catholic Church. At the time of the coup in August 1991, many were critical of the failure of the Patriarchate to pronounce a clear early condemnation of the Emergency Committee. What was nevertheless clear was that the metropolitans and bishops had very different personal responses to what was occurring. While Metropolitans Pitirim and Filaret of Kiev both asserted that the situation was perfectly normal, Metropolitan Ioann of Leningrad was calling on citizens to defend the democratic authorities against the plotters. The pattern of tensions is made more complicated by the fact that a progressive attitude on one set of issues does not rule out a conservative stance on others. That same Metropolitan Ioann, for example, is one of the most vociferous in defense of Orthodoxy against what he sees as the tainting influence of other denominations.

The Political Situation in Russia

Sergei Grigoryants of the "Glasnost Foundation," which organized the above-mentioned conference on the KGB, spoke as follows early in 1993:

> There is no doubt that the secret services ("spetssluzhby") have not changed substantially as far as personnel is concerned...and it is unlikely that the world-view or sympathies of those involved have changed either. But, clearly, in the new conditions new interests have arisen. For example, former and current employees of the KGB are much more heavily involved now in various commercial organizations....So the facts show that although the status of the secret services has changed, their interests and mode of operation remain the same. And the opportunities they now have to influence the situation in the country both financially and politically are visibly growing and subject to no control at all....They are not aiming to restore the old communist regime; but the new society they are creating will operate on the basis of control by "their people" in all spheres, authoritarian discipline, general surveillance and the suppression of all free thought. And this new society could turn out to be much worse than the old decaying socialist system.[7]

One symptom of the phenomenon described by Grigoryants was taken by many to be the new "Consultative Council of Experts" ("Ekspertno-konsul'tativny sovet") in 1993 attached to the government's "Committee on Freedom of Conscience" chaired by Frs. Gleb Yakunin and Vacheslav Polosin. The chairman of the new Council was Yuri Rozenbaum, a jurist who was involved in drafting an earlier and less liberal version of the new Soviet law on religion which was finally adopted in 1990. Other members of the Council were to be nine named individuals (academics, lawyers, journalists and politicians), a representative each of the Russian Ministry of Security, of the Security Council and of the Committee on National Policies, and representatives of nine specified religious denominations. According to journalist Alexander Shchipkov, who for over two years studied the gestation of this Council and related developments in St. Petersburg, it looked as if this committee was to take over some or all of the functions of the defunct Council for Religious Affairs (CRA) which exercised control over religious life in the Soviet Union.

Invited to speak at the February 1993 conference on the KGB, Rozenbaum argued that the churches in democratic Russia would have to function as part of a law-governed state, and that the new Council would enable them to do so. His remarks were received with a degree of skepticism. The Orthodox laywoman and former prisoner of conscience Zoya Krakhmal'nikova wanted to know how the representatives from the denominations were going to be chosen: what guarantee would there be that they would not be collaborators with the KGB? "Why can't you leave the churches in peace?" came an angry query from the floor.

Shchipkov suggests that some at least of the interest groups behind the new Council and similar endeavors (which include plans for new and more restrictive legislation on religion) represent those who want to co-opt one or another chosen denomination and use it to provide an ideological prop for the state. "The chosen religion will have internal pressure put on it; it will be gelded and transformed into a puppet-like instrument. I would suggest that the natural choice will fall upon the long-suffering Orthodox Church."[8] It is clear that some Orthodox bishops would welcome the opportunity to become part of a state church, perhaps even on the terms outlined by Shchipkov. It is equally clear that Patriarch Aleksi himself does not want his church to seek a preferred or established position in the new Russian state. Once again the hierarchy finds itself divided. Inevitable Decentralization? There is, then, widespread fear within Russia of insidious attempts by the old establishment to reintroduce a regime of firm central control. Others both within Russia and abroad would however argue that those who aim to do so do not understand economic and political realities. In his article "Kak nam obustroit' Rossiyu?" (How Are We Going to Rebuild Russia?") published in two Russian newspapers, Alexander Solzhenitsyn argued as follows:

> All our provincial districts...must acquire complete freedom in economic and cultural terms, together with strong (and increasingly influential) local self-government. Our country will not be able to lead a full and independent life unless there emerge perhaps forty centres of vitality and illumination through the breadth of the land. Each would be a focus of economic activity as well as of culture, education, library resources, and publishing enterprises, so that the population of the surrounding area could receive a full share of cultural sustenance...[9]

According to Solzhenitsyn, decentralization is also the prerequisite for the growth of true democracy, which cannot be imposed from the center, but which has to develop in small towns or groups of villages. "Only in areas of this size can voters have confidence in their choice of candidates since they will be familiar with them both in terms of their effectiveness in practical matters and in terms of their moral qualities."[10]

Among observers of Russia in the West there is disagreement over whether that country will continue along the path towards democracy and the successful introduction of a market economy or whether political stalemate and the stagnation of economic reform will mean that Russia, like the Soviet Union before it, breaks up into independent regions.[11] What seems to me self-evident is that if the former is to happen the groundwork will have to be done at the local level: neither political nor economic pluralism can be imposed from above in a country as vast as Russia and weighed down, as Russia is, by so much dead matter from its recent totalitarian past. The growth of genuine pluralism requires tolerance for the opinions of another and respect for his integrity; it requires first of all education and the nurturing of personal spiritual values. In the remainder of this essay I am going to argue that this is the task of the churches, and particularly of the Russian Orthodox Church as by far the largest denomination in Russia; that despite the profound disorientation of the church leadership described above there is much encouraging activity within the church community; and that there are also encouraging signs that the leadership, albeit cautiously and hesitantly, is frequently ready to protect and nurture the spontaneous initiatives of the faithful.

The Priorities for the Church

Priorities are being set both by the official church leadership and by clergy and laity at the grass roots. There is tension, both potential and actual, between what the hierarchy wants and what local Orthodox activists want, but also the potential for cooperation, and gratifyingly frequent examples of actual cooperation too.

Inspiration for Orthodox Activists

Since the 1970s, lay Orthodox activists have found inspiration in the Silver Age of Russian religious philosophy and artistic creativity which spanned the turn of the century and ended only with the Bolshevik Revolution of 1917. Many of those who wrote from an Orthodox perspective at that time were actively involved in social or political work. What particularly inspired the activists of the 1970s was the theme of creativity; and it was in the context of creativity that they were fascinated by the Orthodox understanding of "sobornost' " which as it was developed during the nineteenth century was an understanding of the community reflecting the creative dynamic within the Trinity.

A recent article by Yevgeni Pazukhin from St. Petersburg reflects on the activities of the seminar "37" in Leningrad in the second half of the 1970s which involved young people in just this enterprise of rediscovery of their creative Orthodox heritage. Apparently a number of Orthodox clergy were initially interested and participated actively but later withdrew,

Pazukhin says, because the church was suspicious of too much lay initiative in the spiritual field. For the church leadership, this lay enterprise smacked of Protestantism: "but of course", writes Pazukhin, "this wasn't Protestantism. It was, to use Tillich's phrase, 'the Protestant principle', a very fertile principle, as the history of the western church shows."[12]

Viktor Aksiuchits of the Russian Christian Democratic Movement has recently argued that Russian Orthodoxy is superior to Western Christianity precisely because it is creative. The Orthodoxy he has in mind, however, is that of the "Non-Possessors," the followers of Nil Sorsky who in the late 15th century championed the ascetic path of the monk who renounced worldly goods and pursued spiritual insight and simple toil in monasteries beyond Russia's frontiers. For Aksiuchits, Russia's tragedy is that the "Non-Possessors" lost their struggle with the "Possessors," the followers of Iosif of Volokolamsk, who championed a rich church closely identifying and collaborating with the secular power. The triumph of "Iosiflyanstvo" meant the triumph of pride and passivity in the Russian church, and this in turn prepared the ground for the Bolshevik Revolution.[13] At a gathering of politicians in Moscow in early 1993, Valeri Novodvorsky argued that Russia's tragedy was, "We accepted not the Faustian Christianity of the West, but the magic formulae of Eastern Christianity." "Let us reform our historical church," he urged, "let us include in it a strong Protestant ethic, based on our national traditions, and we will get what we want: a great, prosperous state."[14]

Political Activity

For seventy years, the bishops and clergy of the Russian Orthodox Church were forbidden to comment on any aspect of the political life of the Soviet Union. It was not surprising, then, that after the onset of glasnost' the church's leaders were slow to find a voice. Some observers interpret this as deliberate caution. "Throughout the years of perestroika," writes Yevgeni Polyakov, "the Moscow Patriarchate was trying neither to fall behind nor to overtake the rate at which timid democratic changes were developing, as they were administered in homeopathic doses to the citizens of the USSR by the Communist Party and the KGB."[15] There were nevertheless occasions when church leaders did speak out in surprisingly decisive tones. When citizens were killed in Vilnius in January 1991 in the course of Lithuania's bid to assert its independence from the Soviet Union, Patriarch Aleksi denounced the killings as "a great political mistake—in church language...a sin."

At the time of the August coup in 1991, Patriarch Aleksi II was celebrating the liturgy of the Feast of the Transfiguration in the Cathedral of the Dormition in the Kremlin for the first time since the revolution. He changed the words of the service to make it clear that they were praying for the people of Russia and not for the country's current self-styled leaders. On the second day, he issued a statement asking to hear directly from Gorbachev. Later he excommunicated the coup leaders. After the coup was over, he conducted a service for the three victims who included a Jew —thus sending an important signal to anti-Semites.

For many of the Patriarch's compatriots, this was not enough. The priest Fr. Gleb Yakunin, who spent many years in labor camp for his human rights work in the 1970s, was among the priests with Yeltsin in the White House throughout the three days of the coup. He appeared on the balcony and appealed to the crowd to "take courage and fulfil your duty as citizens." Father Gleb was clearly frustrated at the failure of the Patriarch to speak out clearly in the name of the Holy Synod despite a direct appeal by President Yeltsin. Yevgeni Polyakov deplores the fact that no bishop visited the troops on the barricades. He accuses the leadership of the Orthodox Church of "heroism after the event," and notes that it was only in his second message on August 21 that the Patriarch observed that "conflict and bloodshed have begun." "From my own personal experience and that of others," writes Polyakov, "I can confirm that the clashes in Moscow had already begun on August 19. You didn't have to be Patriarch to see that."[16]

Over the last few years the Russian political scene has witnessed a proliferation of Christian Democratic parties. Fr. Gleb Yakunin was one of the founder-members of the Russian Christian Democratic Movement; Alexander Ogorodnikov, whose followers were distributing food to the defenders of the White House at the time of the August 1991 coup, heads the Christian Democratic Union of Russia. These parties, although constantly suffering from the splits and recriminations which characterize so much of the social and political scene in Russia today, have represented the most obvious forum for the articulation of a Christian—mainly Orthodox— response to current political developments.

At the beginning, the Orthodox leadership was suspicious of the new parties; but over the last two years it has developed a more positive attitude. According to Vitali Savitsky of the Leningrad Christian Democrats, at the time of the spring 1990 election campaign the local church "told believers not to vote for candidates linked with the CDU, and used KGB information on our members to discredit them." After the summer of 1991, however, the church stopped speaking against the CDU; and at least one priest commended the "positive role" of Christian democracy in St. Petersburg. [17]

On December 1-2, 1992, the Patriarchate's Department of External Church Relations initiated and hosted a meeting of four of the five Christian Democratic parties in Russia. Metropolitan Kirill, the head of the Department, said that the low political profile which the Orthodox Church had adopted was not the consequence either of fear or of conservatism, but of the fact that the church wants to give priority to pastoral activity. The church obviously needs to talk to political parties, however, and first of all to those who claim to be Christian, although the church does not identify itself exclusively with Christian Democracy. Referring to the activity of Christian Democrats abroad, he regretted that the Russian parties do not seem to see in the Russian Orthodox Church—the majority church—a natural center for their activity. In discussion, the various parties agreed that they might all cooperate in working out a social program within the Orthodox Church and in determining how to put it into practice. They agreed to set up a series of seminars to this end, the first to be held in January 1993, and at the same time to set up a consultative council of Christian Democrats within the Patriarchate.[18]

Education

In August 1990, at a conference in England, Vladimir Poresh, an Orthodox layman from Leningrad, delivered a paper about his work with a new organization called "Open Christianity" which aimed to introduce atheists and unbelievers to the Christian faith. Poresh wondered whether the church was capable of fulfilling people's hopes that it would become a source of renewal in society. "Today," he said,

> despite the opportunities it now has for going out into the world, the church finds itself in a situation where it is quite incapable of fulfilling its appointed mission of determining the fate of our society...The reasons for the church's weakness and the distortion of its influence on the life of our society do not lie merely in the problems and sins of the church itself...but also in the thorough inadequacy of the church's Word, as addressed to the world, and in the undeveloped nature of Orthodox dogma, when it is required to reach out beyond the inner sacramental borders of the church and address itself to people who live a secular life...[19]

The problem has, of course, been that the Russian Orthodox Church has been systematically prevented for seventy years from coming to grips theologically with the challenges the twentieth century has presented to Christianity in other parts of the world. The Moscow scholar Sergei Lezov notes that just as it is impossible for Western Christianity to be the same now as it was before Auschwitz, so one might expect that it would be impossible for Russian Orthodox theology to be the same now as it was before the Gulag. "There is, however, no Orthodox 'thinking through' of the

Gulag... There is no post-Gulag Orthodox theology, for the simple reason that there is now no Christian theology in Russia at all."[20]

The practical impossibility of addressing contemporary issues which has faced the Russian Orthodox Church for seventy years is compounded by the traditional disinclination of the church to lay down a view on any particular subject which has to be followed by all the faithful. Recently the neo-fascist newspaper *Pamyat'* published *The Protocols of the Elders of Zion*, and was taken to court by a Jewish newspaper. The court approached deacon Andrei Kurayev of the Russian Orthodox Church to give an opinion on behalf of the church as to whether the *Protocols* are in fact anti-Semitic. This is a difficult task, says Kurayev in an interview. No doubt the *Pamyat'* team will field priests of their own who will argue the opposite of whatever he, Kurayev, might say. Then what is the view of the Russian Orthodox Church on Judaism? asks the interviewer. "I have to say that there are two views," says Kurayev. St. John Chrysostom was opposed to tolerance for Jews; St. Makari the Great was in favor. Kurayev then quotes the church historian Vasili Bolotov:

> If I see that different church fathers have different views on a particular question, nobody can force me to agree with the views of the father whom I personally judge to have the less well substantiated view in agreement with the spirit of the Gospel. In the same way, nobody can forbid me to agree with the views of any church father which have not been condemned by a church council and which attract me by their cogency, their beauty or their spiritual power.

Kurayev does not see how the Orthodox Church can take up any one position on the issue. "For me, this is quite unrealistic. There will always be different opinions, different people, and discussions among them." If it is forced to issue binding judgments, the Orthodox Church will be driven into a ghetto

> because if we foster suspiciousness amongst ourselves, develop amongst ourselves a "nose for heresy," and cut ourselves off from dialogue with the world, we will thereby deprive ourselves of any possibility of mission in today's world. And if we don't engage in mission, we will get into a position...where the Orthodox are busy talking about the Jews, while it's the Protestants in this country who are talking about the Gospel.[21]

The Russian Orthodox Church, then, has to overcome certain disadvantages as it enters the field of education. Despite this fact, however, it is taking certain initiatives in the field; and there are also some signs that the church is ready to extend its sponsorship and protection to those grass-roots Orthodox educational initiatives which seem likely to bear good fruit. The priest Father Alexander Min' was murdered in 1990. He was one of the most highly esteemed Russian Orthodox spiritual leaders, and his spiritual children are now active in many areas of Russian public life. Yekaterina Geneva, for example, is director of the Library of Foreign Literature in Moscow, where Father Alexander used to lecture to packed audiences. She has made the library into a center for cross-denominational and ecumenical encounters. It was the venue for the Alexander Min' memorial conference held in September 1992. The Patriarchate was represented at the conference by Metropolitan Yuvenali.

There is also an Alexander Min' University, to which Father Alexander himself delivered the opening address the day before he was murdered. It is just one of dozens of Orthodox higher educational initiatives, many of which have received official encouragement from the Patriarchate. The Humanities Lycée of the Christian Democratic Union of Russia was an ecumenical initiative aiming to develop a Christian conscience in young people. The Lycée had the official support of the Orthodox Church, and participated in December 1991 in an international seminar organized by the church to enable representatives of schools from various European countries to share their educational experiences. The Patriarchate itself has set up its own Orthodox University; Father Andrei Kurayev, mentioned above, is dean of the theological faculty. Meanwhile an Orthodox brotherhood, the "Bratstvo vo imya Vsemilostivogo Spasa," officially opened the St. Tikhon Orthodox Theological Institute in October 1991, with several hundred students following a four-year course. The Institute had already been functioning unofficially for two years, having been originally founded by a "starets" or holy man who was spiritual father to various members of the Brotherhood. From late 1991, the Institute has operated in the humanities faculty of Moscow State University. The Patriarch gave the Institute his blessing and made it clear to the staff that he wanted to support it; and this despite the fact that some of the old guard in the Patriarchate were apparently not enthusiastic about the Brotherhood's educational activity. In the view of Father Vladimir Vorob'yev, the head of the Institute, the KGB was still at work influencing the choice of candidates to train for the Orthodox priesthood and was still trying to ensure that the most uneducated and dullest were chosen. Father Vladimir placed great hopes on the St. Tikhon Institute as a source of a new generation of clergy.

It is, of course, clear that there are many tensions, rivalries and disputes both within and amongst the different educational initiatives. Conservatives clash with progressives, nationalists with internationalists. The monastery at Sergiyev Posad produces champions of a nationalism which often includes anti-Semitic and chauvinist elements. There are at least two other schools of Orthodox theology contending in the educational field: the "Paris" school and the "Petersburg" school, the latter characterized by openness to Catholicism and an interest in ecumenism.[22] The existence of all these tendencies may lead to problems in the short term; but surely diversity is a sign of hope for the building of a "pluralist" future in which respect for the views of minorities will indeed be nurtured.

Interdenominational Cooperation

In the summer of 1992, "Mission Volga" was organized from Finland. It involved 300 missionaries, musicians and teachers of seventeen different nationalities and twelve denominations. The groundwork for the mission's tour of Russia was done by Baptist pastor Peter Konoval'chik. The Holy Synod of the Russian Orthodox Church had decided in the spring that the church would take part, but after lengthy dispute withdrew its official involvement. The Orthodox Church nevertheless encouraged its clergy and people to participate on an individual basis. Among those who did so were two hierarchs: Archbishop Mikhail of Vologda and Archbishop German of Vologial. "Our lives will be lost if we do not know God's love and grace," said Archbishop German in a live television broadcast. "This whole generation could be lost if we do not let the seed of God's word grow." The mission was a fruitful experience. "I learned a lot about the Orthodox Church," said one western student participant. "Faith is a matter of heart and feeling. That is the secret of Orthodox spirituality."[23]

On January 15, 1992, as a lay initiative, an Ecumenical Council was set up in Moscow. The founders were worried by divisions among the churches in Russia at a time of mass influx from abroad of new creeds and sects. Both Metropolitan Kirill and the Catholic Archbishop Kondrusiewicz showed interest in the Council. On 25 January, during the Week of Prayer for Christian Unity, the Council organized ecumenical prayers in St Louis Catholic Church in Moscow. Among the participants were the ecumenist, Sandr Riga, the Baptist Vladimir Oivin, Archbishop Kondrusiewicz and Fr. Vsevolod Chaplin of the Moscow Patriarchate.[24] Once again, official Orthodox participation seems to have gone ahead despite contrary pressure from certain quarters in the Patriarchate. In September 1992, Sandr Riga reported that certain religious groups, including his own organization "Ecumene," had had difficulty getting articles published in the press. Before publishing anything on non-Orthodox groups, the editors of many papers check first with the Patriarchate and then refuse to publish any material which is not approved by that body.

Social Work

Russian Orthodox priests, parishes, political parties and lay groups are involved in a wide range of humanitarian and charitable activity. Just one example will suffice here to illustrate the kind of involvement which is possible at the local level between religious and secular institutions. For some years a representative of the US-based organization Prison Fellowship International has been visiting Russian prisons, including the prison in the city of Zagorsk near Moscow. He describes the underground cells, damp and poorly lit, in which the prisoners are now confined for twenty-four hours a day. Under the old regime, they used to be sent out to work in local enterprises, but the current economic situation, with growing numbers of unemployed, means that there is no work for the prisoners to do.

Zagorsk (now renamed Sergiyev Posad) is home to the Russian Orthodox Monastery of the Trinity and St. Sergius. In 1989, while it was still technically illegal to do so, three brothers from the monastery, Fathers Nikodim, Trifon and Bonifati, took the initiative to start visiting the prisoners. The prison commander gave his somewhat cautious approval. Before long Father Nikodim learned that in prerevolutionary times there had been a chapel within the prison. He found many volunteers among the inmates to reopen it, and soon the walls between the relevant cells had been demolished and the chapel refurbished. During a service at Pentecost, a sparrow flew in through an open window high in the chapel wall. "At Pentecost," said Father Nikodim, who was in the middle of his homily, "God sent his Holy Spirit to the disciples who were gathered in a room much like this. The Holy Spirit descended on them in the form of a dove. Today God has seen fit to grace us with a sparrow, for even though we are prisoners we are loved by him."

When he last went to Sergiyev Posad, the American visitor had just come from a Moscow prison

> where the climate was one of hopelessness and depression. The officers lacked discipline and respect, and depended mostly upon the vodka bottle. What a dismal experience. Just two hours later I was struck by a profoundly different atmosphere as I walked into the prison at Sergiyev Posad...I told (the commander) about my experience at the Moscow prison, "Why is it that this prison is so different even though most of the problems facing you are just the same as theirs?" I asked. "Why is it that your people seem so happy and disciplined?' Tears came to the commander's eyes. 'It's because of them," he said, pointing to Father Nikodim and his friends. "They have touched our heart and brought us peace and God."[25]

Reviving Parish and Monastic Life

The activities of the monks in Sergiyev Posad bring us, finally, to what is arguably the most vital element in the regeneration of Russia: the revival of the parishes and the founding of monastic communities as centers of spiritual formation, moral education, and practical initiatives in the building of true local community. Outlining his prescriptions for rebuilding Russia, Solzhenitsyn observes:

> One would have liked to be encouraged by the positive potential of the Church. But alas, even today, when everything in the country has begun to move, the stirrings of courage have had little impact on the Orthodox hierarchy... The movement towards rebirth in this sphere, as in all others, can be expected to commence— it is already doing so— at the most humble levels, with the activity of rank-and-file clergymen, of parishes united by a common purpose, and of selfless parishioners.[26]

At the Church of Sreteniye Vladimirskoi Bogomateri in Moscow, Fr. Georgi Kochetkov established an experimental parish where the liturgy was celebrated in modern Russia. He set up a carefully graded four-year course for those who wanted to study Orthodox theology, and also a school for children. His parish began producing a magazine called *Pravoslavnaya obshchina (Orthodox Community)*. Eventually, the conservative faction in the Patriarchate had clearly gained the upper hand as far as Fr. Georgi's experiment was concerned. He was removed from the parish and his work there endangered. Nevertheless, initiatives of this sort continue. The group of Orthodox priests, the "Bratstvo vo imya Vsemilostivogo Spasa", mentioned above to take just one example, is a brotherhood at parish level concerned with charitable work, educating children in the faith, and training singers, icon-painters, Sunday school teachers and parish administrators.

In an article called "Russian Orthodoxy: Crisis or Rebirth?," Archpriest Ioann Sviridov, head of the Orthodox Church's education and catechism department, recently picked out the renewal of parish life and the renewal of monasticism as two of the elements vital to rebirth of the church. He welcomes the increasing frequency of communion and the fact that priests now get to know their parishioners by name. He is encouraged to note the appearance of a new type of bishop who rejects privilege and who drives himself into the provinces to participate in parish life. "Such bishops are still in the minority, but to them belongs the renewed church of the future."

The renewal of monasticism, according to Sviridov, is a more difficult problem. It makes no sense simply to restore old neglected monasteries, to put in a few monks, and hope that these places will automatically become

centers of a revived and dynamic spirituality. Historically, Russian monasteries grew gradually around the cells of isolated hermits. The same
pattern of development should be followed today, Sviridov argues. All
over Russia there are monk-like figures in the parishes. They should encourage small monastic groups. "In time, small settlements will arise out
of these communities...and these new institutions are already embryonic
centers of education"[27] To this, one might add that such centers will naturally engage in agriculture and small-scale production like the communities inspired by Nil Sorsky in the 15th century. In 1991, the first convent in
Siberia since 1917 was founded in the village of Mogochino on the banks of
the River Ob on the initiative of Fr. Ioann, the priest of the local church. Six
local women with religious vocations became the first nuns. The local authorities helped with their meager resources, but the convent was basically
being built by hand. The nuns worked in the fields and the kitchen garden; soon they were to be more directly involved with the local community.

The local authorities hope to give the nuns responsibility for the handicapped, the sick, orphans, those who cannot work to feed themselves. There
are no fewer than fifty such people in the small village, and the state is in
no position to help them. That responsibility will rest on the shoulders of
the six nuns.[28]

"Many people are just at the stage of approaching the church," writes
Yevgeni Polyakov.

> They are at the gates of the church. The church must receive
> each of them and give them a warm welcome, while still remain-
> ing the church, not a home for communist or Christian Demo-
> cratic party committees, nor a club for demonstrating national su-
> periority, nor an official villa, with all the conveniences, for bish-
> ops and priests who have brought discredit on themselves.[29]

"So what is happening in the Russian Orthodox Church today?" asks
Father Ioann Sviridov.

> Crisis or renewal? There is no doubt that the church finds it-
> self in a crisis — for in Greek the word "crisis" means "judgment"....
> What is false and artificial is being dissolved: what is genuine will
> remain... The crisis means cleansing and renewal and with that the
> beginning of rebirth. What is most remarkable, however, is that is
> happening before our very eyes.[30]

All aspects of religious life in Russia must be renewed from the bottom
up. As with economic reform and the introduction of pluralism and de-

mocracy, it is dangerous and futile to rely solely on the introduction of reforms by edict from above. At the same time, however, it will be necessary to look to the structures of the church as an institution to protect and nurture the green shoots where they appear. It is encouraging to observe that this does indeed seem to be happening. The historian Nicholas Riasanovsky has described the Russian Orthodox Church as one of the "bonds of unity" which proved to be of decisive importance in the age of division and defeat which followed the collapse of the Kievan state, in particular during the dark first hundred years following the Mongol conquest, that is, approximately from the middle of the thirteenth to the middle of the fourteenth century. Let us hope that the future historians will likewise be able to say that the church was a source of unity and healing in the "first dark decades following the collapse of communist power."[31]

Notes

1. Masha Kamenkovich, "Dawn of the Magicians," *Frontier* (Keston Institute, Oxford, UK), May-June 1991, pp. 1-3.

2. Yevgeni Polyakov, *Moskovskaya patriarkhiya kak vysshaya stadiya sotsializma*, unpublished paper, 1991.

3. Ibid.

4. Alexander Nezhny, *Russkaya mysl'*, December 20, 1991, p. 17.

5. Polyakov, *Moskovskaya patriarkhiya kak vysshaya stadiya sotsializma*.

6. See Mikhail Pozdnyayev, "'I Cooperated with the KGB...But I Was Not an Informer': An Interview with Archbishop Khrizostom of Vilnius and Lithuania," *Religion State and Society: The Keston Journal*, Vol. 21, Nos. 3-4, 1993, pp. 345-350.

7. Gosudarstvennaya bezopasnost' i demokratiya, No. 1, February 1993, *Glasnost'* (Moscow), pp. 5-6.

8. Aleksandr Shchipkov, "Attempts to Revive the Council for Religious Affairs in Russia," *Religion State and Society: The Keston Journal*, Vol. 21, Nos. 3-4, 1993, pp. 367-73.

9. Aleksandr Solzhenitsyn, *Kak nam obustroit' Rossiyu, 1990*, (published in English as Solzhenitsyn, *Rebuilding Russia*, (London: Harvill, 1991), here p. 37.

10. Ibid., p. 71.

11. Compare, for example, Peter Reddaway, "Russia on the Brink?," *New York Review of Books*, January 28, 1993, with Martin Malia, "Apocalypse Not," *The New Republic*, February 22, 1993, pp. 21-27.

12. Yevgeni Pazukhin, "Russkaya religioznaya filosofiya v podpol'ye," *Preobrazheniye*, No. 1, 1992 (St. Petersburg), pp. 16-24.

13. Viktor Aksiuchits, "Bog i otechestvo — formula russkoi idei,"

Moskva, January 1993.

14. "Rossiya, kotoruyu my obretayem," *Novy mir*, January 1993.

15. Polyakov, *Moskovskaya patriarkhiya kak vysshaya stadiya sotsializma*.

16. Polyakov, *Moskovskaya patriarkhiya kak vysshaya stadiya sotsializma*.

17. Roanne Thomas Edwards, "Russian Christian Democracy from a Regional Perspective: the Case of St. Petersburg," *Religion State and Society: the Keston Journal*, Vol. 20, No. 2, 1992, p. 208.

18. Natalia Babasian, Khristiansko-demokraticheskiye organizatsii v sovremennoi Rossii'," *Khristiansky vestnik*, No. 12, December 1992 (Moscow), pp. 16-18.

19. Vladimir Poresh, "Faith and Lack of Faith in Russia," *Religion in Communist Lands*, Vol. 19, Nos. 1-2, Summer 1991, pp. 75-81, here p. 77.

20. Sergei Lezov, "The National Idea and Christianity," *Religion State and Society: The Keston Journal*, Vol. 20, No. 1, 1992, pp. 29-47, here pp. 29-30.

21. Interview with Andrei Kurayev by Natalia Babasian, *Khristiansky vestnik*, No. 6, January 1993.

22. On the various contending theological schools, see the interview with Fr. Valentin Asmus of the St. Tikhon Institute, *Khristiansky vestnik*, No. 13, December 1992, pp. 20-23.

23. "Vessel of Truth," *Frontier*, January-March 1993, pp. 16-18.

24. "Ekumenicheskoye dvizheniye," *Khristiansky vestnik*, No. 1, September 1992, pp. 20-23.

25. "Pentecost in Prison," *Frontier*, January-March 1993, pp. 16-18.

26. Solzhenitsyn, *Rebuilding Russia*, pp. 46-7.

27. Protoiyerei Ioann Sviridov, "Russkaya pravoslaviye krizis ili vozrozhdeniye?," *Russkaya mysl'*, December 25, 1992, pp. 8-9.

28. Andrei Tretyakov, "Siberian Convent," *Frontier*, November-December 1991, pp. 12-13.

29. Polyakov, *Moskovskaya patriarkhiya kak vysshaya stadiya sotsializma*."

30. Sviridov, in *Russkaya mysl'*.

31. Nicholas V. Riasanovsky, *A History of Russia*, 3rd ed. (Oxford University Press, 1977), p. 69.

8

Your Prophets Are Our Prophets

Patriarch Aleksi II

Dear brothers, Shalom to you in the name of the God of love and peace, God of our Fathers who appeared to His righteous Moses in the flames of burning bush and said: "I am the God of thy Father, the God of Abraham, the God of Isaac, and the God of Jacob." He is the one existing (Yahweh), the God and Father of all, and we are all brothers, since we are all children of His Old Testament on Mount Sinai which was renewed, as we, Christians, trust, by Christ in the New Testament. These two Testaments are two grades of the same theanthropic religion, two landmarks of the same theanthropic process. In the process of the formation of the covenant of God with man, Israel became the chosen people of God to whom laws and prophets were entrusted. Through Israel, the incarnated Son of God received his humanity from the Most Holy Virgin Mary. "And this blood affinity is not interrupted and does not cease after the Nativity of Christ... Therefore we Christians, should feel and live this affinity as a communication with the inscrutable mystery of God's sight." This was very well expressed by the eminent hierarch and theologian of the Russian Orthodox Church, Archbishop Nikanor (Brovkovich) of Kherson and Odessa, in his sermon delivered in Odessa over a century ago.

The main idea of this sermon was strengthening the affinity between the religion of the Old and New Testaments. The unity of Judaism and Christianity rests upon a real foundation of spiritual and natural affinity and positive religious interests. We should be united with Jews, without rejecting Christianity, not in spite of Christianity, but on behalf of Christianity and in its name, and Jews should be united with us not in spite of Judaism, but on behalf of true Judaism and in its name. We are separated from the Jews because we are "not yet fully Christians," and they, the Jews

are separated from us because they are "not fully Jews." Because the fullness of Christianity includes Judaism, and the fullness of Judaism is Christianity. The sermon of Archbishop Nikanor was based on the idea of mutual understanding and dialogue between the Orthodox Church and Jewry.
These aspirations to rapprochement and dialogue were not isolated in our
Church. As early as 1861 Bishop Chrisnoph (Retivtcev) of Nizhui Novgorad
called upon the Church to help stop hostilities and establish relations of
dialogue and rapprochement with Jews. Archbishop Nicholas (Ziorov)
addressed himself to the Jews in the same spirit at the beginning of this
century.

> The Jewish people are close to us in their faith. Your law is
> our law, your prophets are our prophets. The ten commandments
> of Moses are obligatory for Christians and Jews. We wish to live in
> peace and harmony with you and to avoid all possible misunder-
> standings, hostilities and hatred between us.

Proceeding from these doctrinal and theological convictions, the hierarchs, clergy and theologians of our Church decisively and openly condemned any manifestations of anti-Semitism and hostility, as well as
pograms against Jews. While condemning the pogram in Kishinev in 1903,
Archbishop Antony (Chrapovitsky) of Volhynia publicly declared:

> The cruel Kishinev murderers should know that they dare to
> act against Divine Providence, that they become the butchers of
> the people beloved by God.

At the famous trial of Mendel Beilis, the experts of our Church,
Archpriest Alexander Glagolev, Professor at the Kiev Theological Academy, and Professor Ivan Trotsky of St. Petersburg Theological Academy,
firmly defended Beilis and decisively spoke against the accusation of Jews
as ritual murderers. Much was done by Metropolitan Antony (Vadkovsky)
of St. Petersburg to protect Jews against anti-Semitic attacks by radical extreme right-wing organizations. Many other hierarchs and theologians of
our Church defended the Jews with courage against hostility and unjust
accusations from extreme right-wing anti-Semitic circles. Among them:
Metropolitan Makary (Bulgakov), Bishop Donat (Babinsky) of Grodno,
Bishop Vissarion (Nechayev), Archbishop Serapion (Mestcheriakov) and
Archbishop Makary (Mirollubov).

It should be mentioned in particular that many of our theologians and
eminent religious thinkers participated in the defense of Jews against any
manifestations of anti-Semitism, e.g. Vladimir Soloviev, Nikolaas Berdyaev,
and Rev. Sergius Bulgakov. Soloviev was convinced that from a Christian

viewpoint the protection of Jews was one of the most important tasks of his life. For him the Jewish problem was not a question of whether we, Christians, were good or bad. Much was done for Christian-Jewish dialogue and rapprochement by our famous Orthodox religious thinkers and philosophers of Jewish descent: Semyon Frank and Lev Shestov.

However, not only our famous hierarchs and theologians participated in this noble endeavor. Many priests at local level actively defended and saved Jews from pogroms and persecutions. During World War Two and Nazi occupation, the clergy and faithful of our Church saved and hid Jews at peril of their own lives. The classical examples are Mother Maria (Skobtsova), Rev. Dimitry Klepinin, Rev. Alexy Glagolev, and many others, of whose feats and selfless ministry for the salvation of Jewish brothers and sisters we should all be aware.

When fighting against Hitler's Germany, the army of our country, at the price of almost twenty million lives, liberated Nazi-occupied countries and thereby prevented the "final solution of the Jewish question" planned and ruthlessly implemented by the Nazis on these territories. Our army thus saved Jews from total extermination.

After World War Two, our Church started establishing relations and cooperation with the whole Christian world and with many international non-Christian religious organizations and unions, including Jewish ones. We took an active part in the activities of the World Council of Churches, specifically in the work of its Commission, "The Church and the Jewish People," and in the work of international conferences—two major international conferences of representatives of the Christian churches and non-Christian world religions took place in Moscow at which the Russian Orthodox Church resolutely condemned militarism, racism and anti-Semitism.

Regretfully, at this difficult time for our society, anti-Semitic feelings and moods are fairly often manifested. These feelings, widespread among extreme radical and right-wing chauvinist groups, find a breeding ground in the general crisis and the growth of national separatism... The task of the Russian Church is to help our people to defeat the evil of separatism, ethnic hostility, and narrow-minded national chauvinism. In this endeavor, so difficult but sacred for all of us, we pin our hopes on understanding and help from our Jewish brothers and sisters. Through joint effort, we shall build a new society which will be democratic, free, open, and just for all those who live in it, a society which nobody wants to leave any longer and where Jews could live quietly and with confidence in an atmosphere of friendship, creative cooperation, and the brotherhood of the children of one God and Father, the God of all our fathers.

It is with joy that I testify here that the idea of dialogue and rapprochement with the Russian Orthodox Church has always found positive response and support from the public and spiritual leaders of Jewish communities in our country. Among the most prominent Jewish leaders mention can be made of Isaac Baer Levinsohn at the beginning of the 19th century (who was a father of the view that the fullness of Christianity includes Judaism and the fullness of Judaism is Christianity).

The Orthodox Church has always found positive response and support from the public and spiritual leaders of the Jewish communities in our country. Among the most prominent Jewish leaders mention can be made of Jacob Baer Levinsohn (beginning of the nineteenth century), who was the father of the Haskalah (Enlightenment) spirituality movement among Russian Jews. He proposed dialogue between Jews and the Russian Church to Archimandrite Christofor, Rector of Kremenels Theological Seminary in Volhynia, where they both lived and worked. Levinsohn's book about dialogue with Orthodoxy, entitled "Enough of Blood", was translated into Russian in 1883 and became very popular and well known. Its popularity scared our reactionaries and they condemned it in the early twentieth century as dangerous for the Orthodox clergy. In connection with Jewish-Orthodox dialogue, several other names should be cited: Rabbi Shomet Alexandrov of Bobruisk (Belorussia) the famous Jewish kabbalist influenced by Vladimir Soloviev and killed by the Nazis in 1941; Rabbi Leb Jehuda Don Yahia of Chernigov (Ukraine), a follower of Tolstoy whom he often quoted in his sermons. It is worth remembering our contemporary Prof. Mikhail Agorsky of Jerusalem, an expert in the history of Jews in Russia who did much for rapprochement. Recently he came from Israel to Moscow to attend the Congress of Russian Diaspora and suddenly died there. Eternal memory to him...

In general Jews in our country had a good and respectful attitude towards our Church and clergy. It is not accidental that at the trial on the case of the so-called Church valuables in 1922, Metropolitan Benjamin of St. Petersburg was defended by lawyer I. Gurevich, a Jew, who stalwartly stood up for the Metropolitan. On the iconostasis of our Russian Church in Jerusalem, we see the words of the Psalmist: "Pray for the peace of Jerusalem!" This is what is now vital for both our nations, and for all other nations, since our God is one Father of all people and His peace (shalom) is one and indivisible for all his children.

This article first appeared in *Moscow News*, February 12, 1992, No. 7, 1992, p. 16. It was reprented in *Glaube in der 2. Welt*, Vol. 21, No. 7-8, pp. 41-45, 1993. Reprinted here by permission from *Glaube in der 2. Welt*.

9

The West Wants Chaos

Metropolitan Ioann of St. Petersburg

"Russia has only two allies: its army and its navy."
— *Tsar Alexander III*

Striving after goodness awakens in human beings as soon as they become conscious of their moral weakness. When this striving after purity and holiness encompasses a whole people, it (the people) becomes the bearer and defender of an idea, an idea that is so strong and noble that it necessarily has significant consequences for the whole course of world history. And this is the destiny of the Russian people. In such a situation, the people and its government necessarily undergo the hardest trials as well as merciless attacks. That also is the fate of Russia.

The history of our fatherland is difficult and strewn with thorns. Its ten centuries are filled with wars and unrest, of invasion by foreigners, and subversion by its own traitors. Whenever Russia declares that it strives after the religious-moral holiness of faith, it inevitably comes in conflict with those who deny the commandments of mercy and brotherly love and who are determined to shape the earthly existence of humanity after the image of a cruel, greedy and merciless herd of beasts...

Back to the Sacred Things of Faith

If we wish to survive, we must return to the great goals, to the personalities whose vision is above all doubt, and to the ideals that are so sublime that no spiritually sound, moral person can possibly criticize them. These are the sacred things of faith. It is not by chance that the Church is the first target of all who want to destroy Russia...

Russia's Wars in History

Let us look once at history. In 988 the Christianization of Russia led by Prince Vladimir gave birth to a centralization: common belief, common holy things, and common understanding of the goal and meaning of human existence. In 1054 the Christian world was shaken to its foundations: The catholic West, led astray by the glory of worldly power, deserted the fullness of Orthodoxy. Russia remained faithful to ascetic stringency and the gifts of churchly grace, to Orthodoxy against all temptations of political expediency. From this moment the war against Russia which continues to the present began.

The Russian people were compelled to struggle ceaselessly. Already in the years 1055 to 1462, historians count 245 invasions and armed conflicts. From 1240 to 1462, hardly a year passed without war. Of the 537 years since the attack at Schnepfenfeld until the end of the First World War, 334 were years of war. During 134 years, there was struggle against diverse antirussian leagues and coalitions. In one of them, Russians battled simultaneously against nine enemies, twice against five enemies; twenty-five times there was a conflict with three and thirty-seven times with two opponents. In most cases, the Russians fought defensive wars. Incomparable are the bravery and steadfastness of our people and the military skills and statesmanship which they have brought to the struggle for centuries. In four hundred years, the territory of Russia grew four hundred fold.... It is true that it led to wars of conquest, but only when the cruelty of its neighbors had exhausted all her patience....

Time and again the enemies of Russia forged plans for the enslavement of Russia. In order to rob Russia of its religious identity and its sacred shrines, it appeared opportune to subjugate it in Catholicism. (The Greek-Catholic union of Brest in 1596 is the best example.)....

The "Protocols of the Elders of Zion"

Three hundred years passed after this Union. In relation to the West, little changed. Then there appeared a highly interesting document, the "Protocols of the Elders of Zion."(....) Some historians hold the document to be certainly genuine, others equally certainly a forgery.... Since its appearance, there has been eighty years with much to think about, as the history of the world so remarkably follows precisely the path the "Protocols" laid down in its plan as if from an invisible dictator.

Judge for yourselves. "Power and deception is our battle cry," proclaim the anonymous authors of this document.

> Force must be the principle and deceit and hypocrisy must be the rule.... We must act as if we were proponents of social questions in order to reach our real goals more quickly.... Above all we have to pretend to be interested in improving the lot of the poor. In reality we must make strenuous efforts to capture public opinion.... As we proceed in this manner we can stir up the masses when we find it opportune, and we will use them as a weapon for the destruction of the throne (of Russia) and for provoking revolution. Each of these catastrophes will be a giant step to the fulfillment of our real goal, the dominance of the world.

The "Elders" make their results dependent in the first case on the destruction of national sacred things.

> We must root out faith, the principle of the divine and of the spirit, and replace them with arithmetical calculation, material needs and interests.... Therefore we have to discredit the spiritual. With every year the influence of the spiritual on the people declines; everywhere freedom is proclaimed: we are only a few years from the time of the full breakdown of Christian faith, of our most dangerous enemy....

For those who remember the terrible destructive role of the mass media in the recent past, it is interesting to read the following words written a hundred years ago by the "Elders of Zion."

> When money becomes the dominant power in this world, then the press will immediately follow in a close second place. We can only reach our goal when we have the press in our hands. Our people must direct the daily press. We are clever and sophisticated and have at our disposal the money we need for this goal. We need the major political newspapers which shape public opinion, the yellow press and the theater. In this way we oppose Christianity step by step and will teach the world what it should respect and believe and curse. Once we have the press in our hand, we can change unrighteousness into righteousness, change dishonor into honor. We can strike a first blow against the up to now sacred institution, namely, the family, one that under all conditions must be destroyed. Then we will be ready to pull out the roots of belief which are still honored today.... Instead, we will create an army of

the passionately obsessed.... In a further step we can then openly struggle against what people respect to the present and which our enemies still honor. We created a crazy, dirty despicable literature, in particular in the so-called highly developed countries.... We already have attacked education, the cornerstone of social life. We have confused and misled the youth.

The Poison of Liberalism

To readers who like to stick to concrete facts, we would say that the "Protocols" have predicted the two world wars, the political forms of government for decades, the development of the world economy, the course of credit and financial politics, and numerous other details of the life of the "Independent Community of States (GUS)" with shattering exactness. Here we have the picture of the political demise of an independent national state as it was described in the "Protocols" at the end of the last century. Compare it with what has happened in Russia today.

> Scarcely had we introduced the poison of liberalism in the organism of the state, until its entire political structure was changed: the state succumbed to a deadly disease, the decay, disintegration and destruction of the blood. We need only to await the end of this agony. Constitutional states arise out of liberalism.... The constitution as you know is only a teaching place for strife, debate, impropriety and fruitless party agitation, with a word, a school which robs the state of its proper distinct character. The "speaking platform" of the parliament renders the government as powerless as does the press. Then we replace the government with its caricature, the president, who arises from the milieu that we created. All countries are tortured. They beg for peace and are willing to sacrifice all for it. But we will not rest until they accept openly and humbly our International World Government. (Omissions by Metropolitan Ioann himself.)

Every intelligent person can draw his own conclusion from what has been said. For my part, I wish to emphasize that the distinctive principles which appeared in the above cited documents are in no way outdated but today are being more precisely honored and more fully developed. And all this appears publicly and on the highest political level.

Russia survived the Revolution and the frightful patricidal Civil War, the awful mass repression, and the terror of collectivization, and nevertheless endured the battlefield strife of the Second World War—during the Great Patriotic War—through miracles of heroism and bravery was able to save its Western allies. It appeared that the time of reciprocal enmity was forever passed and the new blood sealed covenant would be in effect. But this was mistaken! Scarcely had the last armed struggle passed than the Western allies abruptly changed their relation to Russia. No one wished a strong and independent Russia.

The Corrupt West

"We want to plant chaos in Russia," General Allen Dulles said in 1945. He was head of United States political information and later director of the CIA.

We wish to reverse its values through falsehood, compelling it to believe false values. How will we do that? In Russia we will find persons of the same opinion, helpers and allies. This will lead to the tragedy of the collapse of the most insubordinate people in the world, and indeed the final and irretrievable destruction of its arts and literature and its self-consciousness. Theater and cinema will depict and glorify the lowest human instincts. So-called artists who will indoctrinate men with the cult of sex, violence, sadism and betrayal—with a word—every immorality will be supported and promoted.

Chaos and confusion will dominate in state leadership. Unnoticed and yet effective will be the concealment and the unprincipledness of state officials and the receivers of bribes. Bureaucracy and paper war will be turned into virtues. Honor and constancy will be ridiculed. Lies, drunkenness and drug use, insolence, betrayal, nationalism and enmity among the people, foremost enmity and hate of the Russian people, all this will be secretly cultivated step by step....

Only a very few will see what really is happening. But we will make them powerless by exposing them to ridicule and derision. We will find ways to make them into the outcast of society.

Let us look around. What proof does one need in order to understand that against Russia, against the Russian people, a dirty war, well paid, well prepared, unceasing and bitter, is being waged. It is a struggle of life and death. According to the plan of its devilish instigators, our land and people are destined for destruction, and this because of its faithfulness to its historical call and its religious dedication, because through centuries full of rebellion and war, it has defended its religious values.

Rebirth of Russia

Now is the time to take stock and to settle the score of the centuries. May shame and eternal damnation be upon us and our descendants if we do not draw the proper conclusion from bitter experience of the past and if we delude Russia with the mere garbage of conferences, meetings and sessions. May you protect us from all that, O Lord!

It is time that we learn to live trusting in God and ourselves. Nobody beside us can do the difficult but necessary work for the rebirth of Russia.

May God give us insight that we may finally measure our present responsibility, the great importance of the moment, know the whole scope of the catastrophe which awaits us if we in our own selves do not find the power to resist the violent expansion of evil which threatens our land. I pray and believe firmly that Russia will awaken from its sleep. Amen.

Translated by Niels C. Nielsen, Jr. from *Glaube in der 2. Welt*, Vol. 21, No. 7-8, pp. 43-45, 1993. The editor of *Glaube in der 2. Welt* notes that it is not possible to identify all of the sources used by the Metropolitan.

10

Visions in Conflict: Starting Anew Through the Prism of Leadership Training

Walter Sawatsky

One day in 1988 I found myself in Moscow at the Baptist offices, getting reacquainted after a seven year involuntary absence, when in walked a Westerner who seemed familiar. It was Brother Andrew of Open Doors mission, that secretive leader who had become world famous as "God's Smuggler," the one whose organization had brought many Bibles to the USSR. "Why are you here," we asked each other. He was visiting the Russian Orthodox Patriarchate, he said, and had merely dropped in at the Baptist offices to say hello. In response to his challenge a year earlier, the Russian Patriarchate had secured permission to import one million New Testaments legally, the biggest such shipment ever, and he was now making further arrangements with the church leaders for shipping and distribution. The Russian Orthodox Church was cooperating with a western Protestant, primarily Pentecostal, mission society.

In late 1991 American television evangelist Maurice Serullo appeared on his evening show with pictures of what he called a pastors' training conference held in the Moscow Izmailovo Hotel complex only a few weeks before. During the next half hour, Serullo constantly appealed for money to support a major evangelism thrust to the 300,000,000 (sic) people of the godless Soviet Union. Aside from the so-called pastors at his conference, it sounded as if there was no other Christian witness in that vast country except what he was now launching.

I carry those visual images with me in order to keep being reminded that evangelical Protestants and the Russian Orthodox leadership were capable of extensive cooperation, and to be reminded of those missionaries headed for the former Soviet Union who even today know almost nothing about the Christian past, who seem to think that everyone there was an atheist simply because official government policy was so blatantly associated with atheism.

To differentiate is vital, yet for my theme of visions in conflict, it would have been simpler to contrast the Orthodox with the evangelical Protestants by means of stereotypes. Then it would be clear that Orthodox and Protestant Christians (to say nothing of the Roman Catholics) could not really coexist in the same space, as so many from either side do insist. My point will indeed be to delineate those separate worlds, the master visions of the Russian Orthodox, of the evangelical Protestants, and, to a lesser extent, the Roman Catholic vision, in order to show the truth of the difference, and hence the difficulty of a common Christian future after the collapse of the Marxist master vision.

At the same time, however, it is probably more vital to show the degree of conflict among spokespersons within those confessional bodies. For both evangelical Protestants and the Russian Orthodox to think of the other as a monolithic block is truly to miss the main point about what is happening there today. That is, we must try to understand how confessionally committed leaders are seeking to chart a course for Christianity that seeks to build on the past, sometimes to rebuild the ruins, while at the same time being ready for the next century in a more promising fashion than was true a century ago. In doing so those leaders naturally seek to locate their ideas within their own tradition. What will it mean to be the Christian church in the modern world? It is now commonplace to describe that modern world, even in Russia, with the word pluralism.

Orthodoxy and the Russian Idea

The emigre Russian philosopher/theologian Nikolas Berdyaev, a convert from Marxism before 1909, talked about the Russian Idea. Its essential point was that Russians have a profound conviction about a unique historical calling to be the spiritual saviour of the world. If that famous modernizer, Tsar Peter the Great, had decided that Russian society was hopelessly backward and that he must open a window to the progress of the West by building a city and seaport on the banks of the Neva River, other thinkers concerned about the moral cost of western ways and technology sought to chart a different vision.

The distinctly separate road taken by Russian Christianity since its beginnings around 988 had resulted in ascribing greater authority to the ascetic monk than to the grandly robed bishop. The absence of books and the presence of painters of the genius of Rublev had produced a much more sensate spirituality than was true of the more rationalist theology of the Catholic and Protestant West. Here, some argued, was a keen sense of following the suffering Christ, of God as Trinity depicted relationally in the three persons who visited Abraham and Sarah—quite in contrast to the power exuded by the Roman pontiff as God's earthly representative, or the autonomous individualism of classic Protestantism. And above all, for the devout Orthodox, there was the conviction that their church alone had remained faithful to the Christian tradition, whereas others had entered into modern deviations. Theirs was the Orthodox Church, the only one which retained right doxology because in spite of what had happened throughout the course of history, in spite of the failings of the Church's individual leaders, nevertheless it was the liturgy of St. John Chrysostom that was being sung by them today. Educated Orthodox theologians such as the late John Meyendorff kept stressing the concept of development, even for Orthodoxy, but the broad Russian hierarchy's capacity to understand him has remained limited so far.

Although I had been inclined to consign the Russian Idea, along with other such vague notions as the Russian soul, to the romanticism of the nineteenth century, I was reminded of its persistent power as late as October 1992 when a speaker at a conference held in the Russian Academy of Sciences took great pains to spell out the Russian Idea for today as a useful device for developing desirable criteria with which to rebuild Russia. Similarly the vision of Moscow as the Third Rome, taking on the obligation of leader of Christianity after the fall of Constantinople in 1453, seemed to end with the Russian Revolution (unless one wanted to see the Third Rome doctrine in a drastically secularized form).[1] Yet the glossy, multilingual *Orthodox Readings* restated that doctrine in 1989 when reviewing the history of the Russian Orthodox Patriarchate (1589-1989). This penchant for the grand vision, for a utopia, has also been denounced as source of Russia's trouble. Alexander Tsipko by 1990 had reached the point of rejecting all grand organizing visions as too costly in human effort, calling rather for the modesty of small steps that allowed constant course corrections.[2]

That of course implies a reading of the past, a naming of the mistakes that explain the nature of the current Russian and Orthodox vision. Orthodoxy has understood its role in society in terms of the doctrine of *simfonia*, of harmony between temporal ruler as self-conscious servant of God, and the bishop or patriarch as servant of God for spiritual concerns. The late Tsarist family has been elevated to sainthood as if, due to the excesses under Marxism, one could now rebuild the historical myth of the Orthodox Tsar. Under the Soviets, however, the leader of the Russian Orthodox Church, acting Patriarch Sergei, announced in 1927 a policy of unswerving support for Soviet power, a policy declaration not rejected officially till

1990. To include Sergei's subservience under the theory of *simfonia* was intellectually difficult since it now made the church a partner with declared atheists. The general public developed a sense of distrust toward the hierarchy's weakness in resisting the destruction of the church. Some clergy since the mid-sixties have been vocal critics as they experienced betrayal from their leaders or simply became more informed about the actual state of affairs.

One such critical priest, Father Georgi Edel'shtein, called for the removal of many leading bishops, even accusing the very highest bishops of collusion with Soviet authorities to the detriment of the church. The Free Russian Orthodox Church (so renamed May 1990) announced in May 1990 four major conditions to be met by the Patriarchate before it could consider reunion: condemn the 1927 declaration of loyalty and submission, an act of public repentance by the hierarchy and the whole clergy, expose the most politically compromised clergy, and withdraw from all ecumenical bodies.[3]

In this context, Patriarch Aleksi II responded with a series of public gestures. First referring to the October Revolution as a "bitter page" in Russia's history in a speech printed in *Izvestiia*, he went on to assume full personal responsibility for all compromises and actions the church was forced to make. Metropolitan Sergei's statement had been forced from him in the vain hope of saving the lives of some of his fellow bishops, but Patriarch Aleksi declared the declaration to be wrong in ecclesiastical terms. In 1991 just before Lent, Patriarch Aleksi utilized the symbolism of Forgiveness Sunday to drop on his knees before his flock in the cathedral church, saying "Forgive me my children! Forgive me, my dear ones!, forgive me!"[4] Yet at the same time the Patriarch refused to distance himself from ecumenism, rather defending dialogue and warning against extreme nationalism and anti-Semitism.

Much more so than in Protestantism, the Patriarch's statements as leader of the entire church carry great authority. Nevertheless, the fissures within Orthodoxy have become more pronounced as diverse groups seek to influence his voice, or else to create relevant facts by means of their own institutions, including the founding of schools with patriarchal blessing.[5] Here a list of some of those groups shall suffice. The nationalist and anti-Semitic Pamyat' organization established links with the RGC Abroad (Jordanville).

On the opposite side, the intellectuals, many of them with a record of integrity gained as human rights dissidents, tended to push for a democratized church and greater rapprochement with other Christians. Their model priest was Father Alexander Min', murdered in September 1990. Father Gleb Yakunin, one of the best known dissidents who since the mid-seventies had been internationally known for advocating greater freedom for

Orthodox religious practice, attended the Lausanne Committee sponsored evangelism conference in Manila in the summer of 1989. Having been elected to the Russian parliament in 1990 as a reformer, his relations with the Patriarchate underwent new strains while also vainly seeking patriarchal approval for having oversight of a Moscow parish. Before the new elections in December 1993 he was defrocked as priest, though he continues to appeal the action.[6] Father Alexander Borisov was only one of several priests participating in the formation of the Russian Bible Society and the ongoing cooperation with the United Bible Societies. At the same time, the Orthodox seminaries in Zagorsk and Kiev printed pamphlets for public sale in which they attacked the sects, meaning Protestants, as heretics.[7] The theological schools, as we will see below, are positioning themselves to foster specific variations on an Orthodox vision for Russia.

Further, where the Russian Orthodox church used to give the impression of being a united, multi-Slavic church within the Soviet Union, major ethnic tensions have emerged. Indeed, the expressions of conflict between groups in the Ukraine have included bloody street fighting. Russian Orthodox leaders in recent years have needed to deal with more public expressions of the True Russian Orthodox Church (an underground movement stemming from the time of Sergei), the continuing challenges to its legitimacy from the RGC Abroad, and more tellingly by movements for autonomy in the Ukraine and Belorussia. The Uniates finally received legal status in December 1989 and began claiming back church buildings, especially in the Western provinces of the Ukraine. During the early years of perestroika in religion (1988-99) when the Orthodox church claimed to open more than 3,000 new parishes, two thirds were in the Ukraine. This has meant that at least one third of all parishes formerly under the Russian Orthodox Church were claimed by the Uniates, a major loss of revenue.[8]

Perhaps even more painful and debilitating has been the breakup of Orthodox unity in the Ukraine (representing 60% of the membership). An autocephalous Ukrainian Orthodox Church reappeared in central Ukraine in early 1989, seeking ties to the Ukrainian Autocephalous Church of the USA.[9] In response, in 1990 the Moscow Patriarchate granted autonomy (Exarchate) to the Orthodox church of the Ukraine which in October named itself the Ukrainian Orthodox Church. Soon thereafter in the post-communist atmosphere of an independent Ukraine, multiple complaints were sent to the Russian Patriarch about Metropolitan Filaret of Kiev, charging him with having a wife and three children, ruling the church too dictatorially, and, when access to KGB archives was gained, showing Filaret to have been a long-time KGB collaborator.[10] Following a Bishops' council in April 1992, Filaret was at first persuaded to retire, then he reneged upon returning to Kiev. At the end of May, a Ukrainian Bishops' Council in Kharkov defrocked Filaret and elected Metropolitan Vladimir Sobodan of Rostov (a

West-Ukrainian) to replace him. These actions were approved by the ROC Patriarchate and by a Sobor of the Ukrainian Orthodox Church in June 1992. Filaret resisted being deposed, receiving support from the President of the Ukraine, Leonid Kravchuk, former head of communist ideology overseeing the religious affairs officer during the many years of collaboration with Filaret. Filaret also tried to place himself at the head of the Ukrainian Autocephalous Church.

In short, the once apparently strong Russian Orthodox Church under a patriarch now is preoccupied with a different type of survival. The Ukrainian defection (and also a separating Belarus structure) has weakened the mass numbers of the church, and in the unseemly struggle for control of churches and of the Exarchate has poured shame on its recently improved reputation. The Patriarchate in Moscow is struggling to stay on a moderate course between and among the various factions striving to articulate the new Orthodox vision. The task of opening the over 20,000 church buildings returned to it is an impossible financial obligation. As a result local bishops or even parishes have recognized that they will need to take matters into their own hands. That also explains the proliferation of theological schools, and the lack of common approach, although the Sobor of 1990 did set some guidelines.

The Protestant Visions of Russia for Christ

Russian or general Slavic Protestantism is already by definition diverse, the commonality often being little more than being neither Orthodox nor Catholic. It is possible to describe the Protestantism present in Russia for the past two hundred years as a contradictory mix of mystical and rationalist visions of Christianity. That is, Protestant doctrine and polity has relied more on systematic articulation, and Protestantism has usually shown itself to be more committed to the Enlightenment paradigm than would be true of Orthodoxy. Yet at the same time, both the immigrant Protestant groups as well as what emerged naturally on the soil of the Russian Empire were responses to the Pietist renewal of the early nineenth century.

Common characteristics of the Protestant vision of Christianity were its emphasis on *Sola Fidei* (faith alone) in contrast to the "living with tradition" mentality of the Orthodox, and also its emphasis on *Sola Scriptura*. The Protestant impulse for reading and study of Scripture as sole source of authority was probably the strongest impulse behind the Russian Bible Society's formation, even though Orthodox leaders were always the key officers of the society. Evangelical Protestantism in Russia also drew on the anti-authoritarian and anti-ritualistic stream that had characterized Russian religious dissent since the 17th century. Put a different way, evangelical Protestantism provided opportunities for the free and newly literate peasantry finding its voice. The more democratized the society has become since, the more suited the evangelical way of being church has come to be seen.

For our purposes, it will suffice to refer to the vision for Russian evangelical Protestantism as it was articulated during the first twelve years of Soviet power, that golden era of unprecedented freedom for religious minorities.[11] Whether as Baptist, Evangelical Christian, Pentecostal, or even as Adventists, this era marked a time of deliberately fostered and successful evangelism and church growth. Evangelical Christian leader Prokhanov developed an elaborate programmatic statement about winning "Russia for Christ," relying on conscious targeting of unreached areas and using the techniques of preaching tours accompanied by literature distribution.[12]

The evangelical movement was summarily crushed in 1930 and emerged in rather chastened fashion in 1944 under a governmentally approved single national Protestant union known as the All Union Council of Evangelical Christian Baptists (AUCECB). The AUCECB set about a vigorous recovery program characterized by registration/legalization of local congregations, ordaining clergy from the ranks, and riding the post-war emotional revivalist wave. By 1949 the leaders were counseling against any form of mission or evangelism (illegal since 1929 anyway). Nascent evangelism with children and youth was crushed through the Khrushchev attack on religion, though not as fully as in 1930, because of a successful dissenting movement which had organized a competing ECB union by 1965. The Council of Churches of Evangelical Christian Baptists (CCECB) kept appealing to the lost vision of "Russia for Christ" and developed elaborate illegal methods for evangelism. Between 1960 and 1988 the AUCECB rank and file had learned to be content with nurturing their own piety within the confines of the few church buildings permitted them. Gradually, too, the dissenting church union broke apart on issues of leadership style and dissatisfaction with the persisting antagonisms between CCECB and AUCECB.

The Russian national discovery of religion as something interesting and desirable provided renewed opportunity to articulate the vision of major growth in size. Differences within Soviet evangelical circles on how to approach evangelism quickly emerged however. First, there was the passivity of established routines and the de facto development of an identifiable evangelical subculture that made the integration of new converts from secularized society problematic. National differences became more pronounced. Since so much of the new evangelism activity was dependent on the availability of Scriptures, most of which were imported from abroad, competition for Western largesse resulted in an increasingly decentralized church.

Now, in the post-communist Russia and CIS in general, these individualist ways of carrying out an evangelism vision have produced further complications. Western evangelical mission agencies, of both high and low reputation, discovered the former Soviet Union. Frequently individuals from America or another Western country who visited, returned with no more than local church sponsorship to establish an independent church planting project.

Statistically speaking, the Protestant impact might be measured as follows. No one has compiled accurate statistics yet, but those established churches we were counting (e.g. AUCECB with about 205,000 acknowledged members) reported large baptism and membership classes from 1988 to the present, often doubling local membership.[13] If up to four million persons in the former Soviet Union were associated with evangelical Protestantism in 1988, at least six million are now part of that movement (i.e. members and regular attenders) but the Protestant impact has been much greater on society than would be true even of Orthodoxy. That was due to locally organized and also Western sponsored mass preaching rallies, including Billy Graham's visit in November 1992 as a carefully prepared and orchestrated event under the theme of Vozhrozhdenie 92 (Revival 92), the nearly comprehensive circulation of the Jesus film, and the distribution of over 20,000,000 Bibles or portions thereof.

Protestant pluralism appears to have come to stay. Mark Elliott of the Wheaton based East-West Christian Studies center collected data on the existence or establishment of twenty-five Protestant denominations (including remarkable growth by several Korean evangelical churches) plus nearly 2500 parachurch organizations, some of the latter essentially forming their own circle of church fellowships.[14] In addition approximately 700 Western church organizations are now working in the former CIS.[15] Their future direction will depend on the success of major new initiatives in theological education, from systematic Sunday School instruction (first initiated officially in the AUCECB churches in the autumn of 1989) through seminary and perhaps also university education.

Roman Catholic Triumphalism

Aside from Roman Catholicism as the predominant faith in Lithuania, Roman Catholic Christianity was more present (and therefore a problem to Marxist regimes there) in the central East European countries than in the USSR. Thus it was easier for the Soviet authorities to think of Roman Catholicism in terms of the Vatican and its influences on Western governments during the Cold War. The secondary problem for Soviet authorities and their successors with Roman Catholicism is the fact that the Eastern Rite Catholic (or Uniate) church claimed allegiance to the Roman pontiff while maintaining local customs. This was the church that was so long condemned to an illegal existence, that its reemergence continues to be-devil Orthodox and Vatican negotiators.

During most of the past millennium of Christianity when Eastern and Western Christendom lived separately, the agenda for reuniting east and west seemed to be set by Rome. When the decisions of the Council of Florence (1448) for union along the Uniate formula were rejected by the Orthodox, Rome tried to sustain an influence by establishing a school of oriental studies and sending missionary teachers. The entire modern history of Russian Orthodox efforts in theological education intersects at crucial points with the Roman educational approach. Teachers for the newly emerging school under Peter the Great had been influenced by Rome, or indirectly by the Latin instruction carried out in Kiev and at various times in Moscow. Other special schools were introduced during the time of Alexander I, and Catholic and Protestant curriculum influenced the emerging Orthodox seminary and academy curriculum. In short, Catholic influence through education was continually present and the intent was invariably ambiguous, vacillating between fruitful borrowing or outright efforts to convert to Catholicism.

The second major consideration at present for including some remarks on the Roman Catholic vision has to do with the various theories now current to explain the collapse of Communism. George Weigel's *Final Revolution* represents in more detailed fashion than did a *Time* magazine cover story, or the PBS video *Faith under Fire*, the triumphalist claims about a Polish Pope being the key to the moral revolutions of Eastern Europe.[16] In contrast to official submission to Marxist regimes or retreats into escapist piety, Roman Catholic hierarchs in Hungary, Poland, and Czechoslovakia, partly so in Lithuania, had consistently opposed the regimes. The point to make here is that the Roman church seeks to lay claim to a greater record of integrity in its confrontation with Marxism, than was true of Orthodoxy under acting Patriarch Sergei and his successors. The logic would lead to the suggestion that Roman Catholic leadership of churches in Russia/Ukraine might be a surer way to recover the high road of Christianity.

The papacy has immense financial resources that it could direct to a major missionary intervention in Orthodox territory as part of its worldwide evangelization thrust, or it could offer aid to Russian Orthodoxy as sister church. During the past year tensions between the Patriarchate and the Vatican have intensified, particularly as a result of the unexpected naming of five Catholic bishops (four of them ethnic Poles) to new sees in the former CIS.[17] The Orthodox saw this as unwarranted treatment of former communist countries as mission fields and as creating "parallel ecclesiastical structures," whereas a case can be made for the need to provide pastoral structure for Catholic faithful involuntarily dispersed to these regions in earlier decades. Leonid Kishkovsky as ecumenical officer of the Orthodox Church in America was surely right in trying to account for the Orthodox reaction as due to "the sense of fragility and of the unknown" that the previous seventy-four years of trauma had engendered.[18]

Six years after the positive tones of a millennium of Christianity in which Roman Catholic, Russian Orthodox and the Uniates between them were all in readiness for greater freedoms, the tone has been drastically altered. As Joseph Loya puts it, "a critical mass of long suppressed Roman Catholic, Orthodox, and Eastern Catholic antipathies were detonated by a potent charge of political freedom," which he likened to an "ecumenical Chernobyl," and ecumenical "meltdown."[19] Not only was there violence in the streets of Lvov and other cities about reclaiming cathedrals, dialogue at official levels began to break down. At least the seventh plenary session of the Joint International Commission for the Theological Dialogue between Orthodox and Catholic churches meeting in June 1993 was able to set out a series of common prohibitions and affirmations. Not only was there some progress toward common understanding of what type of proselytism is to be avoided, the Eastern Catholic (Uniate) Church was to be included in the "dialogue of love" and mutual respect should characterize relations. The joint statement even stressed that "the formation of priests" (i.e. theological education) should be "objectively positive with respect to that other Church."

When we add the insensitivity to ecumenism of so much of Russian/Ukranian and Western evangelical Protestants and the assumptions behind their theological education efforts, then a Western reader may begin to understand how relevant the conflicting visions are to the preparation of clergy and other church workers. One should also acknowledge that responsible leaders from all the major Christian families in Russia called for a joint conference on "Christian Faith and Human Enmity" for June 1994 in order to signal their members to seek peaceful resolution of deeply felt concerns.

Orthodox and Protestant Theological Education Efforts

Current North American literature on theological education reflects a sense of crisis as well as a sense of discovery. The average tenure of clergy in a parish is so low (less than two years) that almost nothing else so dramatically reveals the impossible expectations faced by clergy in settings where their traditional religious authority no longer intimidates parishioners competent in their own professions. Recent discussion in theological education circles has focused on an ecclesiastical, or even a congregational paradigm as a way of going "beyond clericalism" to more adequately train seminarians to fit in and to lead.[20] Experience-based learning by means of internships or supervised experiences in clinical settings feature large in many recent curricular revisions. At the same time, there is an ongoing debate between the value of producing broadly educated pastor theologians over against someone adequately trained in pastoral care skills.

When tracing out that debate over time, it became evident that there was a lack of serious analytical literature on the vision and impact of theological education. And yet for the church historian, an understanding of how the education of clergy came to shape the patterns for the churching of America seemed more significant than a more traditional focus on colorful leaders or debates between theologians.[21] Most recently we have seen the results of examining a broader slice of the theological education project by examining the Sunday School movement and also the Bible School movement more closely associated with the evangelical Protestant world.[22] This revealed the way in which impatience with theological liberalism at the turn of the century triggered the rapid growth of Bible schools having an intensely pragmatic agenda. That agenda included stressing biblical knowledge and exegesis for all (at the expense of scholarly inquiry) and a predilection to measure achievements by the resultant intensity of spirituality and religious practice. Bible schools were started to train (rather than to educate) missionaries and to hasten worldwide evangelization before the Lord's imminent return. In short order, such temporary schools (characterized by democratic styles and greater gender equality) resulted in the formation of new evangelical Protestant denominations, with the institutes maturing into Bible colleges, then liberal arts colleges, and even seminaries or graduate schools for the denomination in question.

My purpose in highlighting these American developments is at least twofold: to show the way in which the ongoing development of theological education is circumscribed by context, hence placing Russian theological education developments somewhat outside the framework of comparison for our own experts. At the same time, there are predictable patterns of development for which the North American churching of a new country provides precedents. Even more so, the dominant literature in theology and even the dominant theories for theological education will likely be drawn from North America. That is particularly true for the evangelical Protestants. For the latter, a multifaceted approach to religious teaching (from Sunday School to graduate school) is their operative paradigm when assisting in the formation of schools in Russia. Further, to the degree that some American evangelical Protestants challenged reigning theological orientations by organizing their own teaching as an attack on the flaws of the mainline schools, so also in Russia schools are being organized to carry forward the agenda of dispensationalism or of fundamentalism. Some of the independent Orthodox schools identified below reflect the influence of general educational philosophy (Russian and Western) deemed relevant for modernity, rather than the search for faithfulness to tradition. In short, intra- and inter-church conflict in the New Russia may well be fought out in the field of theological education.

Orthodox Theological Education

If Belliustin's widely known depiction of Russian Orthodox parish clergy as ignorant, inebriated and desperately poor creatures was at all representative, then it pointed to the truly massive and difficult nature of the task of theological education and finding sufficient financial resources to pay for it.[23] Nevertheless, thanks to major educational reforms in 1809 and again in the 1860s, it was possible to say that eighty-three percent of all priests held a seminary diploma. That is hardly the case today.

Since the new popularity of Christianity after the millennium celebrations, the image of the priest is decidedly better, if only one could find a priest. As one bishop put it, they had already ordained all the deacons to the priesthood, and still there were desperate shortages. After all one does not create a priest by ordination alone—there are minimal training requirements. In effect, the Russian Orthodox Church had considered the shortage of clergy and insufficient training opportunities as the major problem, at least after it became more evident that the church would survive the Khruschevian effort to eliminate it.

Were one to stylize the Orthodox problem of theological education in the 1970s and 1980s, it would have the following features. Church coffers were relatively full even though all money was collected through free will offerings as in a free church system. The church could afford to train more students and there was no shortage of applicants. Rather the problem lay with state restrictions in not permitting more schools, in restricting scholarship by keeping clergy and other religious scholars out of the state educational system. The state interfered heavily in the student selection process, so that even for the less than twenty-five percent of applicants that could be placed in existing institutions, frequently the most able were refused access.[24]

Hence a primary source of hope as the millennium celebration neared was the growing number of new converts from Russian intellectual circles who had chosen to abandon secure careers in order to commit themselves to the more meaningful, even if publicly demeaning, task of ministry through the church. Such individuals could more easily be tutored or mentored, or even enrolled in the correspondence course since they brought prerequisite academic skills with them. They were also familiar with the antireligious literature available in massive quantities and had learned to read it in mirror fashion for what Christian truth they could wrest from it. Nevertheless the list of complaints about theological education as a problem was a lengthy one.

In statistical terms, after the collapse of the seminaries in the twenties, a few of the former fifty-nine seminaries and four academies were reopened in 1947, a total of eight seminaries and two academies. By 1955 an estimated 1500 students were studying theology. Then five were shut down (Kiev, Minsk, Saratov, Stavropol, and Lutsk) between 1959 and 1964. Between 1975 and 1985, there were increasing signs of expansion again. Where in 1974, at Zagorsk there were forty-six professors, at Leningrad thirty-one and at Odessa sixteen, by 1981-82 this had increased to seventy, sixty, and twenty-two respectively.[25]

Nevertheless, serious expansion of Orthodox seminaries and academies has occurred in the past five years. Currently six seminaries, with an average enrollment of 200 students, are functioning, with the seventh due opening in Tomsk in the summer of 1993.[26] The seminaries are located at monasteries (some newly opened) in St. Petersburg, Moscow (Zagorsk), Kursk, Saratov, Stavropol and Tobolsk. Three seminaries of similar size are now functioning in the Ukraine (Kiev, Odessa and Pochaev) and two others in Belarus (Minsk and Grodno). That represents an increase in seminaries from three (as late as 1986) to twelve. In addition, there appear to be two or three seminaries functioning under Filaret's Autocephalous Orthodox Church. The number of professors at Zagorsk had risen to 140, that in St. Petersburg to forty- five with the remainder averaging ten lecturers each. Following completion of the four year course of study, the majority take orders and are ordained, some of the best students becoming eligible for advancing to the four year Academy program where they can take degrees at the Candidate, Master's, Doctor's levels, the latter quite rare. At present, in addition to the academies at St. Petersburg and Zagorsk open since 1947, the academy of Kiev has been reopened and there are now also some academy students at Minsk.

In order to hasten the training process, numerous two year theological training programs in the tradition of the parish school (eparkhial'ny uchilishchi) have appeared (Vladivostok, Omsk, Alma Ata, Tashkent (recent), Kaluga, Kolomna, Kostroma, Vladimir, Riazan, Smolensk, Vologda and Viatka). These average sixty to seventy students, a new class of about thirty-five beginning each year. In total these schools now represent approximately 2400 seminarians, 250 academy students, 800 in the two year programs, as well as several thousand correspondence students.

Then there are several new theological developments in the main cities. The St. Tikhon Institute of Higher Theological Studies at Moscow State University recently opened with 600 students, 380 of them female. It is a four- five year program. The Catechetical Institute of Vladimir (founded by the newly created Brotherhood of Father Shpiller) with five faculties of study merged with the Moscow school of St. Tikhon, and a two year junior seminary was opened in Vladimir. In February 1993 the Orthodox University (Pravoslavnaia universitet) opened in Moscow with sixty students initially. Located in the Zaikonspasskii Monastery (where once the Greco-Slavic and Latin school of Metropolitan Platon, first begun in 1681 was located, and more recently the Moscow Humanities University), it is divided into three faculties: Biblical Studies, Religion and Philosophy, History and Literature. Yet another Moscow based institution under the charismatic and irenic leadership of Father Kochetkov is called the Orthodox Higher Theological School. Here 400 students (new converts and those who had lapsed) receive evening classes over a four year period. Upon graduation they would be permitted to teach catechism and to be ordained. This institute is thought by some to be almost renovationist because of its innovations with congregational singing, Kochetkov's friendliness to Baptists, and a Hebrew language professor who is the new chief rabbi of Moscow. Since its modest beginnings in 1989 when Father Alexander Min' delivered some public lectures, what is now called Alexander Min' Orthodox University is offering a five year theology course. Its publicity brochure lists a joint venture company in Moscow plus free standing mission societies in Oslo and Paris as source of financial support.

In St. Petersburg, the Religious Philological Institute has begun functioning, a project fostered by the well-known dissident Vladimir Poresh. Although open to all faiths, it includes several Orthodox professors but the highly loved Prof. K. Ivanov was murdered in December 1992. One can imagine that in only a few years there should be considerable new theological discussion in Orthodox circles, in contrast to the earlier seminary record.

The libraries at Zagorsk and St. Petersburg are large (200,000 volumes), although over ninety percent of the volumes are pre-revolutionary in origin, but such resources are more drastically limited elsewhere. For serious study, the institutions associated with the universities may be more promising although Soviet universities did not have serious collections in theology and in recent years have been unable to purchase. The course of study at the seminaries and even at the academies remains very much according to pre-revolutionary topics and resources. In 1985 there were twenty-five subjects for the seminary program: biblical history (New and Old Testament), the Holy Scriptures (New and Old Testament), catechism, dogmatic theology, moral theology, apologetics, comparative theology, practical guidance for priests, homiletics, church regulations (polity), ritual, general church history, history of the Russian church, analysis of the doctrines of Russian schisms and sects, the USSR Constitution, Church Slavonic, Greek, Latin, a modern language (English, French or German), church singing, and Russian.[27]

The list of courses for the academy reveals something about the increased emphasis: Old Testament, New Testament, patrology, apologetics, dogmatic theology, moral theology, pastoral theology and ascetics, homiletics, liturgics, church archeology in connection with church art, history of the ancient church, history of the Russian church, Byzantinology and the history of the Slavic churches, history and analysis of Western confessions, history and analysis of the doctrines of the Russian schisms and sects, canon law, Constitution of the USSR, church singing, Hebrew, Greek, Latin, and a modern language (English, French or German). Thus far there is no indication that these courses and their content have changed particularly. Critics suggested that the subject matter and approach insured that students did not develop creativity or capacity for critical thought. Courses in psychology, philosophy or sociology are now being added for theological academies.

The rapid expansion of theological schools to respond to a serious need is promising but the abilities of the lecturers is very uneven. Currently the so-called "variagi" are regarded as the best teachers. These are members of secular universities, some of whom may have double degrees, now entering the field of theology. Guest professor Dimitri Pospielovsky was asked, for the summer season of 1993, to present courses in Russian Orthodox history for the Soviet period and another on ecumenical relations. These indicate gaps that an outsider might be better able to fill than one of the existing professors.

These concerns for a scholarly sophisticated and critical approach to education have been expressed by Orthodox spokespersons, not merely by western Protestant or secular scholars. Nevertheless, it is vital to keep in mind that the training of priests for highly liturgical churches (i.e. Orthodox and Catholic) is conceptualized quite differently than for pastors who function as preaching theologians. Hence the immersion in the disciplines of the monastery, the valuing of liturgical continuity (over against creativity), and the reflection on dogma and theology in the context of hierarchical subordination would be more central concerns for evaluating seminary education, less so for education at the academy level. For many students too, the attraction of theological education is the opportunity for concentrated focus on the life of the spirit.

Explosion of Protestant Schools

Protestant theological education in the former Soviet Union was much more severely limited than was true of Orthodoxy, and evangelicals had no earlier tradition of schools. Lutherans had relied on the theology faculty at the University of Dorpat in present day Lithuania, or had sent students to Germany during the nineteenth century, but there was nothing in the twentieth century except for a small institute that opened in Tallinn during the 1970s and 1980s. The evangelicals managed to establish two

Bible schools in St. Petersburg and Moscow respectively that lasted for four years (1924-8), several Adventist Bible schools existed initially in Kiev and Rostov, as did several Mennonite Bible schools. Thereafter theological education was limited to possible mentoring with a person of experience, but often the preachers were self-taught or met in small groups to learn together. It is worth remembering that Bibles were in very short supply; that restriction eased for pastors by the early 1970s. It was only in 1968 that it became possible to initiate a correspondence program through the AUCECB for 100 students. In stages this increased to a three year program with 150 students, plus a smaller department for music and choral training. By 1988 about 700 persons had graduated, which represented all the senior presbyters, many leading presbyters plus about fifty students from outside the AUCECB.[28]

The program of study emerged slowly, some of it through translation of works by Mullins and Evans of Moody Bible Institute. Thereby, so remarked Mark Elliott, an essentially Arminian Baptist movement became dispensationalist.[29] Course titles included dogmatics, bibliography (sic), homiletics, exegesis, general church history, pastoral theology, moral theology, comparative theology, history of the Evangelical Christian Baptists, foundations of music and worship, as well as history of the USSR and the USSR Constitution.

Between 1990 and 1993, over fifty Protestant theological schools were founded in the former USSR. This had been preceded by the dramatic success of the Seventh Day Adventists to begin a residential school in the village of Zaokski (160 kms from Moscow). It quickly became a model campus with garden, greenhouses, farm, and printing plant to generate revenues and foster self-reliance, and also gathered a library of 12,000 volumes, a major section of it in English.

When considering only Bible schools or seminaries where students are enrolled for at least one year of study, then there are now nineteen Protestant schools reporting a total of 1667 students (as of February 1993).[30] The eight largest institutions averaged 100 to 220 students each, the remainder around seventy-five. According to data gathered at a February 1993 conference in Moscow, there are slightly more students in the Ukraine than in Russia. Denominationally speaking there are about 535 Pentecostal and 530 Baptist students respectively, although it should be pointed out that the Pentecostal Bible Institute is quite new. There are also 366 students enrolled in nondenominational schools (sponsored by western missions). Through the AUCECB correspondence program as well as other similar programs using TEE methods, there are currently a further 3,184 theology students registered.[31]

These statistics hardly do justice to the human energies, vision, and commitment that have been involved. The Baptist Union in Moscow, for example, had sought to open up a seminary since 1905, had official permission since 1987, but finally announced classes with twenty students for October 1, 1993. While these delays caused frustration in Moscow, Sergei Sannikov of Odessa organized a Bible institute, then secured support from the AUCECB to offer the first two years of the projected four year seminary curriculum in Odessa. By February 1993, there was an enrollment of 160 students, some in a two year Bible College, nineteen in a four year seminary program. Teaching was done in concentrated six week time blocks with guest professors from Britain and America, students also studying English in order to become proficient enough for reading and understanding lectures. In addition, Sannikov organized a publishing house producing educational materials while at the same time overseeing a major construction project. This could not have been done without help from the Baptist world abroad, but even for 1993 he was able to present an operating budget of under $50,000.[32]

Another school located in Donetsk, Ukraine with currently forty-nine students has a different story. It was founded quite explicitly as a training center for mission by an indigenous society called Light of the Gospel mission. Loosely connected to the autonomous ECB churches and individual ECB congregations, its leaders almost by accident were introduced to the director of mission studies at Denver Conservative Baptist Seminary, who happened to be of Slavic origin. For the Denver seminary, the Donetsk Bible College became a "seminary extension" through which faculty offered short-term teaching (three week intensives) at minimal cost. The Bible College consciously worked out a course load that emphasized mission and ministry skills and required experience-based learning with existing new churches.[33]

Yet another school, now located in St. Petersburg and known as Logos Bible College, was the result of the energies of several Soviet German emigrants, who, following their own seminary education, returned to Russia as missionaries. Consciously focusing their curriculum on the pastoral task, their students drawn from various Protestant denominations will be expected to find their own place of ministry later. Faculty in this instance were a mixture of Russian speaking staff from the mission's headquarters in Germany, plus guest professors lecturing in English through translators.[34] Generally speaking, the quality of education is probably only at freshman college level due to the lack of background for students and the unavailability of resources. Since ninety percent of Protestant teaching is by guest professors relying on translation, professors mostly quite unprepared for the context, it is no small surprise that students persist so eagerly in this enterprise.[35]

Some Reflections on Education and the Competing Visions

In the new Russia of today, theological education illustrates both strongly negative and positive elements. The rapidly expanding system of theological schools promises more for the future than at any time since the mid-nineteenth century. Yet the problems are immense. What almost all of the educational efforts described here have in common is insufficient and inadequately trained faculty, virtually no libraries, not even sufficient text-books, and a general lack of physical facilities. Yet they are also character-ized by dedicated staff and a core of very eager students, two vital prereq-uisites for success. The truly amazing accomplishments were made at a time of excessive inflation (twenty-five percent per month or more) and major societal upheaval. By mid 1993, there were voices predicting that the newly opened Orthodox schools would soon close for lack of finances.[36] Nevertheless, the will to succeed is there because of the memories of spiri-tual deprivation and the immense spiritual hunger these future ministers encounter constantly.

What remains to be seen is the degree to which Protestant schools, now so heavily reliant on Western resources, can be contextually Slavic. If there would soon be a major production of Russian language literature commonly shared by Protestants and Orthodox, it is more thinkable that some of the current rising animosities can be reduced. As it is, there are some efforts underway to monitor literature production to prevent unnec-essary duplications.[37] Since thus far there is only one multi-volume Bible commentary series available in Russian and currently used by both Ortho-dox and Protestant, this too marks a small bridge to developing a sense of commonality or at least acceptance.[38] Protestants are also beginning to dis-cuss the formation of a university in Moscow which might serve as oppor-tunity for intensive discourse between Orthodox and Protestant intellectu-als.[39]

Postscript

The preceding sketch including both the broad historical references and the contemporary situation may be new information for many West-ern readers. For others who are reasonably well-read in English language studies of the USSR, there will have been only some interesting nuances in the interpretative and comparative approach and perhaps useful pieces of data from recent developments. But for the majority of leaders in both the Orthodox and Protestant worlds of Russia, such knowledge should not be assumed. Widespread ignorance of their own church history and of the other churches is still the problem today. A critical reading of their own pre-revolutionary and Soviet history is still impossible, due to the lack of literature. It certainly does not appear to be part of the course of studies in most seminaries. Further, for any reduction of the conflict between even a broad Orthodox and Evangelical Protestant vision to occur, there will need to be a serious effort to enter the world of the other—to learn the story of the Orthodox and of the Baptists from some other source that a lecture or booklet on sectarianism or on heresy/apostasy (as the case may be). Rather it requires an exercise in comparative history.

How likely is such a common reading of the past and the future? Realistically speaking, one's first impulse might be to say it will never happen; Protestants and Orthodox will go their separate ways. But on second thought, some stark realities may well portend hope. Severe financial straits for the Russian Orthodox help to explain their fears of being overtaken by well-financed Protestant and Catholic mission efforts—perhaps their well-honed survival instincts may also predispose both clergy and scholars to seek cooperation/assistance from the Protestants. In terms of theological education, the head start of the West in scholarship in most fields will require sustained intellectual encounter.

Protestant evangelicals initially thought that vast numbers of citizens were simply waiting to convert to Christianity, meaning an evangelical Protestant Christianity. We are already seeing signs from such enthusiastic missionaries that the oft repeated phrase "help us recover spiritual values" did not mean what they thought it did. As a result, some of those same missionaries are beginning to ask questions about the culture. That could lead to further questions, to dialogue, to reflection.

Is it thinkable that in the coming decades, Protestant evangelicals as the dominant religious culture in America and the Russian Orthodox might discover each other in Russia? Can one imagine a day when the history courses in American and Russian seminaries would include each other's stories, would affirm that which is held in common—the Nicene Creed as a minimum? Can one imagine a time when pastors or priests in each country will include in their prayers of thanks the saints, in particular the martyrs, from the separate traditions? Given twentieth century suffering, that could multiply the "cloud of witnesses" from which to be inspired manifold.

That may not seem thinkable, except as a utopian wish. But then, neither had many believing Christians ever thought that the Cold War could end nonviolently.

Notes

1.   Makhail Agursky, *The Third Rome: National Bolshevism in the USSR* (Boulder/London: Westview Press, 1987).
2.   Alexander Tsipko, *Is Stalinism Really Dead* (San Francisco: Harper,

1990), especially pp. 128-139, 263-273; cf. Alec Nove, *Glasnost'* in *Action - Cultural Renaissance in Russia* (New York: Unwin Hyman, 1990).

3.   Dimitri Pospielovsky, "The Russian Orthodox Church in the Post-Communist CIS," unpublished paper at AAASS convention, Phoenix AZ, November 1992.

4.   As translated in ibid. p. 14.

5.   One might note that this effort to influence the Patriarch does include the approach of Deacon Kyraev, currently teaching a class on Orthodoxy at Moscow State University with over 300 students attending, who refused to read a paper from the Patriarch's office at the conference, The KGB, Yesterday, Today and Tomorrow (February 19-21, 1993) because he disagreed with it. Kyraev has also been associated with criticisms of Father Alexander Min' and reflects an anti-Semitic bias. (Notes from Moscow Christian Resource Center, in author's collection.)

6.   Sabrina P. Ramet, "Religious Policy in the Gorbachev Era," Ramet, *Religious Policy in the Soviet Union,* (Cambridge: Cambridge University Press, 1992), p. 39.

7.   Mitrofan Znosko-borovskii, *Pravoslavie, Rimo-katolichestvo, Protestantizm i sektantstvo.* (Zagorsk: Sviato-troitskoi Sergievoi Lavry, 1991) 158pp. [pre-revolutionary reprint without date given]. *Gde istinnaia tserkov? Svedeniia o tserkov i sektakh.* (Kiev: Pecherskaia Lavra, 1991) 46pp; *Sovremennye eresi i ikh bor'ba rot iv ravoslavnoi tserkvi* (Kiev: Pecherskaia Lavra, 1991).

8.   Myroslaw Tataryn, "The Re-emergence of the Ukrainian (Greek) Catholic Church in the USSR", Sabrina Petra Ramet, ed., *Religious Policy in the Soviet Union* (Cambridge: Cambridge University Press, 1993), p. 292-318.; cf. *Roman Solchanyk and Ivan Hvat*, "The Catholic Church in the Soviet Union," Pedro Ramet, ed., *Catholicism and Politics in Communist Societies,* (Durham: Duke University Press, 1990), p. 89-90.

9.   *Tataryn*, p. 312-313.

10. I am relying on Pospielovsky, "The Russian Orthodox Church in the Post-Communist CIS" for most of the details, p. 18f.

11. For an overview, see Walter Sawatsky, *Soviet Evangelicals Since World War II* (Scottdale PA: Herald Press, 1981) passim, and this author's more recent survey article "Protestantism in the USSR," Sabrina P. Ramet, ed., *Protestantism and Politics in Eastern Europe and Russia; The Communist and Post-Communist Eras* (Durham: Duke University Press, 1992), pp. 237-275.

12. Wilhelm Kahle, *Evangelische Christen in Russland und der Sowjetunion: Ivan Stepanovich Prochanov (1869-1935) und der Weg der Evangeliums-christen und Baptisten* (Wuppertal: Oncken Verlag, 1978), is still the best treatment. See also the recently published official history, *Istoriia Evangel'skikh Khristian-baptistov v SSSR* (Moscow: AUCECB, 1989), which is still overshadowed by the caution of the previous era, but filled with

sources not available elsewhere.

13. For example, the statistical table in Ramet, *Religious Policy,* p. 355 (prepared by Ramet and Sawatsky) suggests a Protestant membership total of about 750,000.

14. Mark Elliott & Robert Richardson, "Growing Protestant Diversity in the Former Soviet Union," Uri Ra'anan et al, *Russian Pluralism, Now Irreversible?* (New York: St. Martin's Press, 1992), lists twenty-one (I am relying on a pre-published copy). More recently in Mark Elliott's "Protestant Theological Education in the Former Soviet Union," *International Bulletin of Missionary Research,* Vol. 18, No. 1, January 1994, it had increased to twenty-five, including Christian and Missionary Alliance, Pentecostal Holiness and Christian Reformed as planting churches.

15. Sharon Linzey, Holt Ruffin, Mark Elliott, eds., *East-West Christian organizations Directory* (Evanston, IL: Berry Publishing Services, 1993). This is a drastic revision reflecting the explosion of agency involvement since Elliott's earlier directory of 1991. A Russian database of indigenous organizations listed 2500 church related organizations and 28,586 personnel as of March 1994 (Moscow Christian Resource Center, annual report in author's possession; chart excerpted in *East-West Church and Ministry Report,* Volume 2, No. 1, Winter 1994, p. 6).

16. George Weigel, *The Final Revolution: The Resistance Church and the Collapse of Communism* (New York: Oxford University Press, 1992).

17. The sees were Moscow, Belorus, Karaganda (Kazakhstan) and Novosibirsk. See, for example, Patricia Lefevere, "Orthodox-Catholic Ecumenical Developments," *Occasional Papers on Religion in Eastern Europe,* October 1992, p. 42.

18. lbid. See also Leonid Kishkovsky, "Russian Orthodoxy: Out of Bondage, into the Wilderness," *Christian Century,* October 6, 1993, pp. 934-937; a sharper statement by him in *East-West and Church and Ministry Report* (Wheaton), Vol 1, No. 3, Summer 1993, and some evangelical responses.

19. Joseph Loya, "Interchurch Relations in Post-Perestroika Eastern Europe: A Short History of an Ecumenical Meltdown," *Religion in Eastern Europe,* Vol 14, No. 1, February 1994, pp. 1-17.

20. For example, Joseph S. Hough, Jr. and Barbara G. Wheeler, eds. *Beyond Clericalism: The Congregation as a Focus for Theological Education* (Atlanta: Scholars Press, 1988). Cf. Edward Farley, *Theologia: The Fragmentation and Unity of Theological Education* (Philadelphia: Fortress Press, 1983), which has stimulated extensive debate. Briefly stated, the concern is to find a way to focus on the life and faith of the church as expressed in actual congregational contexts rather than on the individual formation of clergy as class. The basic Protestant (or democratic) definition of church as congregation is implicit in most of this literature, even for Roman Catholics. David H. Kelsey's recent book, *Between Athens and Berlin: The Theological Education*

Debate (Grand Rapids: Wm. B. Eerdmans, 1993), serves as helpful review of the discussion. His delineation of the Athenian type of model (education or formation) lends itself to seeing how Russian Orthodox and Roman Catholic seminaries are necessarily linked to the monastic life.

21. See, for example, the recent effort to "explain" rather than recount in Roger Finke and Rodney Stark, *The Churching of America, 1776-1990: Winners and Losers in Our Religious Economy* (New Brunswick, NJ: Rutgers University Press, 1992)

22. See, for example, Virginia Brereton, *Training God's Army: The American Bible School, 1880-1940* (Bloomington: Indiana University Press, 1990).

23. I. S. Belliustin, *Description of the Clergy in Rural Russia: The Memoir of a Nineteenth-Century Parish Priest Gregory L. Freeze,* tr. (Ithaca: Cornell University Press, 1985) (first appearing in 1858).

24. See Jane Ellis, *The Russian Orthodox Church* (Bloomington: University of Indiana Press, 1986), for an extended chapter on theological education, carefully working through the scattered data available, particularly from the detailed report by Ray Oppenheim (American Chaplain in Moscow) and a Dutch student of 1977, Theo van der Voort.

25. Ellis, *The Russian Orthodox Church,* p. 104.

26. Unless otherwise indicated, I am relying on information communicated to me by Prof. Dimitry Pospielovsky by telephone and facsimile on April 12 and May 6, 1993; supplemented by data provided by Irene Barinoff, "Father Florovsky and Religious Education in the Contemporary Orthodox Church in Russia," unpublished paper at Florovsky Centennial Conference. Ann Arbor Michigan, October 10, 1993.

27. Ellis, *The Russian Orthodox Church,* p. 116.

28. *Istoriia AUCECB,* pp. 268-272.

29. Mark Elliott, "Protestant Theological Education," p. 20.

30. Ibid. See also Jack Graves, "Biblical and Theological Education Initiatives in the Former Soviet Union and East-Central Europe," *Overseas Council for Theological Education and Missions,* Greenwood IN (rev'd version of March 13, 1993); Jack Graves published summary "Theological Educators Meet in Moscow," *East-West Church & Ministry Report,* Vol. 1, No. 2 (Spring 1993), p. 9 and Elliott's earlier "Increasing Options for Theological Training in East Central Europe and Soviet Successor States," *East-West Church & Ministry Report,* Vol. 1, No. 1 (Winter 1993), p. 10.

31. Elliott, "Protestant Theological Education," pp. 15, 20.

32. Based on author's personal visit, July 1993, some materials supplied, and report in *European Baptist Press Service,* March 18, 1993. p. 2.

33. Interviews with Alexei Melnichuk, June 1992 and author's personal interaction with students and staff while teaching there June 1992; *On Campus...at Donetsk Bible College,* No. 2, (Winter), 1994.

34. Background statement and syllabus received from Jack Graves of

Overseas Council (April 1993).

35. Elliott, "Protestant Theological Education," pp. 15-16; the author would concur out of his own experiences.

36. So, for example, Vladimir Ivanov, professor of iconography in Moscow, when speaking at a conference in Houston Texas, April 25, 1993.

37. See *Books Translated from English to Eastern European and CIS Languages* published by David C. Cook Foundation in 1992. Of the approximately 370 books in Russian translation and fifty-one in Ukranian translation, the majority are of light devotional content.

38. A thirty-one volume joint project of Soviet evangelicals, the Baptist World Alliance and Mennonite Central Committee, completed in September 1993 (Walter Sawatsky, "Russian Bible Commentary Finished," *East-West Church & Ministry Report,* Vol 2, No. 1, Winter 1994, p. 11).

39. In March 1994 a working group decided to seek registration for the Russian-American Christian University in Moscow, with a first year class of sixty students projected for fall 1994 (Letter of March 31, 1994 from John A. Bernbaum, Russian Initiative Director of Christian College Coalition).

11

The Roman Catholic Church in Post-Communist Russia: Opportunities and Challenges

Janusz A. Ihnatowicz

A Glance at the Past

From an early time there were Catholics among foreigners living in Russia, but there was little or no institutional Catholic presence. When the territory of the Grand Duchy of Lithuania was annexed towards the end of the eighteenth century, Russia for the first time in her history acquired a sizable Catholic population. Of the total population in the newly acquired territories, estimated at almost seven million people, two million were Catholics of the Latin rite.[1] It became necessary to develop a policy towards this minority. The metropolitan see of Mohilev was created by Catherine II, and finally approved by the Holy See in 1783, under whose jurisdiction were placed all Roman Catholics living in Russia.

In addition, after 1795, there were several million Poles living in the Kingdom of Poland also under the rule of the Tsars. Throughout the nineteenth century, large numbers of Poles were transplanted to Russia, willingly or not, and thus its Catholic population increased. On the eve of the October Revolution, there were about half a million Catholics in the European part of Russia alone. They had 150 churches; two seminaries; one Theological Academy. Just in Moscow, there were twenty-seven Catholic schools.[2] There were about 600 parishes in all of Russia.[3] There were very few ethnic Russians, or even children from mixed marriages among them. The doctrine of "Orthodoxy, autocracy, and nationality," as it made possible gaining the privileges of Russian nationality by converting to the Orthodox faith, so also made it difficult, and till the revolution of 1905 even illegal, for a Russian to desert Orthodoxy.[4] People of Polish and German descent predominated in the Catholic population of the Russian Empire. Catholics also tended to separate themselves from Russian society. This was true specially of the Poles, who lived in fear of Russification. Even if they came to Russia out of their own free will, they considered themselves exiles, forced to live in a foreign country, precisely by the Russian occupation of their fatherland.

(If I may use a personal example for this point, my father's family was typical for this tendency. He was born into a rather affluent Polish family which settled in Odessa in an earlier part of the nineteenth century. They considered themselves Polish in nationality, retained Polish as their first language, and consciously placed themselves within the Polish rather than Russian cultural sphere, although, from what I have been told, they did appreciate the great products of Russian literature and Russian music. They also remained Catholics of the Latin Rite, if for no other reason precisely because embracing Orthodoxy would mean going over to the Russian side.) Consequently, the Roman Catholic Church was marginalized; it was seen by its own members and by Russian society at large as a foreign Church. Catholicism was the religion of foreigners.

Under Communism the whole institutional structure of the Roman Catholic Church in the Soviet Union was destroyed even more completely than that of the Russian Orthodox Church. The Archbishop of Movilev, Jan Cieplak, was put on trial in 1923 and sentenced to death; under the pressure of international opinion, his sentence was commuted, and he was exiled to Poland. All four bishops ordained secretly by bishop d'Herbigny in 1926 were soon eliminated. By 1938 only two Catholic churches, served by French priests, remained open because they were under the protection of the French embassy. Of several hundred Catholic priests who were Soviet citizens, not a single one could function legally.[5]

A great number of Catholics could not escape to Poland and remained in the USSR; many of them tried to practice their religion more or less in secret, often suffering persecution.[6] This Catholic presence was increased and strengthened by the deportation, mostly to Siberia, of millions of Poles during World War II. Not only did this increase the Catholic population, but led to a renewal of religious practice through the presence of many priests among prisoners and deportees. (Many of them decided to stay with those who were not allowed to return to Poland after 1945 in order to minister to them, mostly illegally.)

It seems that the Catholics in Russia profited little from the religious "thaw" in the final years of the Brezhnev era and the early time of Gorbachev. Press reports in those years contain little or nothing about Catholic initiatives similar to the actions of the Orthodox dissidents, or about the achievements of the official Russian Orthodox Church, such as construction or recovery of churches; nor is there any data on the increased religious practice among the Catholics.[7] This relative inactivity contrasts with the vigor of the Catholic Church in the Baltic Republics, Belorussia and the Ukraine. There we see rapidly increasing strengthening of religious life among Catholics, manifested in constant demands for the restoration of religious rights, registration of religious communities and the recovery of church buildings, as well as in the renewal of liturgical and devotional life in the parishes that survived the Communist suppression.

This ability to grasp at an opportunity is due largely to the fact that in those Republics, the institutional life of the Church never ceased completely. With the annexation of the Baltic states, as well as the territories of Belorussia and the Ukraine that had been a part of Poland between the two World Wars, the Catholic Church there was strengthened and given a new lease on life by the presence of more priests. Secondly, in those republics, Catholics formed a large minority, living mostly in close-knit communities. Finally, in the old Polish territories, they had not experienced Stalinist persecution. Forty years of suppression, or a little more than one generation, were not enough to eliminate all religious faith and practice in close-knit families.

This vitality enabled the Holy See to press for a normalization of Church life in those territories. Thus on July 25, 1989, Tadeusz Kondrusiewicz was appointed bishop and apostolic administrator for the Catholics in Belorussia. Other bishops were appointed in the Baltic Republics and in the Ukraine.

In other parts of USSR, Catholics constituted a minuscule minority, scattered over large distances. They preserved a vivid memory of Stalinist persecutions, during which being Catholic was interpreted as the sign of being Polish, thus an enemy both of the Soviet regime and of the Russian people and a prime candidate for deportation or execution.[8] It was only with the final collapse of the Communist system and the new religious legislation in 1990 that a more definite movement of renewal appeared.

In response to its appearance, the Holy See could make a move. Earlier, before a need for pastoral care had been demonstrated, Rome, always eager to preserve its reputation of ecumenical sensitivity, especially towards the Orthodox, would find creation of an ecclesiastical administration in Russia rather awkward. On April 13, 1991, several apostolic administrators were appointed for the territories of the Soviet Union. Bishop Kondrusiewicz was raised to the rank of an archbishop and appointed the Apostolic Administrator for the Catholics of the Latin Rite in the European

part of Russia with Moscow as his place of residence. Joseph Werth, a secret member of the Jesuit order, was named the Apostolic Administrator
for the Catholics of the Latin Rite in Siberia. This action placed every Catholic
of the Roman rite living in Russia in the care of a bishop and the organization of normal ecclesial life and pastoral care could now proceed.

Present Day Parameters of Catholic Activity

The pastoral action of the Catholic Church is strictly defined by circumstances that provide parameters of what is possible and what is not, of
what is productive and what would be destructive. Like all other religious
groups in the former Soviet Union, the Catholic Church pursues its work
in a society that for more than two generations was subjected to programmatic, forced atheisation. Therefore among those to whom the Church ad-
dresses its message, three categories of persons must be distinguished: (a)
an admittedly rather small number of those who held on to their religious
faith and practiced it as much as it was possible throughout communist
times; (b) those who had been baptized in infancy, perhaps given some
religious instruction at home, but who for various reasons ceased to practice their faith, and now wish to return to it; (c) those who have been brought
up without any religion whatever; this group certainly represents the vast
majority of the population of Russia.

The spiritual and cultural devastation worked by communist ideology
on Russia and in other countries of Eastern Europe is well known. Communism, says Archbishop Kondrusiewicz, left behind "a spiritual desert."[9]
This devastation involved not simply the psychological and spiritual destruction wrought in individuals; Russian society and Russian culture have
been wounded, and must be healed. The Catholic Church agrees with the
Orthodox Church in believing that Christianity cannot be a merely private
religion; both Churches do not accept the concept of the naked public square.
They believe that the Gospel of Christ provides the most adequate foundation on which to rebuild the society and culture from the devastation inflicted upon them by the communist rule. If this foundation is not laid, the
end of communism may become for the people of the Soviet Union little
more than falling into the slavery of the vices destroying the life and culture of the West; dialectical materialism will be replaced by practical materialism; "a civilization of consumption and desire" will develop.[10]

In his speeches in Poland in 1991, John Paul II repeatedly warned Eastern European nations against this danger, and placed on Christians living
there the duty to be the leaven of a true renewal, spiritual and cultural. The
leaders of the Catholic Church in Russia heed the Pope's warnings and
exhortations. It is the duty of all Christians, not only of Roman Catholics,
to try and fill the spiritual desert left behind by the communist ideology

with the truth of God revealed in Jesus Christ. Yet in trying to fill the spiritual desert, the Catholic Church must be aware of certain conditions under which it operates in Russia.

It is true that the majority of the Russian people do not profess a religion. Moreover, they show a great ignorance of everything religious; few experience a need for God. This does not mean, however, that Russia may be treated as a missionary territory in the strict sense, one in a pre-Christian condition. Christ was known in Russia, and the Christian religion was lived there for centuries. Christianity became an essential part of Russian culture and history, even if communist ideologues attempted to wipe away every trace and memory of it from the minds of the Russian people.

So the problem is not simply to plant anew, but to draw new life from the old roots, to break through the wall of ignorance and disinterest erected by Communism, and to arouse the historical memory of the people. There is an analogy to the post-Christian countries of the West. Though causes and mechanisms of dechristianization were different, the effects are very similar. To Russia may be said what Pope John Paul II said to Europe as a whole: return to your true culture, the Christian culture, this is where your identity, your true nature lie.[11] In other words, Christianization of Russia means recalling Russia to her own history, inviting her to recover her own identity.

To invite Russia to return to her Christian past, means to recognize the special position of the Orthodox Church in her spiritual renewal. Historically Orthodoxy held an undisputed monopoly in the cultural and spiritual life of the Russian people. For that reason, it became the official Church of the Russian Empire. This special position the Russian Orthodox Church still holds, quite independently of legal and political privileges that it may or may not enjoy.

What does this mean for those Russian citizens who are Roman Catholic? What does it mean for the Roman Catholic Church? How does it affect, or should it affect, its pastoral and evangelizing activities? Here history has bequeathed the Catholic Church two problems that make any solution more difficult. One lies precisely in the perception of Catholicism as a religion of foreigners. It is further complicated by the fact that in the past the Catholics themselves tended, as we have mentioned, to isolate themselves from Russian culture and society. But the problem goes even deeper. Catholicism itself lies outside the common culture and ethos of Russia, completely permeated by the spirit of Orthodoxy, its concepts and images. (Here an analogy may be drawn to the position of Roman Catholicism in the culture of Poland, with similar consequences for followers of other religions, even other forms of Christianity.)

What makes matters worse, and this is the second problem facing the Catholic Church, Catholicism is perceived by many in Russia not merely as something foreign, but as something hostile and threatening, both in the national and religious dimension. Here we touch another manifestation of the burden of history weighing so heavily on all of Eastern Europe, and showing so tragically in Yugoslavia.

The history of the Christian world is marked by the effects of the schism between Constantinople and Rome. This schism played a specially important and tragic role in the history of Eastern Europe, through which passes the boundary between Eastern and Western Christianity. In the tenth century both Poland and Rus embraced the Christian faith, the former from Rome, the latter from Constantinople.[12] Soon after, the schism between the two patriarchal sees occurred and was followed by centuries of mutual condemnations and mistrust. In Eastern Europe, where churches of both obediences had to live side by side, often within the same political organism, this religious schism became an important element in national conflicts and rivalries.

By the fourteenth century, western and southern principalities of Rus eventually were absorbed into Polish-Lithuanian Commonwealth and thus their Orthodox population ultimately became subject to Roman Catholic monarchy. Eastern and northern parts became modern Russia, under the sway of Moscow, strongly Orthodox, which with the fall of Byzantium, saw itself as the spiritual leader of Orthodoxy and "the third Rome." The two powers, Poland and Russia, faced off in permanent tension, while peoples of Belorussia and the Ukraine often served as pawns in their political struggles.

Union with Rome, accepted by part of the Orthodox Church in Belorussia and the Ukraine, was one of the elements of this struggle. Its motives and consequences are hotly disputed. One needs only to read what Catholic and Orthodox writers have to say about the person and activities of Josaphat Kuncewicz to see how deep differences in vision are.[13] We cannot discuss the matter here; we need to note, however, that the Union was resented by Moscow, both for religious and political reasons, as it went counter to the double identification of being Russian with Orthodoxy and being Polish with Catholicism, unquestioningly accepted by both Russians and Poles. This identification influenced first mutual relationships between the two powers, whose political and national rivalry was unfortunately seen as a struggle between the two Churches. It later affected Russian policies in occupied Poland throughout the nineteenth century as well as Polish reactions to it.

Victories over Polish insurgency were represented also as a victory of Orthodoxy; Orthodox cathedrals were built in the historically most significant spots of Poland as symbols of Russian power. As a result of the same identification, the Poles would pull them down when they recovered their national independence following World War One. But this identification

affected also members of both Churches. The Orthodox hierarchy in Poland was dominated by ethnic Russians, and the Russian language prevailed in the life of the Church, though only a minuscule proportion of the
faithful was actually Russian. To many of their Polish fellow citizens, the
three million Orthodox in Poland were foreign and suspect.[14] The position
of the Russian Orthodox Church in the Soviet Union during and after World
War Two did not help to improve the situation.

A similar suspicion of Catholicism both for religious and political reasons was common among the Russians. One need only read Dostoevski to
see it. And this mutual hostility and suspicion appears to poison relationships even today. The leadership of the Roman Catholic Church is well
aware of this, and is trying to do all they can to diffuse it as much as possible. Indeed, a desire not to appear to question the special position of the
Russian Orthodox Church, or somehow to infringe on her rights, is one of
the dominating forces of their activity both in Russia and in Rome. (There
is an added motive: the Ecumenical Patriarch has clearly indicated that
continuation of the reunion talks of the Rhodes commission will depend
on the satisfaction of the Russian Church with the situation in Russia.) This
desire explains the seemingly low profile that the Catholic Church keeps
in Russia, quite opposed to the way in which various western Protestant
missionaries conduct their business.

The Roman Catholic Church in Russia Today

The appointment of Archbishop Kondrusiewicz was hailed by some
as a revolutionary development in the history of the Catholic Church in
Russia. By others, it was interpreted as the Vatican's attempt to destabilize
the religious situation in Russia by establishing a competing hierarchy on
Orthodox territory. Both the hope and the charges are unjustified; they flow,
it seems, from a misunderstanding of Kondrusiewicz's position, but also
from a certain lack of historical memory. Archbishop Kondrusiewicz is not
the Roman Catholic bishop of Moscow. An Apostolic Administrator is not
a territorial bishop of a diocese. His appointment does not mean that the
Vatican has created a new diocese in Russia. Such appointments are made
precisely where a territorial permanent organization is not possible or
deemed desirable. Kondrusiewicz has been appointed to serve in Russia
because Catholics live there and have a right to pastoral care by a bishop.

Critical as this development was, canonically it represents less than
the situation before the Revolution. As we mentioned above, ever since
1783 there was a Roman Catholic bishop serving as the ordinary for all of
Russia. This Metropolitan see still exists. It is a sign of Vatican sensitivity
that it was not given to Kondrusiewicz. There might also be another reason for this forbearance. Mohilev is in the independent Republic of

Belorussia; in accordance with its normal policy, Rome wanted to respect the territorial integrity of both countries, by not appointing a bishop whose authority would extend over both. There is no reason to think that the number of persons with a Catholic background has diminished radically since 1917, though during the persecution in the 1930s many hid both their Polish origin and their Catholicism; as a result they did not pass the knowledge of it to their children.[15] Another series of deportations from the territories occupied in 1939 increased the number again. Catholic officials in Moscow estimate that there are about fifty thousand Catholics in Moscow. Bishop Werth speculates there are at least a million Catholics of Polish origin in Siberia alone. To this we must add also those of German origin, like the bishop himself. He believes that about forty thousand Catholics live in the region of Novosibirsk, and another fifty thousand in the area of Omsk and Tomsk.[16]

To provide all these Catholics with regular worship and catechization is the primary goal of the Roman Catholic Church in Russia. Only a small number are reached by such actions at present. By the summer of 1991, there were about thirty registered Catholic communities in the European part of Russia and some more exist in Siberia. This is merely the tip of the iceberg and the beginning of a longer process. Only those who have preserved best their religious awareness and possess strong initiative would demand legal recognition in the early, uncertain times. There is surely a much larger population of baptized Catholics, belonging to the first two groups mentioned earlier, without the same degree of concern or initiative. There are even more who have lost contact with the faith of their parents, the faith in which they themselves had been baptized.

Church workers observe a surprising indifference to religion in many old people who had been baptized in infancy and given some rudimentary catechesis as children, but who for various reasons ceased to practice their faith. They are pleased to receive whatever care and service they can, but are quite unresponsive to suggestions about a return to the sacraments of the Church, or prayer. And there is probably an even larger group of middle-aged and young people from families where a Catholic background was preserved in some measure at least, but who were not even baptized. One must also not underestimate the residual fear that changes are only temporary and that communism will return which keeps many from religious practices; this fear is often voiced in conversations. Nor must the simple lack of knowledge of new freedoms and possibilities be discounted. (A case in point is a good illustration. In the spring of 1993 an old woman arrived in St. Petersburg. She lives in Siberia, and recently she heard that there was a Catholic priest in St. Petersburg. So she decided to travel there in order to go to confession for the first time since the Revolution before she died. She journeyed thousands of miles, not knowing that close to her own city there was a Catholic parish, even a Catholic bishop.)

For this work to be successful, some minimum of personnel and property is necessary. Naturally the former is more important, but a lack of the latter makes pastoral action more difficult for all concerned. The material base is minimal. The territory under the care of Archbishop Kondrusiewicz covers some three million square kilometers. As of the summer of 1992, there were about thirty registered parishes, but only two church buildings were fully in possession of the Roman Catholic Church. (These were the two churches, one in Moscow and one in St. Petersburg, which alone remained open throughout the times of communism, due probably to their French ownership.) Since then two or three others have been returned, none of them in a fully usable condition. Thus in the Immaculate Conception Church in Moscow that had been converted to an electric cable factory, the ground floor was returned to Catholics but the factory occupies the rest. In St. Petersburg, the Church of St. Catherine has been returned, but as seven years ago it was severely damaged by fire, the Catholic community has so far been able to use only the sacristy which it managed to restore.[17] The same situation obtains in Siberia, where Bishop Werth is responsible for a territory of twelve million square kilometers; there are small church buildings in Novosibirsk and Tomsk, but elsewhere premises have to be rented for services.

The most serious problem is the lack of personnel capable of pastoral care and evangelization. During communist times, a few priests worked more or less secretly. Many of them were Polish priests, who when they had been freed from labor camps decided to remain in the Soviet Union; there were also a few younger men ordained clandestinely to minister to their fellow Catholics. As recently as the 1980s they still faced imprisonment for their activities. According to Bishop Werth, the first Siberian Catholic Priest, Fr. Joseph Svednistky, ordained in 1982, was arrested in 1984. Until the arrival of three priests in 1991, Siberia had no priests at all. At present there are some thirty priests in Siberia, and a similar number in European Russia. The majority of them are foreigners; others come from Lithuania or Belorussia.

With such a small number of priests over so vast a territory, the question of lay catechists becomes a burning issue. At present there are a number of religious sisters, from Poland and Slovakia and other countries, who divide their time between charity work and catechization. But everywhere, especially in out of the way communities, there is an urgent need for Russian speaking catechists. It must be remembered that whatever their ethnic or national origin, most of the faithful and specially the young have Russian as their first language. Unless it can function in Russian, the Catholic Church will not be able to reach the younger generation.

This brings us to the most significant change in the situation of Catholics in Russia. As our historical survey showed, the Roman Catholic Church in Russia was originally the Church of Poles and other ethnic groups, who often considered themselves exiles in a foreign country. This is no longer the case. Even if they are conscious of being of Polish descent, most, especially younger men and women, consider themselves citizens of Russia, and in this political and cultural sense Russians. They have no wish to be isolated from the rest of their compatriots by their religion. Few of them know Polish. (In this sense, the situation is analogous to that in the United States.) It is, however, more than just the question of language. These young men and women do not want to be considered foreigners in what they consider to be their own country, just because they are Catholics. Few would like to replace Orthodoxy with Catholicism, but they wish the Catholic Church to become, and to have the right to become, Russian.

Russification of the Roman Catholic Church is necessary if it is to survive in Russia. Otherwise it will not be capable of reaching and holding young people. The future of the Church lies in its ability to attract and retain them. Aware of this, the Catholic Church spends much energy and inventiveness in reaching the young, and in providing those who will evangelize them now and in the future. This is specially urgent, as the territories of the former Soviet Union are the object of great missionary activity by various Protestant communities and various non-Christian cults. One means of attracting and retaining the young is to challenge them intellectually. This is why an increasing amount of resources and personnel is engaged in various forms of the apostolate of education and information.

St. Thomas Aquinas Academy (College) of Catholic Theology in Moscow is the most ambitious example of such apostolate to date. In its first year of operation (1991-1992) 150 students were registered; now there are three hundred students enrolled. Students following a three year program receive basic training in philosophy and theology. The Academy has sixteen branches throughout Russia, including two in Siberia. The Academy fulfills two needs. Its graduates will form a group of educated men and women capable of taking up the task of evangelization and catechesis. But it also is an immediate response to the more personal spiritual need of a large number of the "new intelligentsia" of Russia. About eighty percent of the students are recent graduates from various university departments, from engineering to history, or from Russia's high schools. They are men and women who will assume positions of leadership in Russia. Why do they enroll in the Academy? "To know Christ better," is the usual answer. And their desire to know Christ must be powerful, for they are willing to give twelve hours a week to classes, to which they often must travel long distances, even from the various satellite centers of Moscow.

Besides intellectual instruction in philosophy and theology, the Academy offers to its students a more profound Christian spiritual formation.

In other words, its goal is to develop a group of Christian believers capable of understanding and communicating their faith in an articulate manner, but also willing to live it in their daily lives. In this way, the Academy hopes to make a contribution to the future of Russian society. This is how Archbishop Kondrusiewicz sees its role: "If these people of culture— teachers, philosophers, engineers and technical experts—have a serious and authentic knowledge of theology and the foundations of the faith, the whole society will benefit. These are the people whose task it is to rebuild the heart of our society."[18]

For this reason, though it is sponsored by the Catholic Church, the Academy has an ecumenical character. Ten percent of its students are Orthodox, as well as two of its twenty-four faculty members. There are also Protestant students and some who describe themselves as atheists. Those who want to know Christ are not limited to the students of the Academy. Communism left behind it a feeling of spiritual emptiness. Many, especially among the young, "are now searching for new ideals in which to believe; most of all they are searching for the truth."[19] This search leads many to an interest in religion. Paradoxically, this interest, as one of them put it, is often sparked by their memory of atheist propaganda in Soviet schools. They become interested in something that the regime fought with such effort.

The Catholic Church, within its rather limited means, tries to respond to this desire to know Christ. When asked, priests organize talks for students of various scholastic institutes. The Academy has established a publishing house for religious literature; a monthly periodical *Truth and Life* is published and has a rather encouraging circulation. Preparations are being made for opening a Christian radio station in Moscow; there are already religious programs broadcast on Channel 2 of the Russian Radio. By their very nature, such initiatives will reach not only those who identify themselves to one degree or another as Roman Catholics. They are designed to reach the third category of people mentioned at the beginning of this paper, those who have been brought up without any religion whatever, but who are seeking the truth. Indeed, they often are the first stage of evangelization of the unevangelized.

They also tend to be ecumenical: members of the Orthodox Church take part in them. Such actions offer, therefore, real prospects for cooperation among the churches; indeed their success will depend on such cooperation and pooling of resources. All these initiatives are a manifestation of the Catholic Church's desire to remain in the mainstream of Russian life. Yet precisely this desire and the actions resulting from it are interpreted by some members of the Russian Orthodox Church as an attempt at undermining the special position of Orthodoxy in Russian society. Because they often lead Russians to ask for baptism in the Roman Catholic Church, they are condemned as proselytism.

The Catholic Church is very conscious of the fact that Russia is a land where a sister church, the Russian Orthodox Church, has a long and noble history, and where it suffered much and gave brave witness. Both the Roman Catholic bishops in Russia and the majority of the priests show a great openness to and respect for their Orthodox brethren. In fidelity to the teaching of the Second Vatican Council, they recognize the theological richness and dignity of the tradition of the Christian East preserved in Orthodox Churches. They obey willingly various practical directives flowing from the revaluation of Orthodoxy by that Council. They involve themselves willingly in various ecumenical ventures, as hosts or as guests; without hesitation they follow the Holy See's instructions in such matters as participation in Orthodox liturgical services or receiving sacraments from Orthodox priests.[20]

Archbishop Kondrusiewicz often reminds his co-workers, that they are not missionaries here, but are pastors ready to serve those who want to belong to the Catholic community. Not proselytism but dialogue and cooperation are the goal. They make their own the words of the declaration that Pope John Paul II signed together with Patriarch Dimitrios:

> We renew before God our common commitment to promote the dialogue of charity in every possible manner....In this spirit we reject every form of proselytism, every attitude that could be perceived as a lack of respect.[21]

And the Pope's words spoken to the Orthodox community of Poland:

> Dialogue obliges all of us...let us combine our efforts and the aspirations of the hierarchy and the whole People of God, in order to form, in the Spirit of the Gospel of Jesus Christ, Christian collaboration... maintaining and developing the wealth of the spiritual, liturgical and national tradition. May this spirit deeply pervade the daily life of the two communities and become a new way of living together in reconciliation and charity.[22]

Catholics in Russia are well aware that there is need of such reconciliation, need of mutual forgiveness. They understand that there is a long history of mutual estrangement and suspicion, of hostility and violence on both sides. Such wounds do not heal quickly. Much patience is needed on both sides. Yet there are certain things that are not negotiable for the Catholic Church. The duty of evangelization is one of them. No Christian community may allow itself to become so turned inward as to be satisfied with providing only for the needs of those who are already "within the fold."

The Second Vatican Council summarized well the common belief of all Christians when it said: "The Church on earth is by its very nature missionary, since, according to the plan of the Father, it has its origin in the mission of the Son and the Holy Spirit."[23] All Christians feel themselves bound by Christ's missionary command (Matthew 28: 18-20). Hence evangelization, proclaiming the Gospel to those who do not know Christ, inviting them to become Christ's disciples, is an essential element in the Church's activity everywhere and always and under all circumstances. The Roman Catholic Church, in Russia as everywhere else, takes this duty and this challenge seriously.

The question is only: where does evangelization end and proselytism begin? Evangelization is an activity of proclaiming the Gospel to all the world; it is surely the duty of every individual Christian and every Christian community. Proselytism means attempts by propaganda, enticements, or moral pressure to draw the faithful belonging to a Christian denomination to join another, which just as surely is reprehensible. Concretely, what should the attitude of the Catholic priest be towards those who come asking for instruction and baptism? There are significant numbers of young people who approach Roman Catholic priests with this request. Some of these young men and women come from ethnically Polish or Lithuanian families, and thus have presumably Catholic roots, but others do not have this background; often they are ethnic Russians. And here lies the rub. Is accepting them into the Roman Catholic Church a form of proselytism?

There are those in the Russian Orthodox Church who believe that the proper, indeed exclusive, role of the Roman Catholic Church in Russia is to serve religious needs of foreigners living there. They object to the Russification of the Roman Catholic Church, protesting such actions as holding liturgical services and preaching in Russian. They argue that a Russian, which often means anybody whose native tongue is Russian, asking for baptism should be sent to the Orthodox Church. This is something that the Catholic Church will not and may not do. This inflexibility is based primarily on a theological principle, but also on an understanding of the situation of the people involved.

First, on the level of principle, whatever might have been done in the past, the Catholic Church today espouses a strongly personalist vision of religion, rejecting the concept of a "national church" in the sense that one has an obligation to belong to a particular denomination in virtue of one's nationality. And conversely, no one may be refused admission to the communion of the Roman Catholic Church simply on the basis of his origin or cultural heritage. It is not an act of proselytism to receive those who by a free and mature decision have decided that God has called them to serve him in the Catholic Church, no matter where they come from or what their past was. It is not proselytism, but the necessary consequence of the duty to evangelize. (I believe that the Orthodox Church holds a similar position when conversions to the Orthodox faith are concerned.) This, of course, does not negate the fact that such individual decisions are not the most perfect way of restoring the unity of the Church willed by Christ; it should be accomplished by the recovered communion of all sister churches, not individual conversions.

Secondly, on the practical level, it is questionable whether the majority of those asking for baptism in the Roman Catholic Church in Russia should be classified as Orthodox faithful. Even if some of them had been baptized in the Orthodox Church in infancy, few if any practiced their Orthodox faith. Most of them come from an atheist background; the majority did not even have grandparents who were believers. Their only connection with Orthodoxy would be their nationality, their cultural background.

At the same time, the Russian Orthodox Church would seem to be the natural place for these young Russians to embrace the faith. Their history, their whole culture is so strongly united with Orthodoxy. Why then do they seek to find Christ in a church which in its liturgy, its theology, and its culture represents the western mind? The reasons offered by them in interviews are many. They deserve a serious study by pastors of both churches. Here I wish to suggest one possible, though largely unacknowledged, reason. It is precisely the "foreign" background of the Roman Catholic Church, its western character, that makes it of special interest to these young Russians. One could say that the interest in Roman Catholicism among Russian "new intelligentsia" corresponds to the enthusiasm with all things western, from literature and philosophy to chewing gum, electronic gadgetry, and porno shops, so strongly affecting Russia today. Becoming a Catholic is also an act of embracing the idealized Western world.

Saying this, I do not wish to reduce the interest in Catholicism to a temporary fad or to question the religious authenticity of such decisions. Certainly there are "romantic conversions" caused primarily by an infatuation with the West. They will have no lasting character. It is also a challenge for the Church to provide these young people with other reasons and intellectual and spiritual means of sustenance when the novelty of "being Western" begins to wear off. For most, I believe, their choice of Catholicism is the conclusion of an authentic pilgrimage to Christ. When seen in the light of faith and hope, the existence of this small group of Russian Catholics will not be a source of conflict but perhaps a means of healing.

The history of the Christian world is marked by the effects of the schism between Constantinople and Rome. This schism played a specially important and tragic role in the history of Eastern Europe, as it was dominated by the not always peaceful coexistence of the two churches. It is possible that Russia may become the place where a new modus vivendi develops between the two "Sister Churches." In post-communist Russia, Catholics and the Orthodox must live together, facing the awesome task of undoing the spiritual and cultural desolation wrought by the seventy years of communist rule. I am optimistic, because, whatever her past and present difficulties, and there are many, Russia is spared the hatreds and conflicts that make the situation in such countries as the Ukraine or Yugoslavia so intractable. If in turning to the West, these young Catholics do not reject their Russian heritage, they may contribute to the enrichment both of the East and of the West by, in a sense, joining Byzantium and Rome again. And if reason and patient charity reign in both Churches, this Russian experiment may in the long run be an instrument of overcoming the burden of the past between Orthodoxy and Catholicism, and between Slavs of both obediences.

Notes

1. Kloczowski, L. Mulllerowa, J. Skarbeck, *Zarys dziejow Kosciola katolickiego w Polsce* (Krakow: Znak, 1986), p. 178.

2. Data from archbishop Tadeusz Kondrusiewicz.

3. Roman Dzwonkowski, "Ksiadz w spoleczenstwie," *Znaki Czasu*, No. 25, 1992, p. 125.

4. See Michael Florinsky, *Russia: A History and an Interpretation* (New York: Macmillan, 1953), Vol. 2, pp. 754, 797-800.

5. Dzwonkowski, "Ksiadz w spoleczenstwie."

6. A striking testimony of their devotion and suffering is found in *Memoir: From the History of the Moscow Chapter of the Sisters of St. Dominic 1921-1932* by Anatolia Mowicka. It is found in the Hoover Archives at Stanford University (Alfred Poninski Archive, Box l). An English translation by Claire S. Allen has been published in a Houston publication, *The Samaritan Review*, Vol. 9, No. 3, 1989, pp. 1-13.

7. E.g. in 1987 permission was given for the construction of thirty Orthodox churches, eighteen were returned. In 1966 10,261 children had been baptized, in 1986 this number rose to 40,469. Quoted in *Science and Religion*, January 1989. No such Catholic gains reported.

8. See an interview with a survivor, Edward Mozejko, in *Tygodnik Powszechny*, Vol. 46, No. 31, 1992, pp. 1-5.

9. *Observatore Romano* (English), No. 13, March 31, 1993, p. 8.

10. Pope John Paul II, Homily in Wloclawek, Poland, 1991, in *Observatore Romano* (English), No. 25, June 24, 1991, p. 4.

11. See his homily in Wloclawek, Poland, June 7, 1991, n. 5. *Observatore Romano*, No. 25, June 24, 1991, p. 12.

12. The name "Rus" is preferable to the anachronistic "Russia".

13. For contrasting assessments, see e.g., Alexander Schmemann, *The Historical Road of Eastern Orthodoxy*, trans. Lydia W. Kesich (New York: Holt,

Reinhart, 1963), p. 325, and Jan Jarco, "Kosciol na Bialorusi" (The Church in Belarus) *Znaki Czasu*, No. 16, pp. 30-34.

14. See Kloczowski, *Zarys dziejow Kosciola katolickiego w Polsce*, p. 298.

15. See Edward Mozejko's report on arrests of Poles in western Russia on the eve of the German invasion in 1941, *Tygodnik Powszechny*, Vol. 46, No. 31, 1992, pp. 1, 5.

16. See *Observatore Romano* (English), No. 12, March 24, 1993.

17. *Observatore Romano* (English), No. 11, March 17, 1993, p. 10.

18. In an interview in *Observatore Romano* (English), No. 9, March 3, 1990, p. 8.

19. Bishop Werth, in an interview in *Observatore Romano* (English), No. 12, March 24, 1993, p. 9.

20. See e.g. Decree on Eastern Churches, nn. 24-29; Decree on Ecumenism, nn. 14-18. Among post-conciliar documents, e.g. Directory Concerning Ecumenical Matters (Ad Totam Ecclesiam), nn. 39-54.

21. *Rome Declaration of December 7, 1987.*

22. Address in Bialystok, June 5, 1991. *Observatore Romano* (English), No. 24, June 17, 1991.

23. Decree on the Church's Missionary Activity (Ad Gentes) n. 2; *Vatican Council II*, A. Flannery, trans.-ed., (Northport N.Y: Costello Publishing Co., 1988 rev. ed.), Vol. 1, p. 814.

12

The Role of Religious Communities in the War in Former Yugoslavia

Paul Mojzes

The starting point of this chapter is two premises. The first is that war is the worst form of human interaction. The second is that cooperation among people of diverse characteristics (such as race, religion, nationality, gender, etc.) is more important than national sovereignty, national "Lebensraum," traditions, customs, historical boundaries, and so forth. If these premises are acceptable then one may claim that the contribution of the religious communities to the outbreak of the present war in the former Yugoslavia is major while the contribution of the religious communities toward cessation of hostilities and reconciliation is minor.[1]

The focus of this chapter will be exclusively on the contemporary because of my conviction that the historical overview has been offered *ad nauseam* with no new light shed since each religious community has its own distinct version of history and because at the present moment history is being mythologized in ever more bizarre and divergent directions, the distinct purpose of which is not to determine what happened in the past and interpret it for the present but to provide ammunition for one's claims in the present situation and to recall grievances against other groups in the past so that one may avenge them in the present.[2]

Likewise I will leave out my own analysis of how this war broke out and what fuels it as I have addressed this elsewhere.[3] I do not claim that the present war in ex-Yugoslavia began as a religious war or is currently a primarily religious war but it is my contention that the war is currently ethno-religious as these two realities have become so enmeshed that they cannot be separated.

The interaction of nationality and religion to the point of overlapping and identicalness is a well known phenomenon in much of Eastern Europe and especially in the Balkans.[4] The communist regimes in Yugoslavia and elsewhere tried to rupture this close identification for both good and bad reasons. A generation or two grew up under Tito which believed that ethnic and religious distinctions were not unbridgeable and that virulent nationalism was laid to rest at the end of World War Two. We now know that this was not so; ethno-religious identification returned with a vengeance. For most of the readers this was discovered basically after the Great Transformation in 1989, but it was discernible much earlier.

For one, political scientists noticed that the phenomenon of "national Communism" was a powerful disruptive factor of the international Communist movement, and it was nurtured with the hope that it would erode Soviet hegemonism. This it did but one wonders whether the results are not somewhat akin to nurturing Islamic fundamentalism as an antidote to Arab socialism or Saddam Hussain as an antidote to Ayatollah Khomeini's Islamic revolution. In any case Communists were unable to dispose neither of nationalism nor of religion despite their efforts in both directions. As the communist pterodactyl perished and left the nest empty, the eggs hatched an entire flock of birds of prey who are now viciously pecking at each other in the fight to dominate the nest or at least one's segment of the nest.

The large religious communities played a divisive role both during the communist and the post-communist period.[5] Yugoslavia in reality was divided not merely into three communities: Eastern Orthodox, Roman Catholic, and Muslim but into smaller ethno-religious units. The Roman Catholic Church of Slovenia reinforced Slovenian nationalism, Roman Catholic Church u Hrvata supported Croatian nationalism, the Serbian Orthodox Church supported the idea of Serbdom among Serbs and Montenegrins and tried even to incorporate the Macedonians.[6] The "schismatic" autonomous Macedonian Orthodox Church contributed to the strengthening of Macedonian national awareness, and Islam contributed to the affirmations of Slavic Muslims in Bosnia and Herzegovina and adjacent areas (e.g. Sandzhak) and Albanians in Kosovo, Macedonia, and Montenegro.[7]

Orthodox ecclesiology provides for the formation of national churches but Catholic and Islamic ecclesiology eschews such approaches. So for theological, political, and national reasons, Roman Catholic leaders would frequently use the vague term "our" Church but a closer examination would reveal that "our" was quite limited to their own national unit. Likewise Bosnian and Albanian Muslims had little interaction.[8] The Roman Catholics of Slovenia perceive themselves as having a quite separate religious dynamic of interaction with their nation than the Catholic Church among Croats and vice versa. If Roman Catholic ecclesiology allowed it, these churches would in no time call themselves Slovenian Catholic Church and Croatian Catholic Church.[9]

To put it bluntly, the leaders of each religious community enthusiastically and uncritically supported the continuous inflation of the nationalism of their respective membership and frequently attacked the others for allegedly being even more uncritically nationalistic then they were. This is analogous to a blind person calling a deaf-mute handicapped!

Most of the religious communities contribute to the sacralization of their respective nationalities and religion plays the role of a political ideology. "The greater the participation in religious activities in a region, the greater the tendency toward national homogenization and separatism."[10] Let us now look at several specific cases.

Contribution of Religious Communities Toward Hatred and War

Roman Catholic Contribution to Nationalism[11]

Recently two Roman Catholic authors, Geert van Dartel and Jure Kristo, have claimed that the Roman Catholic Church, unlike the Serbian Orthodox Church, does not identify Croat-Catholic and has a more reconciling, ecumenical posture than the Serbian Orthodox.[12] I believe this to be an error and indeed aim to prove it by the very data that are used in support of these contentions.[13]

Josip Beljan in *Veritas*, writing about the role of the Pope and the Holy See declares that they, in an unprecedented act, became the amplifier of Croatian independence and sovereignty as a reward to the Croatian people on account of thirteen centuries of their loyalty to Rome.[14]

> God has by way of his Church, by way of the Holy Father, looked at his faithful people, spoke out on their behalf, directly intervened in history, in the struggle, warring together with his people for their liberation.... With this war God also returned to his people, in its heart and home. (God) Returned to the entire mass media, political, social, and state life of Croatia, from where he was driven out forty-five years earlier. The cross of Christ stands next to the Croatian flag, Croatian bishop next to Croatian minister of state. Croatian priest and teacher are again together in the school. Present at masses in churches are officers and Croatian soldiers. Guardsmen wear rosaries around their necks.... This was truly again a real war for "the honored cross and golden liberty," for the return of Christ and liberty to Croatia.
>
> The Church is glad for the return of its people "from the two-fold" slavery—Serbian and Communist. This is a great "kairos" of

God's grace for the entire Croatian people.[15]

He continues,

> Here was not a battle for a piece of Croatian or Serbian land
> but a war between good and evil, Christianity and Communism,
> culture and barbarity, civilization and primitivism, democracy and
> dictatorship, love and hatred. Thank God, it all ended well, due to
> the Pope and Croatian politics.[16]

Another example was an interview carried out by a journalist of the
now defunct *Danas* with Franjo Cardinal Kuharić over a gun-toting
Franciscan chaplain accompanying Croatian troops in battle. To the question whether he condemns such activity Kuharić wove a lengthy answer
saying that ideally chaplains ought not to go into battle but since the head
of the Franciscan order, in whose jurisdiction this friar belongs, did not
condemn him neither will the Cardinal. The conclusion that can be drawn
from the Cardinal's response is that such action is permissible. And, indeed, many priests have fought in battles.[17]

Jure Kristo characterizes the leadership of Cardinal Kuharić as skill-
fully steering the Croatian people to sovereignty. He states for instance
that in the late 1980s

> Unlike his communist compatriots, (sic) Cardinal (Kuharić) was
> not timid about the defense of national sovereignty. Catholic bish-
> ops were convinced that by defending Croatian sovereignty they
> were doing something good. Hence, they used every opportunity
> to stand in defense of Croat national interests. One such opportu-
> nity was the debate about constitutional amendments concerning
> the name of (sic) official language in Socialist Republic of Croatia.[18]

They pressed the exclusive use of the Croatian literary language rather
than Croato-Serbian or Serbo-Croatian. Apparently the bishops and other
Catholic leaders did not have the foresight that this would be threatening
to the Serbian population who would interpret it as the denial of their cultural rights.[19] Did not the Catholic bishops have enough wisdom to promote the rights of the Croatian people in such a way as not to threaten
minority populations? Did they not act anti-constitutionally in their advocacy of a move that would tear apart the federal structure? Surely they
knew of many precedents where civil wars broke out for the preservation
of a federation.

Kristo proceeds to point out other unconstitutional initiatives of the
Catholic bishops. Namely as soon as they succeeded in having their aims

of unseating the Communist Party of Croatia and replacing it with the Croatian Democratic Union or *Hrvatska Demokratska Zajednica-HDZ* (which Krišto calls a national movement rather than a political party — which, indeed, is how the *HDZ* wishes to be represented in order to obtain a near monopoly over Croatia), they switched attention to Bosnia and Herzegovina and supported the political activity of the *HDZ* among Croats in blatant contradiction of the existing law which forbade the creation of political parties based on exclusively national or religious basis.

Writes Krišto, "Hence, the Catholic Church made offers to strike that provision from the books. At the same time, the faithful were encouraged not to fear organizing themselves on the national and religious basis."[20] Indeed, they and other nationalists prevailed. Exclusively national-religious parties were created by all—Muslims, Serbians, and Croatians. They became the three major parties of Bosnia and Herzegovina. Those who know the national and religious problems of that state know how fragile the balance of the ingredients was and that the *only* non-violent alternative is for a government that can somehow keep all three national-religious groups working together in a secular context. The Roman Catholic bishops initiated the process of national-religious confrontation. The outcome of that political move is nothing short of catastrophic, and the Roman Catholic leadership bears a considerable responsibility for the ensuing tragedy. It does not take great wisdom to see that their initiatives in this complex region could only lead to war. The communists, it appears, were far more realistic about the national-religious threat than the Roman Catholic and Croatian leadership.

Another manner in which the Roman Catholic leadership contributed to the tension in Yugoslavia was their support of the Albanian cause in Kosovo. This they did ostensibly in the name of protection of human rights. It is true that the human rights of Albanians in Kosovo were severely curtailed by the bloody politics of repression on the part of Milosevic's regime and that no decent human being could be silent on this issue, but the leadership of the Roman Catholic Church was not evenhanded and did not speak out on behalf of other repressed minorities (especially not on the territory of Croatia!). Their speaking out about the Kosovo situation was bound to aggravate the Serbians who do have some legitimate grievances about the fate of Serbians in Kosovo, though they pressed their interests in a very brutal and unacceptable manner. The Serbians would naturally interpret these appeals as an anti-Serbian and anti-Orthodox move by the Roman Catholic Church.

When the first free elections in Croatia yielded the victory of the HDZ and the Roman Catholic Church was finally publicly rehabilitated after years of oppression, the Catholic Church at first seemed to display practically unlimited support of the new regime's super-patriotic Croatianism.

The church leadership was present at the opening of the Sabor (Parliament) sessions, politicians and clergy did not fail to use picture opportunities in order to be seen together in the media, and much was done to reinforce the notion of the unity of the church, nation and state.

Also, the church leadership vigorously promoted the cult of Alojzije Cardinal Stepinac, a controversial figure. Insofar as the Catholic leadership rejected the labeling of the entire Croatian people by some Serbian extremists as genocidal and indicated that Stepinac was badly treated by the communists they were right, but they showed too little willingness to express regret for the massacres against Serbians in World War Two in which a number of Catholic clergy were directly involved and for which Stepinac had a certain culpability. Geert van Dartel mentions that Bishop Pihler in 1963 did issue an apology asking Serbians for forgiveness.[21] However, during the tense times prior to the outbreak of the war, Serbian bishops often pleaded with their Roman Catholic colleagues to issue a more emphatic statement of regret and condemnation of the war crimes by Croats over Serbs in World War Two, but more often than not Catholic bishops reacted by minimizing the casualties and responding that many Croats were killed after the War by the Partisans.[22] This too, of course, would have been interpreted by the Serbians as a threat as they wondered whether the Croatians are planning a similar ethnic cleansing as they did in World War Two.

So, did the Roman Catholic Church of Croatia contribute to the outbreak of the war? I would answer that with an emphatic yes. The Church leadership (some more than others) together with President Franjo Tudjman made provocative and foolish moves. They pushed their agenda with no regard to the consequences of their behavior and certainly have to be seen as being among the culprits of the war.

Serbian Orthodox Role in the
Disintegration of Yugoslavia

Since the Serbs had far more vested interest in keeping Yugoslavia together than the other nationalities, it may seem odd that the Serbian Orthodox Church leaders contributed to the outbreak of hostilities, but they did. They did so by their role in the Kosovo conflict, in whipping up the claims of the uniqueness of Serbian victimization by others, and later in their uncritical support of Serbian nationalist aspirations.

Already in the late 1970s, the Serbian Orthodox Church started warning about the Albania "menace" in Kosovo.[23] The population explosion of the Albanians and the exodus of the Serbs was labeled in a hyperbole as genocide of Serbs. Before too long this claim would be generalized that the Serbs are threatened on all sides by conspiracies.[24] As the Yugoslav government cracked down on Albanian demonstrations and repeatedly repressed dissents evoking concerns by non-Serbs about violations of the rights of the Albanians, the Serbian Orthodox Church went on a propaganda counter attack by issuing appeals regarding alleged rapes, murders, expulsions, and destructions of Serbian cultural monuments and sacred sites—in other words "ethnic cleansing" — by Albanians. This strengthened the Serb resolve not to give up Kosovo and produced powerful anti-Albanian dislike among Serbs.

Another nationalist conflict was fanned by the Serbian Orthodox Church in its strenuous opposition to the separation of the Macedonian Orthodox Church. The Patriarch of Belgrade claimed jurisdiction over nearly all Orthodox Churches in Yugoslavia, namely Serbia, Montenegro and Macedonia. Already at that point it became obvious that Serbian Orthodox Church leaders and Serbian communist leaders saw eye to eye on the Macedonian questions, just as the Macedonian Orthodox Church hierarchy saw eye to eye with the Macedonian communists. Tension also arose in the Orthodox Church in Montenegro where a pro-Serbian branch negated the separateness of the Montenegrins and a pro-Montenegrin branch asserted that the Montenegrins ought to insist on the autonomy of their church, as it was in the past. These two groups occasionally came to literal blows. Neither of these two conflicts are yet resolved. Instead they resulted in another schism in 1993.

As it became evident that Yugoslavia was heading toward disintegration after Tito's death, Serbs perceived a threat to their national interests. The leading role in this crisis was played not by the Church but by the scholars of the Serbian Academy of Sciences (*SANU* for *Srpska Akademija Nauka i Umetnosti*) who issued a Memorandum in 1986. In that document, Serbian academics countered the charge that Serbians dominated all other nationalities in Yugoslavia and pictured the reality in reverse, namely, that the Serbs suffered most for the sake of Yugoslavia but were the greatest losers and most heavily victimized by the Communist system and Tito's government. It was charged that the inter-republican borders were established unilaterally by Tito, a Croat, with no reference to demographic factors and in order to weaken and damage Serbia. The Yugoslav constitution of 1974 was blamed for weakening the Serbs and a great constitutional hassle was created with the Serbs wanting to change and the other nationalities wanting to uphold the constitutional provisions of 1974.

The Serbian Orthodox Church soon vigorously joined SANU in voicing Serbian grievances, in particular incensed by what they regarded as the lack of Croatian Catholic willingness to atone for their wartime crimes against the Serbian Orthodox population in Croatia and Bosnia. Prominent Serbian Orthodox bishops and theologians started vigorously speaking up on behalf of what they considered threatened Serbdom in areas where in World War Two massacres of Serbs took place, in particular the concentration camp of Jasenovac in Croatia. It was lamented that no Roman Catholic official came to the commemorations of the victims of Croatian fascist "ethnic cleansing" during the dedication of the Serbian Orthodox Church in Jasenovac.[25] Cries of "never again" could be heard from both nationalist and church circles. The Serbian Orthodox Church kept reiterating its age old claim that the Church always was, is, and will be, even when all others fail, the defender of Serbian national interests. The gravest threats to Serbdom and Orthodoxy, they pointed out, were Muslims and Catholics. The crimes of the Nezavisna Drzava Hrvatska (abbreviated to NDH and standing for Independent State of Croatia) and the "ustashe" (Nazi Croatian crack units similar to the SS) were frequently linked to the Roman Catholic Church and its leadership.[26] The Serbian Orthodox fully sided with other Serb nationalists who saw in the Croatian independence movement many "ustashoid" elements.[27]

By the late 1980s the anti-Albanian and anti-Slovene and anti-Croat feelings were conflated and the Serbian Orthodox Church saw initially in Slobodan Milošević's "antibureaucratic revolution" the salvation and liberation of the Serbian people. Only in 1992 did some Orthodox leaders, especially Patriarch Paul I, see Milošević's populism as a threat to the well-being of the Serbian people. Patriarch Paul I and several other prelates openly criticized the government of Milošević at anti-government demonstrations in Belgrade and elsewhere and charged that the government is harming the interests of the Serbian people.

Some authors demonize the role of the Serbian Orthodox Church for allegedly always supporting the state in contrast to what they perceive as the much more independent role of the Catholic Church among Croatians. This author does not see any significant difference in the relationship of these two churches toward the nation which they represent. It is true that the Serbian Orthodox hierarchy was more servile to the former Yugoslav government than the Roman Catholic hierarchy was, but there are a host of other plausible explanations for that. In respect to the rise of national chauvinism, both churches contributed heavily. It is symptomatic that parallel to the notion *Crkva u Hrvata* is its match *Srpska crkva* as a synonym for the Orthodox Church. The term Serbian seems to carry more weight that the term Orthodox. An interesting editorial in *Teološki Pogledi* (Theological Views), the official theological journal of the SOC, indicates that there are those who mistakenly favored only the Serbian national identity as a measure of their adherence to the Christian church and that in the period of the decline of communism some people started identifying the church with the state, blaming the SOC for the errors of government policies and claiming that this brought about God's wrath upon both the Serbian church and state. But Dr. Ignjatije Midi, the author of the editorial, rejects this equation.[28] Yet in typical Orthodox fashion, he rejects a sharp division of the worldly (political) and spiritual (ecclesiastical) domains.[29]

The SOC Metropolitan of Sarajevo, Nikolaj Mrdja, was the first in Serbia to point out that organized rapes were being carried out by Serbian extremists. However, at Christmastime in 1992, the SOC hierarchy issued a sharp statement categorically denying that Serbians have organized rapes and challenging anyone to name a single concentration camp where such rapes occurred, while simultaneously charging that many Serbian women had been raped by Muslims and Croats.[30] This case indicates the delicate position of the SOC, namely to truthfully point out events that it cannot conceivably condone and the need to become the protector of the national reputation when the entire Serbian nation is demonized by the outside world.

Like the Roman Catholic Church in Croatia, the Serbian Orthodox Church favors obligatory religious education in schools.[31] Unlike the Croatian Sabor, the Assembly (Skupština) of the rump Yugoslavia defeated the motion with a large majority. The SOC worries about the situation of Serbian children being catechized by Roman Catholic teachers in Croatian schools but seems unconcerned about the fate of non-Orthodox children in the event of mandatory Orthodox catechism in schools of Serbia. Serbian theologians also undertook the defense of Serbians and attacked Croatians (and others) when Croatian views critical of Serbs appeared in foreign journals.[32]

Bosnian Muslims: Ethno-Religious Ambiguity

The Bosnian Muslims are in the unique and somewhat awkward position of being the only group of Muslim believers in the world who are also considered Muslim by nationality. Some claim that national consciousness among the Slavic Muslims of Bosnia and Herzegovina came late. Others maintain that the Muslims were the mainstream of Bosnian life, having come peacefully to Bosnia in the ninth century and having created a Muslim civilization, culture, language, script, and so forth.[33] However, most scholars contend that Christians of the former Bosnian Church underwent a mass conversion to Islam from 1436 onward.[34]

One thing is sure: most contemporary Slavic Muslims do not remember their pre-Islamic religious or ethnic origin. Since they were the ruling class during the rule of the Ottomans, they were detested by their neighboring Slavic Christians, Orthodox and Catholics. When the Turks withdrew from the Balkan Peninsula, the so-called "poturice" (Turkicized people) were expected to return to their Christian origins thereby swelling the ranks of the Orthodox and/or Catholics. When this courting of the Muslims turned out to be unsuccessful, the Christian population continued their resentment and the Muslims had to work on their own identity.

Some preferred to call themselves Yugoslavs, some *"Bošnjaks,"* others Muslims. The Croats and the Serbs vigorously continued to claim that all the Muslims had been converts of their respective religion and nationality. It is most likely that in fact both Serbian Orthodox and Croatian Catholics as well as Bogumils of the Bosnian Church converted and in any case repressed their previous identities so effectively that most of them do not care to regard themselves as one or the other.[35]

I am not well informed about the engagement of Muslim religious leaders with enhancing Muslim nationalism in Bosnia. My own personal travels through the region and the general opinion of observers is that Islam is more a cultural than religious identity for most Muslims in Yugoslavia and that they may well be one of the most secularized Muslim communities in the world, gravitating toward Europe rather than the Muslim world. It is said that the current President of the Bosnian government, Alija Izetbegović, at the time when he was a communist prisoner wrote a pamphlet that some describe as Islamic fundamentalism, because allegedly he aimed to establish Bosnia as an Islamic state in which the Muslim majority would take over and rule with the help of the shariyat law.[36] It is evident, however, that since he was elected to a responsible government post, he has consistently pledged himself to a secular, multi-national, and multi-religious state in which everyone's rights would be respected.

It is also evident that since the Western world has not given any effective assistance to the Muslims who are the major losers thus far in the war in former Yugoslavia, that eventually these Slavic Muslims may be driven into the arms of Islamic fundamentalists who seem more eager to assist them than others. If this takes place it will be less a conscious and free decision of the Bosnian Muslims and more an act of a desperate people on the verge of extermination.

Macedonian Orthodox Separatism

This is another area which the author did not research. It is general knowledge that the Macedonian Orthodox Church was supported in its schism from the Serbian Orthodox Church by Tito's government in order to make a more determined effort to prove the separateness and identity of a Macedonian nationality. Since in Eastern Europe one cannot imagine a nationality without its own religion, it was important to establish an autocephalous or at least autonomous Macedonian church. This was done to deter Bulgarian, Greek, and Serbian claims that Macedonians are not separate but are parts of their nationhood. Though one of the last nations in Europe to become free of Turkish overlordship (1913) and one of the last ethnic groups to proclaim its own national consciousness, the Macedonians in turn have made some outrageous claims about uniting Greek, Bulgarian, and Yugoslav Macedonia into a Great Macedonia, a move which has cost them especially Greek resistance to recognition as an independent, sovereign state upon the fall of Yugoslavia.[37]

Macedonian Orthodox higher clergy have dutifully carried out the task of promoting Macedonian sovereignty and been fairly effective ambassadors abroad. It is interesting that the Macedonian Orthodox hierarchs have nurtured fairly good relationships with the Vatican and the Croatian Catholics — one presumes on the old European principle of being friends with the enemies of your enemy. There seems to be a minor reconciliation with the Serbian Orthodox Church since no Orthodox Church in the world was willing to grant autocephaly to the MOC and some accommodation will have to be worked out with the SOC which has very reluctantly granted it autonomy under the domain of the Serbian Patriarchate.

Protestants: Inability to Withstand War Propaganda

The Protestants, being less than one percent of the population, are quite marginalized. Generally the larger churches tended to be churches of national minorities (Hungarians, Slovaks, Germans). Among the larger Yugoslav nationalities, the number of Protestants was quite insignificant and played only a marginal role.

In the past, the free church Protestants, who tended to attract membership from a variety of national groups (e.g. Baptists, Pentecostals, Seventh-Day Adventists, Methodists) tended to nurture exemplary harmonious relationships between the members of various nationalities, and there was hope that these good relationships could survive the war. They were also outspoken in maintaining that God is not a nationalist and that religion ought to reconcile rather than divide people.[38] But that would have been too good to be true. For one, these formerly unified churches that acted wherever they had members on the territory of Yugoslavia now found themselves in separate countries and had to break up along the new nation-state principles.

Then many of the Protestant leaders in Croatia became so morally outraged at what they perceived, along with the rest of the Croatian people, as Serbian aggression that they condemned this aggression and urged foreign military intervention against Serbians, often criticizing foreigners, especially Americans, for inaction.[39] This incensed their fellow-religionists in other states and formerly close colleagues now regard them no longer as peacemakers but warmongers.[40]

On the whole, the Protestant communities tend to accept the official propaganda of their respective new states and often interpret the events the way this propaganda channels them. This does not mean that they

uncritically support all the policies of their governments but it does show
that even they are unable to bridge the enormous abyss that now separates
Croats and Serbs, Serbs and Macedonians, etc.

The Reconciling Role of Religious Communities

We already noted that the reconciling role of the religious communities is undeveloped in comparison to the divisive role. Calls for peace and
reconciliation are not lacking but many of them do not go beyond plati-
tudes and claims that this or that religion has always stood for peace. Frequently the call for peace was tempered by strong defensive language rejecting culpability of one's own side and blame directed toward the other
groups. Very few positive statements have been uttered about other religions and nationalities during these times, which is not surprising given
the cruel treatment dished out to each other.

Of course, like most people the churches regret the war (though not
many mourn the disintegration of Yugoslavia). Few members of the religious communities can give a sound assessment of the situation that is not
merely a reflection of what they hear from their mass media.[41] These assessments rarely receive wide circulation. And even fewer are those who
decide to become activists on behalf of peace. Most people see themselves
as being victims of forces far too great for their modest abilities. Survival in
tumultuous times is the overwhelming desire—active peacemaking is neither a tradition nor do people have enough psychic energy left for conflict-
resolution. Most are too shell-shocked by the brutality of the war and the
troubled times for their communities and their own persons to be able to
stem the confrontational mood throughout the country.

Several remarkable statements have been made, however, by leaders
of religious communities, both by themselves and in meetings with others.
The most significant such occasions were the meetings between Patriarch
Paul I of SOC with the head of the RCC Bishop's Conference Franjo Cardinal Kuharić. Their first meeting was in Sremski Karlovci (Serbia) in May
1991, the second in Slavonski Brod (Croatia) in August 1991, the third one
in Geneva in September 1992, and the fourth a meeting at which the Reis-
ul-ulema of the Islamic Community Jakub Selimovski also was able to be
present, a meeting convened by the Conference of European Churches and
the European Catholic Bishops' Conference in Switzerland in early 1993.

The most powerful text that emerged out of the Geneva meeting is
partially reproduced here as follows:

> Following our prayers and conversations, we appeal with one
> mind and voice to the faithful of our churches, to the responsible
> organs of the state, to military commanders and troops, to all
> peoples and men and women of our common geographical and

spiritual area, as well as to all international forums and institutions engaged in the search for a solution or in the provision of aid to our region and in our states; and we do not only appeal but demand, on the basis of our spiritual position and moral responsibility:

1. Immediately and without condition to cease all hostilities, all bloodshed and all destruction, in particular to stop the blasphemous and insane destruction of places of prayer and holy places, Christian and Muslim alike; and that negotiations between the warring parties be initiated without delay.

2. Immediately and without condition to liberate all prisoners of war and hostages, as well as to close all prison camps and to free all those incarcerated in this evil war.

3. Immediately and without condition to cease the inhuman practice of ethnic cleansing, by whomever it is being incited or carried out.

4. To permit all refugees and deportees to return to their homes and to ensure all bishops and priests of our churches as well as Islamic spiritual leaders free access to their flock and undisturbed exercise of their office.

5. That normal communication and unrestricted circulation be re-established, as well as the possibility of free movement and settlement for all people, whatever their religious or national affiliation, and

6. That all suffering people be assured undisturbed and equal access to humanitarian aid.

Equally with one mind and voice we condemn all crimes and distance ourselves from all criminals, irrespective of which people or army they belong to or which church or religious affiliation they claim. We especially express our horror at the perpetration of extremely immoral misdeeds, at the mistreatment of older and younger women and girls, which only monsters can perpetrate, no matter what name they give themselves. Before God, before humanity and before our own conscience we pledge that we will use all evangelical means and the full influence of our office and responsibility in church and society to work, in our own states and peoples, decisively and openly for peace, justice and the salvation of each and every one, for the dignity and inalienable rights of every individual and every people, for humanity and tolerance, for forgiveness and love. We ourselves call, individually and together, for repentance before the God of love, for conversation and for service to him, that we can live anew as neighbors, friends and brothers, Peace to all![42]

Of great importance was the distancing which the prelates took from those who would wage war in the name of their religion, saying that to do so is the greatest crime against one's own religion. The Christmas message 1992 by all the Orthodox bishops presided over by Patriarch Paul I is likewise very peace oriented. In it the Bishops give an answer why such destruction ensued after the proclamation of democracy and multi-party elections.

> The reason is that the proclaimed principles were accepted only externally, formally, but in the soul matters stayed unchanged due to espousing the notion that one can help oneself and one's people more by doing evil than by good, and that one can defend oneself and one's people from crimes and criminals by doing the same, namely by means of inhumanity and crimes....[43]

The bishops proceeded to point out that these attitudes brought about the unhappiness of all the nations involved in this war and invoked love toward all as mark of Christian discipleship.

The Roman Catholic Archbishop of Belgrade, the Slovene France Perko, also rejected the linkage between war massacres and religion yet admitted that the coupling is now closer. While urging patriotism instead of nationalism, the Archbishop conceded that many believers see themselves more as nationalists than Christians due to the deficiency of evangelization.[44]

Looking at the leadership in religious communities it is difficult to find prelates with a distinct orientation toward peace. The top leadership of the three communities — Orthodox, Catholic, and Islamic — are more conciliatory than some of their colleagues, but no one emerged with a Christlike, Gandhian or Martin Luther King, Jr. type strategy of resisting evil. There are miniscule groups of dissenters who oppose the war or who look for alternate peaceful ways in Belgrade, Zagreb, Mostar, and Sarajevo.[45] In Sarajevo, for instance, there is a small group of Catholic, Orthodox, and Muslim clergy led by Marko Oršolić, a Franciscan, who founded the International Center for Interreligious Dialogue, Justice, and Peace and who are working toward converting one of the military barracks into a dialogue center after the war, but they are not only isolated but also despised by their own religious community. Some have already been assassinated by members of their own groups; Oršolić, a Croat, is being attacked in the Croatian press as a "communist."[46]

One of the American peace activists reports that most of the clergy, especially higher, in former Yugoslavia have been inundated by foreign ecumenical and fact-finding delegations and they feel overburdened by high expectations that the churches can be agents of reconciliation while they do not see themselves as having that much influence. The activist reports that it is fairly difficult to find key middle level or higher clergy who wish to meet with their opposites from other churches. The most that one can expect at the present moment is relief work by the churches, an effort for which they are neither trained nor particularly well suited. While some of the church centers seem to be able to effectively distribute relief based only on need, there are reports of abuses; certain local churches distribute aid only to regular churchgoers of their own denomination or use aid to promote church attendance.

Conclusion

It is difficult to have hope regarding a better future for the devastated and brutalized people of ex-Yugoslavia, including the religious segment and its institutions. Most people with whom I spoke or corresponded expect it to become worse before it will become better. In Dante's "Inferno" there is a sign over hell: "Abandon hope all those who enter." The people in former Yugoslavia are, indeed, closer to hell than to heaven—at least regarding life here on earth. The most the religious communities are able to do is to suffer along. Perhaps some of them learn a lesson that stimulating national chauvinism and separatism rather than tolerance, pluralism, and concern for fellow-human beings regardless of nationality and religion is a recipe for hell.

Notes

1.   The term "religious communities" will be used here instead of the more customary term "churches" because the word "church" is unsuitable for Islam (as well as Judaism but the latter plays a negligible role in the present conflict). The term "religious community" is used here in the sense of an organized institutional formation of adherents of a religious orientation, such as Serbian Orthodox, Macedonian Orthodox, Roman Catholic, and Islamic.

2.   Among the more hilarious products of recent nationalistic "historical" investigations is that the Croats originate in ancient Iran, that the Serbs originate in the Caucasus and yet earlier in ancient Mesopotamia,

that Islam came to the Balkans independently centuries prior to the Otto-man Turkish conquest or that the present Macedonians are somehow directly linked with Alexander the Great of Macedon.

3.   See "Nationalism, Religion, and Peace in Eastern Europe with Special Reference to Yugoslavia," *Occasional Papers on Religion in Eastern Europe* (hereafter OPREE), Vol. 11, No. 6, December 1991, pp. 12-31, and "War Between Religions," *OPREE*, Vol. 12, No. 2, March 1992, pp. i-vi; "The Reign of Ethnos: Who is to Blame In Yugoslavia?," *Christian Century* (November 4, 1993), pp. 996-999, and "Intervening in Bosnia," *Christian Century* (April 14, 1993), pp. 388-390.

4.   I prefer the use of the word "ethnicity" over "nationality" because some ethnic groups do not have a state of their own, yet possess a yearning for self-governing and sovereignty and because I believe that the nation-states of the former Yugoslavia are not nations in the modern sense but are somewhat akin to tribalism, i.e., that the claim of being a Serb or Croat is closer to the claim of being a Yoruba or an Ibo than being a Swede or a Norwegian.

5.   Professor Vjekoslav Bajsić, a Roman Catholic theologian who is teaching at the Roman Catholic Theological School in Zagreb explained already in the late 1970s in an interview with this author that the only institution that was holding Yugoslavia together was the Yugoslav Communist Party (and the army which was under its control) while the religious communities played centripetal roles. Thus when the Communist Party of Yugoslavia fell apart along the six national component parts, there was no longer a force that could hold the country together.

6.   An awkward linguistic term even in Croatian which transliterates even more awkwardly into English: "in Croats," but could be more freely translated "of Croats" or "among Croats."

7.   This I know from personal experience as I interviewed prominent Roman Catholic theologians in Slovenia and Croatia who were members of the same Bishops Conference but did not know even rudimentary data about each other's life while being able to provide detailed analysis of the situation of their church among their nationals. Another illustration of the ethno-religious separatisms is the case of a village in the Zagreb Archdiocese which had an overwhelmingly Slovene population and was served by a Croat priest. This priest caused great distress among the villagers as only one of the about twenty masses celebrated per week was in the Slovene language despite the repeated petitions of his parishioners. They finally requested transfer of their village into the Ljubljana archdiocese. This took place as recently as 1991/92.

8.   I found in 1969 that the Supreme Islamic headquarters in Sarajevo were quite uninformed and uninterested in Islam among Albanians.

9.   Illustrative of this nationalistic character of religion is the unhap-

piness among Croats over the decision of the Vatican to separate the Bishops Conference of Croatia from the Bishops Conference of Bosnia and Herzegovina—both of whom are Croatian, though no regret was shown over the split of the Slovenian Bishops conference.

10. Ivan Cvitković, "God is Dead," in *Breakdown: War & Reconstruction in Yugoslavia* (London: Yugofax, 1992), p. 52.

11. I will zero in on the Roman Catholic Church among Croats (Katolička crkva u Hrvata or frequently simply Crkva u Hrvata) because I have more data on it and because there is a war in Croatia.

12. Geert van Dartel, "The Nations and the Churches in Yugoslavia," *Religion, State, and Society*, Vol. 20, Nos. 3 & 4, 1992, pp. 275-288. Geert van Dartel is a Roman Catholic activist from Holland who studied in Zagreb under the late Josip Turčinović, one of the most liberal Catholic priests who was rather exceptional in his ecumenical stance and van Dartel mistakenly ascribes it to the entire Roman Catholic Church in Croatia.

13. Jure Kristo, "The Catholic Church in Times of Crisis" and "Diverse Functions of Catholicism and Orthodoxy in Social Upheavals (1989-1992)," unpublished manuscripts.

14. Josip Beljan, "Priznata vjernost," *Veritas*, No. 9-10, (September-October, 1992), pp. 24-25. *Veritas* is a popular Catholic review.

15. Ibid., p. 24. Translated from Croatian into English by Paul Mojzes.

16. Ibid., p. 25.

17. Marko Oršolić, a professor at the Franciscan Theological Seminary in Sarajevo, told me that most of his former students are armed with machine guns defending the city.

18. Kristo, "Diverse Functions," pp. 7-8.

19. This would later be aggravated after the victory of the Croatian Democratic Union by the immediate removal of signs that were both in the Latinic and Cyrillic script, which in an economically weak country is an expensive move, which could only be interpreted by the Serbians as a decision to obliterate evidence of Serbian presence from Croatia (one should note that in Serbia to this day, signs and newspapers appear in both alphabets).

20. Kristo, "The Catholic Church in Times of Crisis," p. 12.

21. Van Dartel, "The Nations and the Churches in Yugoslavia," 286.

22. The Austrian Catholic theologian, Dr. Philipp Harnoncourt, provided information in January 1993 to this author that he personally heard at a meeting in Vienna convened by Cardinal Koenig to work on reconciling the two churches, a plea by the Orthodox Bishop Irinej Bulović of Novi Sad and Bačka that the Roman Catholic Bishops could do much to allay Serbian fears by condemning the destruction of 500,000 Serbs during World War Two. However, the Catholic Bishop Djuro Kokša responded that the charge is exaggerated — there were only 50,000 killed, he claimed—and

then did not proceed to apologize even for that number. This author likewise never heard a Croatian Roman Catholic priest make any statement
that could be considered as a condemnation of the atrocities of the past
war.

23. The province is a Serbian national shrine on account of it having
been the center of the medieval Serbian kingdom and the site of the fateful
Kosovo Polje battle in 1389 as well as the location of the first Serbian Patriarchate.

24. To the contrary, the Serbs were the largest of the national groups in
Yugoslavia and were dominant in the federal army and bureaucracy.

25. This author does believe that it was the real aim of Pavelić's regime—to have a pure Croatian "Great Croatia." I am stressing that in order to point out that the Serb attempts at "ethnic cleaning," which I under
no circumstances support, are in fact retribution for what happened in World
War Two (namely, we are witnessing the ending of that war on the Balkans
as well as the beginning of the next round of warfare). The Serbs are carrying out what is popularly known as *"milo za drago"* or tit for tat.

26. Among the Serbian publications emphasizing the tie between
Croatian nationalism and Roman Catholicism were Dragoljub Živojinović
and Dejan Lučić, *Varvarstvo u ime Hristovo* (1988), Vladimir Dedijer, *Vatikan
i Jasenovac* and Milan Bulajić, *Ustaški zločini genocida* (1988).

27. It seems, indeed, that too little care was given by the nascent
Croatian independence movement to clearly reject the symbols of the fascist NDH.

28. Ignjatije Midić, "Umesto uvodnika" (Instead of an Introduction),
Teološki Pogledi (Belgrade), Vol. 23, Nos. 1-4, 1991, p. 12.

29. Ibid., p. 15.

30. *Glasnik* (Belgrade), Vol. 23, No. 12, (December 1992, p. 201. Also
"Noch einmal: Moslem-Frauen," *Glaube in der 2. Welt*, Vol. 21, No. 2, Febru-
ary 1993, pp. 10-11. See also "Gewalt gegen Frauen als Mittel der
Kriegsfuhrüng," *G2W*, Vol. 21, No. 1, January 1993, pp. 16-19.

31. Lazar Milin, "Omladina i religija: pitanje veronauke u skolama"
(Youth and Religion: The Question of Catechism in Schools), *Glasnik*, Vol.
73, No. 8, August 1992, pp. 133-142.

32. Lazar Milin, "Srbi u očima hrvatskog književnika Vlade Gotovca"
(The Serbs in the eyes of the Croatian writer Vlada Gotovac), *Glasnik*, Vol.
73, No. 5, May 1992, pp. 85-89.

33. Statement by Smail Balić at the international Jewish-Christian-
Muslim dialogue in Graz, Austria, January 4, 1993.

34. Vatro Murvar, *Nation and Religion in Central Europe and the Western
Balkans—The Muslims in Bosnia. Hercegovina and Sandzak: A Sociological Analysis* (Brookfield, WI: University of Wisconsin Press, 1989), p. 12. This author
regards many of the speculations and hypotheses of Murvar and Balic as

farfetched, just as he is unimpressed by Serbian and Croatian mythological history.

35. Professor Esad Ćimić, a former Marxist sociologist of religion of Muslim heritage, caused quite a controversy when he rejected the innovation created during the later years of Tito's regime to call muslims "Muslims," by joking that he thinks of himself as a Croat and his brother believes himself to be a Serb.

36. Since I did not read any of his writings I cannot substantiate this claim, but Serbs frequently refer to the alleged fundamentalism of Izetbegović. Croats on the other hand criticize him for having been too naive and trusting of the Serbs and not arming the Bosnian Muslims in time, thus causing them to suffer disproportionate war causalties.

37. Institut za Nacionalna Istorija, *Istorija na Makedonskiot Narod* (Skopje: NIP "Nova Makedonija," 1969), 3 vols.

38. Peter Kuzmič, "Bog nije nacionalista," *Danas* (1989).

39. Peter Kuzmič, *Glas Slavonije* (Osijek).

40. Bill Yoder, "The Evangelicals of Ex-Yugoslavia," unpublished essay to appear in *Religion in Eastern Europe*.

41. One such sound interpretation is that of Vjekoslav Bajsić. Interview with Bajsić, January 11, 1993, in *Zagreb*.

42. See full text in *OPREE*, Vol. 12, No. 5, October 1992, pp. 50-51.

43. *Glasnik*, Vol. 73, No. 12, December 1992, pp. 198-199. Trans. from Serbian into English by Paul Mojzes.

44. "Krieg erst am Anfang," *G2W*, Vol. 21, No. 2, 1993, p. 11.

45. In Zagreb Jerry Shenk, an American Mennonite theologian and activist, tried to teach pacifism at the gathering of a group of religious people convened by the Fellowship of Reconciliation.

46. Interviews with Oršolić during the first week in December 1992 in Baltimore and Rosemont, PA.

About the Book

The collapse of communist rule in Russia and Eastern Europe ended the greatest persecution of religion since the fall of the Roman Empire. Not only did popular elections and a market economy become a priority for the new democratic agenda, but freedom of conscience and religious liberty were viewed as indispensable. Believers were suddenly free to practice their faith openly without threat of persecution. Christian leaders—some of whom had shown courage in communist times—were called upon to lead the renewal of civil society under the rule of law.

But the course of development in post-communist Russia is uncertain. So, too, is religion's place and role. Newly strengthened, divisive ideologies such as nationalism and continuing economic chaos are constraining religion's constructive and prophetic role.

In an attempt to address this revolutionary change—and uncertainty—this volume brings together historians, social scientists, and theologians from Europe and the United States who ask the deceptively simple question, "What is happening now to religion in Russia?" Drawing upon Eastern Orthodox, Protestant, and Roman Catholic points of view, they examine the religious attitudes, activities, and institutions of post-communist Russia and explore the ways in which religion will significantly impact emerging social and political questions there. The volume is essential reading for scholars of Russian politics, society, and religion and for anyone interested in the emerging culture of the former Soviet Union and Eastern Europe.